William Alexander Pickering

Pioneering in Formosa

Recollections of Adventures among Mandarins, Wreckers, & head-hunting Savages

William Alexander Pickering

Pioneering in Formosa
Recollections of Adventures among Mandarins, Wreckers, & head-hunting Savages

ISBN/EAN: 9783337177485

Printed in Europe, USA, Canada, Australia, Japan

Cover: Foto ©ninafisch / pixelio.de

More available books at **www.hansebooks.com**

PIONEERING IN FORMOSA

RECOLLECTIONS OF ADVENTURES
AMONG
MANDARINS, WRECKERS, & HEAD-HUNTING SAVAGES

BY

W. A. PICKERING, C.M.G.

LATE PROTECTOR OF CHINESE IN THE STRAITS SETTLEMENTS

WITH AN APPENDIX ON
BRITISH POLICY AND INTERESTS IN CHINA
AND THE FAR EAST
AND
Twenty-five Illustrations
FROM PHOTOGRAPHS AND SKETCHES BY THE AUTHOR

LONDON
HURST AND BLACKETT, LIMITED
13 GREAT MARLBOROUGH STREET
1898

All rights reserved

TO

VICE-ADMIRAL

LORD CHARLES T. M. SCOTT, C.B.

AND THOSE MANY NAVAL OFFICERS
WHO HAVE AT ALL TIMES AND IN SPITE OF MUCH
DISCOURAGEMENT
AIDED AND DEFENDED BRITISH ENTERPRISE IN CHINA
AND THE FAR EAST

THIS BOOK IS DEDICATED

IN GRATEFUL MEMORY OF 'AULD LANG SYNE'

PREFACE

SINCE I BEGAN this descriptive account of Formosa, important changes have taken place in the Far East.

Owing to the utter collapse of the Chinese army, Formosa, by the Treaty of Shimonoseki, has been handed over to the Japanese, who, after an interval of 300 years, have been able to re-occupy the island.

There can be little doubt that the change of government will ultimately benefit the Japanese, the inhabitants of Formosa, and the civilised world generally, but hitherto the conquerors have not achieved any great results.

This, however, cannot surprise anyone who is acquainted with the real state of things. The Chinese governed the portion of the island under their control merely for the benefit of the officials, and in many parts of Formosa within the Chinese pale anarchy prevailed for generations. However much the Chinese inhabitants may have been oppressed by their own mandarins, it is certain that they will not submit quietly even to just and good government, when exercised by a nation whom they have been accustomed to call 'dwarf slaves.'[1]

The Pekinese authorities must feel deeply the disgrace

---

[1] 'Oé-lo' in the Fuh-kien, or 'Ainu' in the court dialect. This epithet must be a relic of ancient times, before Japan was settled by its present inhabitants, who perhaps came from the south.

of surrender, and will doubtless intrigue amongst the two or three millions of their countrymen inhabiting the plains; and the Hak-kas of the lower ranges, who have never really been amenable to any rule, will gladly keep up an opposition, under the guise of patriotism and loyalty to the 'Son of Heaven.'

While there will be little difficulty with the semi-civilised and the savage aborigines, only the severest measures will subdue the Chinese, and much allowance must be made if the Japanese have to inflict punishment which in these days, and amongst civilised people, would be termed barbarous.

At any rate, Great Britain might have spared the necessity of the danger, as since 1860 she has had several opportunities of annexing Formosa, but has, with a culpable supineness, foregone the opportunity of possessing a fertile island and, in the Pescadores, a point of vantage for her fleet.

It is of little use to cry over spilt milk, and our duty is to be alive to the present position of affairs in China. The population of this country have an immense stake in China and the Far East, and now, instead of, as in 1860, having nearly a monopoly of influence at Pekin, we are confronted by the powerful opposition of Russia and France, combined with the jealousy of the Germans.

The public journals daily contribute trustworthy news which show that, at every point where our expansion of empire for the vital interests of our people is concerned, Russia and France are ready to thwart us. The Chinese Empire is sick unto death, and the inevitable partition cannot long be delayed. Unless England secures her proper share of the Celestial Empire, we shall not only lose the markets which are more and more absolutely

PREFACE ix

essential for the very existence of the masses in the three kingdoms, but we shall also be endangering the safety of our colonies of Hong Kong, the Straits Settlements, and also our possessions in Burmah and the Malay Peninsula. In these countries and islands, the backbone of the population, the source of revenue and prosperity, are the Chinese, of whom in the Straits, Malay States, and Hong Kong we have, at a moderate estimate, three-quarters of a million adults, the majority of whom, leaving their families at home, are entirely at the mercy of the Powers which rule the Celestial Empire. Were England to neglect her duties, and allow the French and Russians to be paramount at Pekin, I feel certain that in case of war the Chinese of our colonies could be so manipulated, either by promises of favours or by threats of punishment to their families in China, that we should find it very difficult to keep down rebellion within, and at the same time defend our coaling stations and most valuable colonies from external attack.

Entertaining these opinions, I shall be glad if the book I now venture to publish should conduce towards interesting my fellow-countrymen in the affairs of the Far East. I have spent the greater part of my life amongst the Chinese, and am conversant not only with their dialects, but also with many of their customs and their mode of thought. Sir Robert Hart, who for many years has been the personification of the Chinese Government with relation to Europe, has borne testimony that I have enjoyed almost unique opportunities of becoming acquainted with the Chinese of all classes, races, and languages.

In this connection, I would urge that the present time is most critical as regards our interests in China.

Although the present Inspector-General of Customs has most loyally served the Chinese Imperial Government, and although to him it is owing greatly that the Chinese Empire has been preserved from dissolution, yet at the same time Sir Robert Hart, I venture to declare, has done more than any British ambassador at Pekin to uphold our prestige. There can be little doubt that, owing to advancing years, and also to the jealousy of his influence felt by Russia and France, Sir Robert's term of office must soon come to an end; after that, affairs must become precarious indeed.

Any opportunity to assert our proper position in China, if now lost, will never be regained. Our diplomatists have never been able to cope with the strategy and *finesse* of Chinese statesmen, and what hope can we have (except in the inevitable gunboat) when the good counsels of Sir Robert Hart are wanting to the Chinese, and when, in addition to the astute members of the Tsung-li-yamen, we have the ministers of Russia and France working them as puppets to defeat British progress and commercial interests in that immense field of profit, the eighteen provinces of the Chinese Empire?

Now or never is the time to change our policy of sending men to Pekin who can declare that they will never allow the interests of twenty-nine millions of people to outweigh those of three hundred millions, and to select the most capable men we have to be abroad at Pekin for the benefit of the English people who pay their salaries. Our plenipotentiaries should be supported by an overwhelming naval force in the China seas, so that, in case diplomacy fail, we may be able to assert, *vi et armis*, that preponderance of influence in the Far East which our necessities demand, and which we moreover deserve by having borne the burden and heat of the day in opening out China for the benefit of the whole world.

Our treaty rights, and our immense interests in those parts of the empire still left to the Pekin Government—interests which are so essential for the benefit of our working classes—depend entirely upon our being ready and willing to enforce them: whilst in those spheres under Russian, French, and German influence, our commercial freedom is subject to their will.

It appears to me that, by means of Admiral Dewey's successes in the Philippines, Providence is affording our nation one more favourable opportunity. A cordial understanding between the United States, Japan, and Great Britain in the Far East would probably more than retrieve our past loss of prestige and commercial influence in China.

It is sad for old China hands to witness the apathy of our countrymen upon such vital questions. Englishmen cannot plead ignorance: during the past ten years the most experienced travellers and talented critics, such as Messrs. Colquhoun, Michie, Douglas, Norman, and the *Times* correspondent, Mr. Chirol, have written books, articles, and many warnings, showing the real state of things in the Far East, and the dangers imminent from neglect on our part to secure our just rights.

I, in my small way, have done what I could; and in the Appendix to this book I have reprinted all my warnings and prophecies for years past, which, I have some hope, may not have been written in vain.

In conclusion, I would acknowledge the great assistance rendered by my collaborator, 'Mark Sale,' who has enabled me to bring this book before the public in a more acceptable form than my own literary faculty would allow.

May 12, 1898.

NOTE
ON ORTHOGRAPHY OF PROPER NAMES

ALL the vowels are pronounced as in Spanish and Italian, and each distinctly sounded. *G* always hard, as in *Gertrude, Gilbert*; *ch* always as in *church*.

Ch,' K,' P,' T,' Ts' : these initials are all strongly aspirated.

CONTENTS

CHAPTER		PAGE
I.	I ENTER THE CHINESE IMPERIAL MARITIME CUSTOMS	1
II.	LIFE AND ADVENTURE AT FOOCHOW	9
III.	DESCRIPTION OF THE ISLAND OF FORMOSA . .	24
IV.	HISTORY OF THE ISLAND	40
V.	RELIGIONS OF THE CHINESE INHABITANTS . .	50
VI.	THE ABORIGINES AND THEIR RELIGIONS . . .	64
VII.	THE PROGRESS OF CHRISTIANITY IN FORMOSA. THE GREAT STORM	76
VIII.	CORRUPTION AND RAPACITY OF CHINESE OFFICIALS	89
IX.	MY FIRST VISIT TO THE SAVAGE TRIBES OF THE INTERIOR. THE END OF GENERAL BURGEVINE .	98
X.	COWARDICE AND PLUCK. VISIT TO THE SAVAGE VILLAGES. MY LIFE AT TAIWANFOO . . .	113
XI.	ADVENTURES IN THE VICINITY OF TAIWANFOO .	130
XII.	SECOND TRIP INTO THE INTERIOR	142
XIII.	MY VISIT TO THE BAN-TAU-LANG TRIBE . .	154
XIV.	AN EXCEPTIONAL CHINESE MERCHANT. GENERAL LE GENDRE TO THE RESCUE	167

CHAPTER		PAGE
XV.	Wrecks and Wreckers	176
XVI.	The Triumph of Diplomacy	194
XVII.	The Beginning of the Camphor War	202
XVIII.	Further Camphor Troubles. A real Ghost Story. The ultimate Triumph of the Tao-tai	220
XIX.	My Farewell to Formosa	239
	Appendix	247

LIST OF ILLUSTRATIONS

PORTRAIT OF THE AUTHOR	*Frontispiece*	
MAP OF FORMOSA	*To face p.* 24	
TAKAO, SOUTH SIDE—MESSRS. ELLES & CO.'S HOUSE AND GODOWNS	,,	28
FORT ZELANDIA (BUILT BY THE DUTCH ON THEIR OCCUPATION OF FORMOSA, 1630), ANPING (PORT OF TAIWANFOO)	,,	31
INSIDE CITY, TAIWANFOO	,,	32
TAIWANFOO, PART OF CITY WALL	,,	33
DOCUMENTS IN THE LANGUAGE OF CIVILISED ABORIGINES, PRESERVED FROM TIME OF DUTCH OCCUPATION, 1650	,,	41
PARADE GROUND, TAIWANFOO, WHERE 187 BRITISH SUBJECTS WERE EXECUTED, 1842	,,	46
GRANARY WHERE 187 BRITISH SUBJECTS, *EX* TRANSPORTS 'ANNIE' AND 'NERBUDDA,' WERE IMPRISONED BEFORE EXECUTION, 1842—TAIWANFOO	,,	47
PEPO-HOAN CIVILISED ABORIGINES	,,	64
FORMOSAN CHINESE ('MAN'), HOK-LO . . .	,,	66
THE GREAT STORM . . . . *From a drawing by the Author*	,,	85

Pepo-hoan and Chinese Group, Formosa .	. To face p.	100
Anping (Port of Taiwanfoo), View of Old Dutch Fort, 1650	,,	105
Mount Morrison, Formosa	,,	118
New Ground broken by Rain—Central Mountain Range	,,	121
Bamboos, Formosa	,,	132
Land Subsidence, Action of Subterranean Torrent between Kwan-te-bio and Bak-sa	,,	142
A Pepo-hoan Fishing Party with Bows and Arrows	,,	144
Aborigines, North Formosa	,,	148
Camphor Depôt, Go-ch'e	,,	205
From a drawing by the Author		
The Scene of the Ghost	,,	225
From a drawing by the Author		
Tamsui (Treaty Port, North Formosa)—British Consulate	,,	231
W. A. P., 1869	,,	232
British Consulate, Taiwanfoo	,,	236

PIONEERING IN FORMOSA

CHAPTER I

I ENTER THE CHINESE IMPERIAL MARITIME CUSTOMS

IN the year 1862 I was third mate on a Liverpool tea-clipper lying off Pagoda Island, in the river Min, some nine miles below the City of Foochow. I was twenty-two years of age, and I had been on the sea since the year 1856, when my indentures were signed,[1] and I, a shivering lad, was handed over to work out a four years' apprenticeship on board one of the old Blackwall East Indiamen.

Now, at twenty-two one is confident and sanguine as to one's ability to succeed in any and every line of life. I had by this time come to the conclusion that a sailor's life was but a dog's life even at the best. But, more than this, five or six years' voyaging between the many Ports of Burmah, Siam, China, and the Malay Archipelago had fascinated me with the glamour of the Orient, and I was eagerly longing for some opportunity to present itself which would open out for me a prosperous career amongst the people of the Far East. Therefore when in Foochow River the Customs officer boarded us, and in him I recognised an old shipmate of my apprentice days, it

[1] The Managing Clerk who signed as witness to my indentures, and who was beloved by all the apprentices for his kindness, still survives, I am delighted to hear, in the person of the respected founder of the well known shipping firm, Messrs. Gellatley, Hankey & Co.

B

occurred to me that the time had arrived; and truly, as results proved, this unexpected meeting was the turning point of my fortunes.

Poor old Johnston—so clever, and so futile, as far as his own interests were concerned. He had been a great favourite with the apprentices on board the old 'Lady McDonald,' and was a fine specimen of the shrewd, solidly educated, 'kindly Scot.' He was a thorough old-fashioned 'sailorman,' which implies a great deal. As he often told me, it had been the hope of his parents that he might even 'wag his pow in a pu'pit,' and nothing but his devotion to the national beverage kept him 'before the mast'; otherwise he was qualified to command a vessel. Having served ashore or afloat in most parts of the world, Johnston possessed an inexhaustible fund of anecdote, and we youngsters of the 'half-deck' would listen breathlessly while he spun interminable yarns of adventure among South Sea cannibals, of revolutions in South America, or of the stern justice meted out by the 'Vigilance Committee' in California.

One of my old comrades died in command of a 'Castle Liner'; another, leaving the sea soon after his 'time was out,' has amassed a large fortune in the City; while I, thanks to an appreciative Government, am able to live 'at home at ease,' having had all that a man could crave of danger and adventure, and of wanderings in strange lands.

Old Johnston, who was chiefly instrumental in securing my success in life, after a few more years' service as 'tidewaiter,' ended his life far away from old Scotland, and was laid to rest on the barren shore of China.

But in 1862 the end was not yet. Old Johnston had by some strange happenings drifted into the newly established Imperial Maritime Customs, one of the institutions of New China which tend perhaps more than any other to bring her within the family of nations. He was

I ENTER THE CHINESE CUSTOMS

enthusiastic on the subject of the advantages and emoluments of the Service. 'You must join us, my lad,' he declared. 'Why, bless my soul, with your knowledge of languages, and your adaptability, you'll go ahead like steam. Only learn the language and you'll soon be on the high road to fortune. It is a sin that a young fellow like you should be living the life of a mere dog on board ship. What good are your brains to you here, I'd like to know? Join us, my boy, and exchange your salt-junk and mouldy biscuit for fresh fish, flesh and fowl, all of the best; your dreary midnight summons to "shift over stunsails," or to "close reef the topsails," for warm uninterrupted "nights in." Come! take the goods the gods offer you, is my philosophy: Plato could have no better. Say you'll join us, and I'll manage the rest.'

The offer was a tempting one. I was thoroughly disenchanted as to the romance of the sea. I was already interested in the strange people of China—'ever living backwards,' as it were, on the wisdom and the mandates of their ancestors. The difficulties of their language attracted me; the climate seemed all I could wish. I laid the matter before my Captain, who was also my friend; his advice seemed wise, since it coincided with my inclinations. He interested himself with the Customs authorities, and gave me my discharge with a very favourable testimonial; and I agreed to 'eat the Emperor's rice' at a monthly salary amounting to about 15l. of English money. Such wealth dazzled me. Feeling profoundly that all was 'right with the world,' I entered on my duties with a light heart.

It was about the year 1860 that, with the consent of the ambassadors of the European Powers, the 'Maritime Customs' service at all the treaty ports in China had been placed under the supervision and control of Europeans paid by the Chinese Government. This new department was equally disliked by the Chinese local authorities and the European merchants. The former, to their disgust, instead of being allowed to make large fortunes by peculation, saw the import and export duties collected honestly by Europeans, placed in a bank, and correct returns sent to the central Government at Pekin.

The Europeans, instead of being able, by paying a round sum as a bribe to the Mandarins, to clear a vessel, and so escape the regular tariff duties, were now obliged to pay nearly as much on a single lighter of tea or silk as they would otherwise have done for the whole shipload.

Since the days of which I am writing, the Chinese Maritime Customs Department, under the able management of Sir Robert Hart—an Ulster man—has become one of the finest services in the world. It is the mainstay of China as far as import and export revenue is concerned, and has also been the chief means of maintaining peace between the Celestial Empire and the Western Powers. It has studded the coast of China with splendid lighthouses, and on its security China has been able to negotiate and punctually pay interest upon loans in Europe.

The official residence of the Imperial Maritime Customs staff at Pagoda Island was at that time an old hulk, the 'Spartan,' moored in the River Min, it being a more desirable residence both on the score of hygiene and safety than a house on shore.

We were a queer cosmopolitan set; almost every nationality was represented, more or less worthily, amongst us. There were subjects of most of the States which now compose the German Empire, with excitable little Spaniards and Portuguese; Chinese, with their pigeon-English; Frenchmen who cried '*Vive l'Empereur*,' and who a few years later, in 1870, roared '*La Marseillaise*' with equal fervour; Irish-American Fenians, who spent their evenings in poring over maps of the 'distressful country' apportioned as she should be, and studying Gaelic that they might be ready for the halcyon time when the

I ENTER THE CHINESE CUSTOMS

usurper should be ousted and they should rule, the rightful lords of peasantry and pigs.

All the day long, as the vessels lay anchored in the river, we tidewaiters boarded them and kept tally of their imports and exports, being treated hospitably by most of the captains, but strictly boycotted by a few.

In every spare moment I set myself to master the language. I began to pick up colloquial Chinese in the local dialect. 'What call you this, and that?' was my constant query to every Celestial who would reply, until I could chatter to them in their own tongue, and they slapped me on the back in their astonishment, declaring as a profound compliment that I was 'not a barbarian, but a man.' Then, as time went on, I began to study the written character. The hieroglyphics upon the sides of the teachests and bales were my spelling books; my enthusiasm grew with my difficulties. I waited with most sanguine hopes for quick promotion as a reward of my exertions.

Fortune came at last in the shape of the Assistant Inspector-General of Customs, Mr. Robert Hart, who visited our station in a coasting steamer which I boarded on arrival. Mr. Hart was endeavouring with but indifferent success to make one of the Chinese boatmen comprehend his instructions to take his luggage to the 'Spartan.'

I was pacing up and down the deck within earshot, and, when Mr. Hart's patience was giving out, I stepped forward, raising my cap, and gave the desired commands to the bewildered Chinese in his own particular dialect. It was well. The Inspector-General turned an observing eye upon me.

'Who are you?' he inquired sharply.

'A tidewaiter, at your service, sir,' I replied.

'Who taught you Chinese?'

'I picked it up myself since I joined the Service.'

'How long is that ago?'

'Five months, sir.'

'Five months!' His pocket-book came out. He wrote down my name. He would not forget me when he returned to headquarters.

I was jubilant. At twenty-two one credits the world with a long memory for one's peculiar merits. I felt my fortune was as good as made. But I knew that, however useful the local *patois* might be, if I wished to merit promotion I must acquire the Mandarin or court dialect of Chinese. Wherefore, one-fourth of my salary henceforth went to hire a native instructor. I redoubled my efforts, and spouted forth Pekinese even in my sleep.

Some of my comrades were so interested in my progress that one day, they, with me, forced themselves into the District Magistrate's Yamen at the town of Min-ngan, in order to prove whether my Pekinese was genuine. Luckily for us the Mandarin was delighted with the polite phrases I had learned from my Manchu teacher, and treated us very hospitably; otherwise we might have paid dearly for our impertinence.

But my Fenian brethren looked upon me with distrust. Such wiles to court the favour of the detested powers that be were alien to their creed. I was going over to the ranks of the oppressor and the tyrant.

But the days went by, and no sign came from headquarters. At last I took my courage in both hands and sent a Chinese letter to the Commissioner of Customs, Baron de Meritens. He was graciously interested; Mr. Hart confirmed my account of myself; a grant came to pay the salary of my instructor, and I was most kindly encouraged to persevere by all means in my studies.

At the end of the following year Mr. Maxwell, the Commissioner of Customs for Formosa, selected me to accompany him to that island, where he was engaged in establishing custom houses in the southern ports; and I, eager to put my newly acquired knowledge to practical use, gladly accepted the duty.

I ENTER THE CHINESE CUSTOMS

So, in 1863, custom houses were established at the ports Tamsui, Kilung, and Takao, where some years before the great houses of Jardine and Dent had established themselves and were carrying on trade under difficulties.

I remained at Takao, as tidewaiter at the Customs there, until I had become conversant with the vernacular as spoken in Formosa ; and in 1865 I was placed in charge of the Customs at Anping, the port of Taiwanfoo, the capital.

Shortly after my arrival at Takao I found opportunities of visiting the savage aborigines in the interior, and in my official duties at Taiwanfoo I became acquainted with many of the Chinese officials.

In 1867 I received what I considered a very advantageous offer to take charge of the Taiwanfoo branch of an English firm—Messrs. McPhail & Co. (subsequently Messrs. Elles & Co.), who were carrying on the business formerly belonging to Messrs. Jardine and Dent. I gladly availed myself of this opportunity to be in the employ of my own countrymen rather than in the service of the Chinese Government.

Thus it came to pass that I settled in Formosa, where my Chinese studies proved to be of considerable service to me in many strange ways ; where I was destined to probe deeply into the unfathomable nature of the wily Celestial ; and where it was my fortune to have adventure in plenty by land and sea, and peace infinitesimal, for nearly seven long years.

My new employers placed horses and servants at my disposal, encouraging me to travel into the interior, both amongst the Chinese settlers and the aboriginal tribes, in order to find out the resources of the country and to ascertain the facilities for trade. I thus daily increased my knowledge of the languages and habits of the people, and was enabled to explore many districts and make acquaintance with tribes of Chinese, Sek-hoans, and savages hitherto unvisited by Europeans.

I remained in Formosa until the end of 1870, when I was invalided home, and during my stay in England I received the appointment of Chinese Interpreter to the Government of the Straits Settlements. In 1877 I was gazetted Protector of Chinese for the Colony, which post I occupied until the year 1890, when I retired from the colonial service on pension.

With these prefatory details, I will proceed to give a brief account of this interesting and but little known island, its history, its people and their religion, and some of the adventures which befell me during my residence in Formosa.

CHAPTER II

LIFE AND ADVENTURE AT FOOCHOW

IT was in the middle of 1863 that Mr. Maxwell was appointed Commissioner of Customs for the island of Formosa, under the Foochow Commissioner.

Baron de Meritens desired Mr. Maxwell to employ the remainder of his stay in Foochow in searching all the ports and creeks between Foochow and Ningpo, for the purpose of seizing all European vessels found harbouring in them, it being well known that a flourishing illicit trade was carried on in defiance of treaty obligations.

For this scrutiny of the coast, the Customs authorities had chartered a diminutive steamer called the 'Mercury,' which, in spite of her Liliputian size, had been brought out round the Cape by her daring owner and captain.

Our chief-tidewaiter, with a *posse* of Irish-American subordinates, was told off to accompany Mr. Maxwell upon his expedition round the coast, while I was included in the party on account of my knowledge of the local dialect, which would be useful for the purpose of communicating with the fishermen of the coast, in order to obtain information from them as to the whereabouts of possible delinquent vessels.

Thus one brilliant morning we steamed forth, bound for Nam-kuan and the Samsa Inlet, some seventy miles north of the river Min. The Captain was evidently filled with the greatest pride and belief in the capabilities of his ship; we were all young fellows glad of this pleasant break in the monotony of our life as tidewaiters; the weather was superb; and we all anticipated a pleasant picnic, with the additional excitement of capturing possible prizes.

Alas, for our bright visions! Soon after leaving the river a strong breeze arose. The sky clouded, and heavy seas began to break over our frail craft. To crown all, at this crisis our machinery broke down, and the little 'Mercury' drifted unmanageable in the trough of the waves.

We were all bundled down below and the hatches battened down above us, which is not an agreeable experience, giving one much the sensation of a trapped rat, without the chance of a swim for life.

Meanwhile the violence of the waves increased. Things looked pretty desperate; but providentially the sailors contrived to rig up a rag of a sail, and by taking cunning advantage of the wind we were able to scud under the lee of an island, where, when the elements abated, the engine was patched up sufficiently to take us back to Foochow.

A week or two later, when all deficiencies in our boat's machinery had been made good, we sallied forth again.

Upon this occasion no untoward events frustrated our plans. The weather continued fine, and we were able to search the two ports, without, however, dropping upon any smugglers.

We boarded some fishing boats, whose crews volunteered the information that there were several barbarian vessels anchored in the port of Wen-Chou, further to the northward.

To Wen-Chou our Chief thereupon decided that we should steam, and, upon arriving at the anchorage in that port, we perceived four vessels, the captains of which unsuspectingly boarded the 'Mercury' directly we dropped anchor.

Mr. Maxwell calmly proceeded to hoist his Chinese Customs flag, and exhibited his official authority to them, declaring to the astonished skippers that he seized their vessels for breach of the Tien-tsin Treaty.

Tidewaiters were forthwith appointed in charge of each vessel : the national flags were hauled down, and the Imperial Customs flag was hoisted in their place.

It appeared that the vessels were respectively : the 'Japan,' a British brigantine ; the 'Russalka,' a Russian schooner ; the 'Chloris,' a Danish brig ; and the 'Amoy Trader,' a Prussian schooner.

The Chinese authorities of Wen-Chou received orders, which we brought with us, from the Governor-General at Foochow, commanding them to render us all necessary assistance. They were consequently obliged, very unwillingly, to furnish us with a guard in case of any resistance from the captains.

All these four vessels were chartered by Chinese merchants ; therefore, as their supercargoes were on shore, they were detained by the Mandarins as hostages for the good conduct of the respective skippers.

I was placed on board the 'Amoy Trader' in company with an American named East, who was my senior in the service, a fine-looking fellow six feet high.

We proceeded to reconnoitre in our new quarters, and to make the acquaintance of those on board the 'Amoy Trader.'

We found the Captain to be a big, surly looking German, very naturally in a high state of exasperation at the unexpected turn affairs had taken. He had been trading on the coast for several years, and had accumulated a fair sum, especially through the illicit trade between Wen-Chou and other closed ports. The present voyage was positively to have been his final venture ; and then, had all gone well, he had planned to return home to Dantzig to end his days in the Fatherland on a moderate competency.

He had with him, on board, his wife, a meek, gentle little frau, whose mission appeared to be to try to pour oil upon the troubled waters of her morose husband's wrath.

It can be imagined that we were most unwelcome guests. As soon as the Captain returned from his interview with Mr. Maxwell on board the 'Mercury,' he worked himself into a frenzy of anger, abusing us vigorously in Low German; and so uncontrollable did his rage become, that he had to be held down by the united efforts of his poor little wife and the mate to prevent him from doing himself some injury in his madness.

We were not invited to partake of any meal, so we arranged to have our food sent on board to us; and, as it was fortunately dry weather, we were able to contrive our beds upon the cabin roof.

During the evening the three other unfortunate skippers came on board for mutual condolence and sympathy. They made a night of it, keeping up their drooping spirits with schiedam and cherry cordial. We consequently got but little rest from the noise, besides having to endure, with what patience we could muster, strong abuse of the Maritime Customs and all things appertaining thereto—abuse delivered in a language which, though foreign, was sufficiently akin to my Midland-county Saxon *patois* to be extremely irritating.

Everything has an end at last—even the dram-drinking capacity of a seasoned salt. After crying, drinking, and singing until they were quite exhausted, they separated to their respective vessels, and we managed to snatch some sleep.

The next morning was Sunday. We were early summoned on board the 'Mercury,' and Mr. Maxwell informed us that the little steamer, with the head-tidewaiter on board, would tow us down to Foochow, whither, if all went well, we should arrive that night or the following day. He instructed us to keep a keen watch that our German Captain played no tricks with the tow rope, nor attempted to run away.

Mr. Maxwell added that the head-tidewaiter would

forward from Foochow a more powerful steamer to tow the other vessels down.

We assured him of our best endeavours. We were young and self-reliant, and we were each armed with a Smith & Wesson's revolver.

Upon these arrangements being made known to the Captain of the 'Amoy Trader,' he became at first furious, and then, when words failed, sank into a sullen mood.

He had imagined that he would have got clear with a fine; but these severer measures meant ruin to him, as his vessel would inevitably be confiscated. He retired to his cabin, followed by his tearful little wife, who tried in vain to comfort him.

Meanwhile we got under way, and about seven o'clock we were towed out of the river, between the islands at its mouth.

When we launched into the open sea both I and my companion breathed more freely. Ours was a disagreeable position. We hailed the prospect of a speedy arrival at Foochow, when we should be relieved from our uncongenial duty. Our hopes were destined to disappointment.

There was scarcely a breath of wind, the heat was intense, whilst a very heavy ground swell added to our discomfort.

Moreover, it soon became evident that every pitch of the sluggish, heavily laden schooner jerked the little 'Mercury' astern. Our progress was simply *nil*.

After an hour or two more of vain endeavours, the tow rope slackened, and the steamer dropped alongside.

The head-tidewaiter jumped on board, carrying the small half of a bottle of Martell, a paper of cracker biscuits, and a few cigars.

Addressing East, as senior, he said :

'This state of things is no good. You must take

charge of the vessel, and make the best of your way down to Foochow, whilst we go ahead to procure a bigger steamer. The Captain of the " Mercury " says that the sea-breeze is about to spring up. With that in your favour, you will probably be in the river Min as soon as we shall.'

We blankly objected that we had no knowledge of the coast, nor any charts to guide us.

Upon this the morose Captain was summoned from his cabin, and informed by the head-tidewaiter that he must take charge of the ship's navigation. Moreover, that it entirely depended on his conduct as to what treatment he would receive from the Commissioner of Customs on reaching Foochow.

The skipper fumed and stormed, but gradually calmed down, and ultimately promised to do his best.

Away puffed the little ' Mercury,' freed from the encumbrance, and we were left to ourselves.

There were only catspaws of air, and these appeared to be blowing right into the only passage that we could discover.

As the smoke of the tiny steamer gradually faded from sight, the Captain thrust his hands deep into his pockets and began to chuckle. He turned upon us with malicious glee, and said in his broken English :

'*Now*, what you fellows do? I not navigate the schooner. Himmel! not *I!*'

We tried to reply with ease which we were very far from feeling :

'All right, Captain. Don't trouble yourself. We'll do our level best, if you lend us your chart.'

'Ho, ho !' he cried, laughing bitterly, ' I no let you see my kart. You fellows smart enough to get me in this mess ; you just get us out now.'

We thereupon hurried off to the mate, and requested him to get sail on the vessel, promising him that he should be suitably rewarded if he loyally assisted us in working the schooner and in managing the Malay crew.

We easily made terms with him. He, being a Dane of Schleswig, had no sympathy with the German Captain, who, he assured us, was a brute, a tyrant to his wife and to all on board.

We got sail on the schooner with all speed. A breeze sprang up; unfortunately, not the predicted sea breeze, but a wind from the southward, dead in our teeth.

We began to exercise our seamanship in working through the channel and in tacking between the islands. Although the shore appeared steep-to, yet we grew nervous, as we were obliged to make as long tacks as possible, and we had no knowledge of probable hidden dangers.

The mate could give us no assistance in this ticklish business, for it was his first voyage in the 'Amoy Trader,' and he had never been to Wen-Chou before. He could only assure us that the Captain and his little 'frau' knew the coast 'like a book.'

Well, audacity must save us since knowledge would not! We were going finely through the seething waters —that is, the old tub was making a lot of noise at her bows—and we began to think it time to tack, as the rocks were pretty near.

At that moment up rushed the Captain, frenzied.

'Oh, my goodness! my goodness! What you do here? What ever you do here? You put my ship ashore! You kill mine wife! You kill me! We all die! Ah, Donner und Blitzen!'

East replied philosophically:

'Well, Captain, I guess we're doing our best. If you won't do something, we must. The blame is yours.'

We hastened to put the schooner round on the other tack.

The Captain's wife joined him, and timidly urged him

to be wise and take over the charge; but as we reached off clear of danger, the man relapsed into his former dogged, sullen humour.

'Well, skipper,' I said, 'I have no doubt that, as you say, we shall run the old craft ashore sooner or later. We don't know the coast, and we have no chart, so it is about certain that we must come to grief. But that doesn't matter so much to us as it does to you. We have no ship, nor wife, nor cargo to fuss about. We have only the clothes on our backs to lose; our wages are paid all the time. If we go ashore, we have at least a better chance than you, for we are both young and active, we can swim, and we can talk the natives' lingo. Therefore we should probably fare better than you would do if it comes to such a crisis.'

The little frau backed up my words, again entreating him to listen to sense.

The man at last seemed to relent. He said:

'All right! Get out of that, and let me take charge of the schooner. I'll take her, and save our lives.'

We were immensely glad to be relieved from our anxious post. We hastened below, to discuss the biscuits and brandy and to enjoy a well-earned smoke.

The whole of that night and the next day was occupied in getting clear of the islands. The wind perversely fell light again, and we drifted with the current to the north and east.

As the hours went on the skipper grew somewhat more genial. His wife, poor soul, had been invariably gentle and conciliatory to us. We were invited to their table, where they fed us well upon queer German dishes, composed of pork and yams, sweet soups and vinegar, with other strange foods dear to the Teutonic palate, accompanied by a fair allowance of Schnapps, Hamburg sherry, and cigars.

After two days of aimless drifting hither and

thither, out of sight of land, the Captain broached a proposition to us at dinner.

This precious scheme was that he should, with the favouring south-west monsoon, run up to the Amur River, and sell the schooner and her cargo to the Russians at Vladivostock, who would be certain to give a good price. Then we were to share the proceeds equally.

We were astonished, but we did not interrupt him for some time, whilst he said smooth things of the plausibility of his plan. At last, I replied, half banteringly :

'Yes, Captain, that sounds very well; but if you would sell the schooner in that way, I should be afraid that you might sell us with her. We can speak neither Russian nor German. No, no. I am going nowhere but straight ahead to Foochow, and as long as I have my revolver, and can use it, I will let no one take me except where I want to go.'

Nothing further was said at the time, but I observed that subsequently I was treated less liberally.

We contrived to make our way towards the land again, but the wind continued unfavourable.

Upon the fourth day our ingenious Captain proposed another little plan—that he should sail his vessel to Hong Kong. He would promise us a substantial reward if we would let him run away with us.

He argued that the glass was falling; it was typhoon season, and if we were to continue knocking about at sea, waiting for a favourable wind to fetch Foochow, we should very probably be caught in a typhoon, and all hands would go to the bottom.

East seemed not altogether indisposed to take the proposed trip to Hong Kong. When I saw he was wavering I grew exceedingly angry.

'You fool!' I said to him. 'This rascally Dutchman, who would ask us to betray our trust, would not hesitate to sell us when we reached Hong Kong. When he had

C

done with us, he would just kick us on shore. We should lose our berths, we should lose our characters, and nobody would sympathise with us, for we should richly deserve what we got. I'm not going back to sea again now I have a good job on shore; and, moreover, I'm not going to be false to those whose rice I eat. So now you know *my* mind. You can all do what you like, but I'll take my chance, if I have to fight the lot of you!'

I rushed from table, and laid down on deck to cool my wrath. Afterwards I went to talk things over with the mate, who cynically decided, for his part, to side with those who gave the best terms. Then I had a mighty row with East, giving him my mind very fully on the question, and I thought he seemed convinced that it would be foolish to join the Captain in his desperate scheme.

From this hour my life was 'not a happy one.' No more schnapps or tobacco was bestowed upon me, and I felt the want of both comforts, as our slender stock was finished.

Worse than all, when I went to get a drink of water at the scuttle-butt near the cabin, I discovered that salt water had been mingled with it; and this was neither pleasant to drink alone nor as tea.

East, I observed, was treated as hospitably as ever, and I found that the skipper had bottled off a quantity of fresh water for their consumption in the cabin.

These inconveniences, however, only made me the more determined to oppose them all, and to get to Foochow by any possible means.

On Sunday we found ourselves becalmed off an island called Tong-Ying, I think. A light air sprang up from the north-east, which, to my joy, began steadily to waft the schooner on her course. The breeze strengthened gradually, and before sunset I felt convinced that we could not be far distant from the entrance to Foochow River; yet, to my perplexity, in spite of the fair wind, we were not shaping our course towards the land.

Since the last intrigue of the Captain, I had not been friendly with East, who spent all his time chatting with the skipper and his wife, on deck and below; but I had converted the mate and the crew to my views by promises of liberal rewards for their rectitude from the Commissioner of Customs when we should reach Foochow.

I was very uneasy; the wind was steadily freshening from a quarter which during the south-west monsoon generally presaged a typhoon. I went aloft on the foretopgallant yard, and thence I could plainly distinguish, away on the starboard bow, the White Dogs Islands at the entrance to the River Min.

I argued that we ought in consequence to have kept right away before the wind to make for them. I was convinced now that there was an intention of passing Foochow, and things looked very black.

I climbed down on deck, and went off to my bunk to fetch my revolver from its resting-place beneath my pillow. To my dismay it was gone.

I rushed to the fore part of the house, and caught up a little capstan bar which lay handy. Then I proceeded aft to the stern gratings, where the Captain, his wife, and East were having refreshments and a smoke.

'Captain,' I said strenuously, 'there's the White Dogs Islands broad on our starboard bow. Why don't you keep away before the wind for them? If you don't, we'll have to haul up on the other tack before long.'

The Captain leisurely removed his long pipe, and smiled sardonically at my excitement.

'Don't you make a bobbery, young man,' he replied; 'we not going to Foochow.'

'Oh, yes, you are,' I responded wrathfully, 'or I'll see why.'

The skipper laughed maliciously.

'What you do, one man? Where your revolver?' he asked.

'Never mind!' I replied grimly. 'I know all about that. This, you'll find, will do as well.'

With which I banged the handspike on the stern gratings, causing confusion and damage amongst the bottles and glasses.

Then did I in my wrath speak many strong words to that recreant East. I began to storm and upbraid him for a fool and a coward.

'If you *will* listen to that Dutchman, you are ruined for life,' I shouted. 'What does he know or care about duty, so long as he can manage to get back home with his dirty dollars? Don't mind him a bit! See, the mate and the crew will obey us. Come! show yourself a man before it is too late. My father taught me that I must do my duty to my employer at all costs, and I mean to do it now. That Dutchman doesn't know the meaning of duty or honour. Surely now a Yankee and an Englishman can stand shoulder to shoulder, and defy a dishonest old Dutchman and his frau! Come on, I tell you!'

The skipper, who understood my tirade imperfectly, but sufficiently, jumped up in a towering rage, and smashed down his clenched fist upon the breech of a brass gun close to where he was sitting, cutting open his knuckles in his frenzy.

With every German and English epithet at his command, he abused all Englishmen.

'You cursed Englishman!' he roared. 'You always talking, talking, about duty, duty, duty! What is mine duty? Mine duty make dollars—many dollars! That mine duty!'

East appeared to be impressed by my appeal to his better nature, and the skipper, seeing it, went off into a fit of rage.

His trembling wife took charge of him, and I half

LIFE AND ADVENTURE AT FOOCHOW

dragged East to the fore part of the house. Then we summoned the mate and crew aft, and asked them the crucial question, which master they would serve.

The Malays said they would obey us. The mate decided that he also would stand by us, if we would pay him well.

East agreed to his terms. The yards were trimmed, and our course was shaped for the White Dogs. It was now nearly dark: therefore we shortened sail, that we might not get too near the land before daylight: the old craft, however, was not a clipper.

By the time all this was complete, the skipper had come to himself, and, in a very subdued frame of mind, was permitting his poor wife to dress his injured hand.

The wretched man seemed to have lost heart since his plan had failed. He returned me my revolver, and volunteered in spiteful tones the information that a typhoon was approaching.

There was indeed every appearance of this; but as the wind was still steady from the north-east, I was rather pleased than otherwise, as I calculated that the skipper would be only too glad to hurry into Foochow River to escape the coming storm.

He, however, doggedly refused to take charge. He argued that he was now ruined for life; that what he had endeavoured to do would be brought up against him; that he had lost his last chance, and that he did not now care what became of his ship and all on board.

This put us in a nice predicament. We dared not attempt to make the passage: all we could do was to keep the schooner under the shortest sail possible until daylight.

When at last the dawn broke, we found that we were close to the mouth of the river; but not a pilot nor a fishing-boat was in sight, as the typhoon was rapidly coming on. The skipper remained inexorably despairing. We were all welcome to drown, for aught he cared.

We had but slight hope of hitting the entrance, and we were feeling pretty blank, when the little German wife cried out suddenly:

'Mein husband, mein husband! *I* can pilot the ship as well as you can. *I* will take her in!'

Whereupon this plucky little soul laid hold of the wheel, whilst we strong men obeyed her orders; and, with half a gale behind us and a flood tide below, we scudded at a steamer's pace through the hazardous entrance and on up the river to Kuantao, where a Chinese pilot came on board, and hurried us up to Pagoda Anchorage, where we arrived just before the mighty cyclone burst in all its force over the country round.

Directly the Chinese pilot had taken charge, our poor little heroine brought her husband to us, and entreated that we would say nothing to the authorities of his wild attempt to run away.

'Mein husband,' she pleaded tearfully, 'is ruined for life. His work of all the long years is lost. He is distraught with rage and despair. Have pity on us!'

I was deeply touched with the woman's goodness to her bearish husband, and the remembrance weighed with me that her courage and prompt seamanship had probably saved our lives. East and I mutually promised to say nothing of the attempt to escape, but to put in a good word for them to the Commissioner of Customs.

The Captain besought us also, as a very great favour, to permit him to fly his own national flag at his mast-head when nearing the anchorage.

He explained to us that he had traded out of Foochow for so many years. He was known and respected by everybody there. The disgrace would be too bitter if the Customs flag should be hoisted without his beloved 'spread eagle' ensign!

East promised him this favour also; but, to my astonishment, as soon as we came in sight of the shipping, the

Chinese flag alone floated at the mast-head. We found that the three other confiscated vessels had arrived before us, having all been towed down from Wen-Chou.

I was indeed delighted and thankful to get back safe on board the old 'Spartan'—to have again a good wholesome meal, of which I had been deprived for á few days.

The captured vessels were all declared confiscated property, without a word of protest from their respective Consuls. All, however, but the 'Amoy Trader' were, I believe, permitted to be redeemed by payment of a heavy fine. The unfortunate Captain of that schooner, and his wife, were turned on shore with only their personal effects, and they were dependent upon the charity of the other Captains for a temporary home.

East was directed to submit a written report of the voyage to the Commissioner of Customs. This document I never saw; but the mate and the Malay crew were, I believe, rewarded.

Tide-waiters were placed on board each of the vessels until their cases had been decided. It was my lot to be on board the 'Amoy Trader' when the Captain and his wife came to collect their effects.

I fully expected to be abused for my unwilling share in their misfortunes; but to my surprise they came up to me, saying mournfully—

'You good Englishman! You keep your word. You say nothing; but that —— Yankee, he write to Foochow, and tell all about it!'

East, I discovered, had given himself great credit for bringing in the schooner; and he doubtless got his reward, which I did not envy him.

I, for my part, quietly pursued my studies, and was recompensed by the increasing appreciation of Mr. Maxwell, who, the following year, selected me to accompany him to Formosa.

CHAPTER III

DESCRIPTION OF THE ISLAND OF FORMOSA

THE 'Ilha Formosa,' to give it its Portuguese name, or 'Tai-wan,' according to its Chinese appellation, is one of the largest islands in the Eastern seas. It is situated between 22 and 26° North latitude, and 120 and 122° East longitude, being separated by a channel some hundred miles in width from the adjacent mainland of China, of which it was a political dependency until 1896, when it was ceded to the Japanese, upon the conclusion of the war.

It forms the end of one of the many chains of islands, which, from the western part of Russian America to the southern archipelagos, seem to fringe the eastern coasts of the Asiatic continent with a succession of long loops, and it terminates that of which the Japanese group, the Loochoos, and the Meiaco-Sima group, are the component parts.

The length of this important island is about 235 miles, by 70 to 90 in its widest part, and it is intersected by a range of lofty and densely wooded mountains which follow the general direction of the island from north to south, forming a huge backbone or ridge, the highest peak of which, Mount Morrison, is more than 12,000 feet high. The island runs from north-east to south-west, and its shape is that of a long oval running down to a point at the south, with a circumference of some 450 miles.

When the Portuguese first visited this great island, in the sixteenth century, they were so enraptured with its

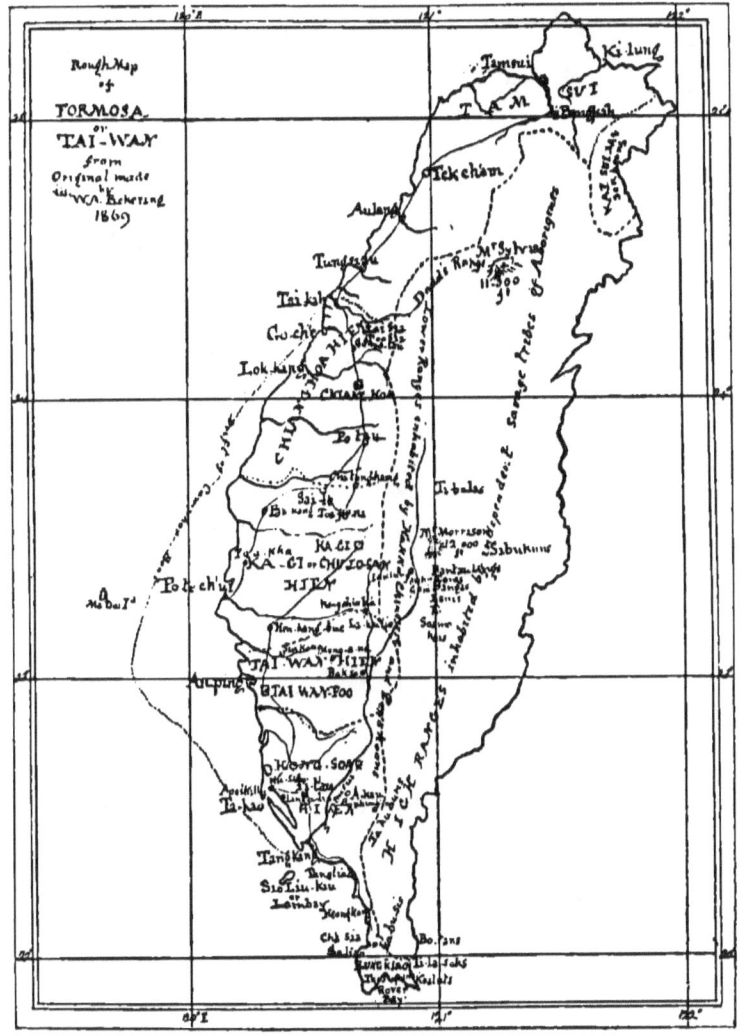

tropical beauty that they bestowed upon it the name of Ilha Formosa, or the Beautiful Island. Few names have been more correctly chosen. Formosa is indeed majestic in its beauty.

Coasting along the little known eastern side, the voyager is repeatedly struck by the magnificence of the scenery. In the far background a range of mountains rises to a height of about 12,000 feet, whilst between it and the water are numerous peaks of an elevation at least half as great. Domes, spirals, and wall-like precipices succeed each other in imposing variety. A luxuriant vegetation clothes their sides, down which dash cascades that shine like molten silver in the tropical sunlight.

These lordly mountains descend, in a steep slope, to the blue waters of the Pacific Ocean, where the Kuro Siwo, or Japanese Gulf Stream, flows to the north-east at the rate of some fifty miles in the twenty-four hours, thus preventing any such alluvial formation as is found on the west coast of the island. At intervals from December to March these highest ranges are tipped with snow, and the scenery in the valleys is entrancingly beautiful.

Anon, on rounding a headland, a deep gorge is revealed, and, in the shelter of the overshadowing heights, one sees a dim outline of some native village; for, behind those mountains, in their impregnable territory of forest and crag, lurk the savage tribes of aborigines, their hand against the Chinese, and every Celestial hand against them.

Following the coast southwards, one rounds the South Cape, of which the two most prominent hills are named Nansha and Ma-ke-tou, which are frequently capped with clouds.

There is a quaint Chinese legend which affirms that two spirits, in the guise of men, the one clothed in vermilion, the other in white, used to play chess upon these hills; but of this there is now no evidence, except the existence of a large flat-topped stone, shaped like a chess-board.

The coast at this point is rugged and dangerous, and, in my day, woeful indeed was the fate of any mariner who might chance to be wrecked upon this inhospitable shore. The Koaluts, a savage tribe, would unfailingly make short work of him, for the sake of preserving his skull for a trophy. But of these native wreckers, and their treatment of survivors, I shall have more to say in a later chapter.

We now approach the western coast of the island, where Chinese occupation may be considered to begin. Viewed from this side of the island, the slope of the mountains is much more gradual, and is intersected by valleys which imperceptibly lose themselves in the large undulating plain stretching from north to south, upon which the Chinese have settled. It is not difficult to explain the attraction which the south-western portion of the coast undoubtedly had for the early Dutch settlers; for, viewed from shipboard, it must have been strongly suggestive of their beloved Holland.

Unlike Dutchland, however, the most extraordinary feature of this coast is the rapidity with which the land is gaining upon the sea.

In 1624, shortly after achieving their independence, the Dutch sent a fleet from Java, and took possession of this western coast of Formosa. They settled at the spot now occupied by the capital, Taiwanfoo, and built a fort on the seashore, off which their ships were lying. This fort they called 'Providentia.' They also built another and larger fort upon an adjacent island, and gave it the name of 'Zelandia.' Providentia is now inside the city of Taiwanfoo, four miles from the sea, and Zelandia is the Anping settlement connected with Taiwanfoo by a plain some three miles wide and ten miles long.

There is an old Dutch picture which depicts Fort Zelandia with the richly laden argosies of the Dutch East

DESCRIPTION OF THE ISLAND

Indian Company, drawing many feet of water, anchored close to the fort; and so rapid has been the encroachment of the land that the British Consulate stands where the war junks used to lie, and mud banks have formed an increasingly shallow bar half a mile beyond the spot where, within the memory of the present inhabitants, the gunboats had their anchorage.

This rapid encroachment of the land upon the sea is due to several causes, principally to the extraordinary violence of the typhoons which occur during the south-west monsoon, the period from June to October. The velocity and violence of the winds during the height of these storms is beyond belief; the rain falls in torrents, and is swept, in steam-like masses, along the ground, whilst the rivers appear to be lifted bodily from their beds, rushing down from the mountains with overwhelming force, and bearing an enormous amount of sediment to the sea-shore, where the violence of the south-west winds prevents this accumulation from being carried out to sea, thus forming a great delta upon the western coast. These typhoons do not extend far into the Formosa Strait. There is but one case on record of their having reached Amoy; and northward of Formosa they are of rare occurrence. But to the east of Formosa they extend as far as the Bonin Islands, and probably right across the Pacific.

Another cause of this continued alteration of the outline of the coast is the frequent occurrence of volcanic shocks. It is probable that Formosa was once a portion of the Chinese coast, but was severed by an earthquake at some remote period. The island now inclines, however slowly, to reunite itself with the mainland.

This stratum of mud banks does not tend to make the western coast comparable, on the score of wild and romantic beauty, with the less-known eastern side. Beyond the shallow stretch of water, with its banks of sand and mud, there extends a fertile alluvial plain, about 180 miles in length, with an average breadth of about 30 miles. This plain is dotted with isolated hills, which have doubtless within a comparatively recent period been small islands. Beyond this plain the mountains rise, in appearance not unlike a succession of terraces, which probably suggested to the Chinese the name they have given the island—Taiwan, the Terrace Beach, or Bay of the Raised Terraces.

There are several rivers descending to this plain; but, owing to the very short distance they have to run, and to the quantities of deposits they wash down from the mountains, they are so obstructed by shoals and bars as to be useless for navigation. Some of these rivers have beds three miles in width, in the dry season containing merely a small rivulet in the centre, whilst in the wet season they are roaring torrents. The sand of these riverbeds appears to be composed of slate fragments, the stones being water-worn slate, rounded by marine action probably, in the days when the sea extended inland, possibly to the range of slate hills at the base of the mountain range.

The most southerly port on the western or Chinese coast is Takao. The harbour is shallow, and the part where vessels lie is becoming daily more contracted, as the drift sand fills up the lagoon, and is carried out by the force of the tide to the entrance. Crossing the bar, the entrance to the harbour is through a chasm of some seventy-five yards wide. To the northward is a rocky bluff composed of limestone masses, beyond which rises, some 1,800 feet in height, the rugged, barren sides of Ape's Hill, so called because it is inhabited by a community of large monkeys; whilst on the south side is a smaller point of 180 feet, called the Saracen's Head, bounded on the seaface by a line of precipitous cliffs rising directly from the water's edge. Between the two heads is a small, greenlooking mound separated from Ape's Hill by a chasm, and from the other point by a deep channel about sixty yards wide, which forms the entrance to the inner harbour.

TAKAO, SOUTH SIDE - MESSRS. ELLES & CO.'S HOUSE AND GODOWNS

This is some six or eight miles long by two or three across in the widest part, forming a calm, placid lagoon, bounded on the north by a flat, rich-looking plain, covered with banyan and pandanus or screw pine, and cultivated with sweet potatoes, and on the south by a low sand bank, reaching from Saracen's Head to an extension of the plain, whereon the town of Takao is situated.

In this inner harbour one sees with curiosity a number of quaint boats, used by the Chinese who fish in these waters. These 'catamarans,' as they are called by Europeans, are simply large rafts of stout bamboo lashed together, and propelled either by the ordinary Chinese paddle or by a large bamboo sail fitted in the usual manner. They have a slight railing round them, and also a large tub in which the passenger sits; and though they look most frail and insecure, as the waves repeatedly dash over them, yet they are doubtless the safest kind of boat to cope with the heavy swells which lash the whole of the Formosan coast. In appearance they somewhat resemble the Brazilian jangadas, or corkwood rafts, which are found in the neighbourhood of Pernambuco.

Takao presents the ordinary unsavoury characteristics of a small Chinese town. It is chiefly inhabited by fishermen, with here and there a semi-European residence occupied by some foreign settler. It is only saved from being quite uninteresting by the varied and beautiful foliage of the bamboo and banyan groves, which grow luxuriously even in the barren sandy soil. To the north a magnificent view is to be obtained from the summit of Ape's Hill, which is a huge mass of ancient coral limestone, and contains some curious caves and rifts, filled with shells and bones of fishes. One crosses a small bay, wherein is a sulphur spring, and, following a path which winds irregularly up the hill from this point, one is amply repaid for the steep climb by the glorious view which is revealed. Seawards roll the breakers, forming a high white line of surf, roaring stertorously, and beating upon the shore as though in an impotent rage with its encroaching enemy, the land. Landwards there is a mass of rich tropical vegetation bordering the river, with all the varied beauty of colour and form of pandanus or screw pines, palms, mimosas, and similar trees. Beyond, again, spreads a level fertile plain, giving pleasing evidence of the usual rich cultivation of the Chinese, sown with emerald-hued rice and slender sugar canes, and dotted here and there by groups of bamboos, which add further variety to the foliage, or perchance by a small village—to which distance lends picturesqueness—whilst far away the view is bounded by the low range of hills. On very clear days, notably at sunrise, the purple tops of lofty mountains are to be seen far away to the east, forming a noble background.

There are but few towns near Takao: the chief and largest is that of Pi-t'au, to which one has access by first proceeding by boat to the little village of Ling-a-liau, and thence by a good road, either on horseback or by chair, for about seven miles through the richly cultivated fields of the plain. Another town, which was once the district capital, but is now partly deserted, lies five or six miles to the north of Takao. A band of robbers having made themselves an impregnable retreat in the hills above, from which they could command the town, the mandarins wisely removed their establishments to the safer locality of Pi-t'au.

There is capital snipe-shooting to be had among the marshy river districts in the neighbourhood of Takao, and good fishing.

Following the western coast slightly further north, we arrive at the port of Anping ; the capital of Formosa, Taiwanfoo, lying about three miles inland. This port is merely an open roadstead with an anchorage of some six fathoms, and a series of flat sandy banks, whereon the

FORT ZELANDIA (BUILT BY THE DUTCH ON THEIR OCCUPATION OF FORMOSA, 1630), ANPING (PORT OF TAIWANFOO)

DESCRIPTION OF THE ISLAND 31

surf breaks violently, dividing it from a shallow muddy lagoon stretching away to a flat plain. Along these mud and sand banks lies the village of Anping, clustering around the ruins of the old Formosan stronghold of the Dutch, whereon, over the main entry leading into the fort on the northern side, one can still decipher the inscription—TE CASTEL ZELAND, GEBOWED ANNO 1630.

This fort consisted of a central keep, built upon a small and probably partly artificial hill, in the shape of a bastioned fort upon a square of about sixty yards each way. At about a hundred yards distant on the northern side, this was surrounded by a wall which followed the course of the coast line and met the keep at its western and northern angles. The walls, though hollow in the centre, were of great thickness, built of a peculiar small brick, brought expressly from Batavia, and were extensively loopholed.

This once impregnable old fortress has succumbed to the gradual forces of time and repeated shocks of earthquake. Not one of the angles of the central keep remains; the walls are split and broken, and a large banyan tree, growing upon the top of the wall of the keep, waves gnarled and knotted branches, rustling a soft requiem to the long past glories of Zelandia. Its chief use now is as a landmark for ships making the port of Anping.

Crossing in catamarans through the surf on the bar between the shipping and the shore, one lands on the beach near the fort, round which clusters a squalid little fishing village. Passing through this we reach a large alluvial plain, which is apparently of recent formation, as during the south-west monsoon it is still always partially covered with water. Through this plain run canals, which form a medium of communication with the prefectural city of Taiwanfoo, three miles away.

The city is nearly five miles in circumference. It is enclosed, in the customary Chinese manner, by a high battlemented wall, quadrangular in shape, with four gates and watch-towers over them, forming in fact a poor and small imitation of the Great Wall of Pekin. This wall is about twenty feet high, built of brick, and is plastered with mud. It is now but of little use for purposes of protection, as, owing to the violent rains and the frequent shocks of earthquake, it is in a very dilapidated state, riddled with gaps in various places, through which a hostile army could pass into the city with comparative ease.

A walk around these walls, however, repays one. Looking to the seaward of the city wall, one sees a large and extensive suburb, which contains the public markets, and, though dirty and offensive, after the manner of Chinese towns, it is here that the business of the place is done. Turning one's face to the interior of the city, it is a pleasant surprise to note the luxuriance of the foliage, the green lanes, the open, park-like spaces—lovely groves of bamboo and wide-spreading aged banyan trees giving a refreshing and rural aspect to the large and straggling town. Amongst the green branches of the trees one gets a glimpse of the houses of the mandarins, the chief citizens, and several temples dedicated to the three religions of the Chinese Empire—Confucianism, Buddhism, and Taouism. Many of the houses, though forming streets, have a rural seclusion secured to them by thick bamboo fences or cactus hedges in front. The only real street in the town —one in which there are some fair shops—is that leading from the west gate to the Tao-tai's yamen or palace.

Adjoining the Tao-tai's yamen is a large examination hall, fitted with stone benches and seats of slabs of granite sufficient to hold one thousand competitors for the degree of Siu-Tsai or Bachelor of Arts. In this place there is a large and curious tower, built of red bricks, rising to a height of about fifty feet, wherein the devout Celestials were wont, with reverent hands, to place the god who watched over literature, named Wên-ch'ang.

INSIDE CITY, TAIWANFOO

CALIFORNIA

TAIWANFOO—PART OF CITY WALL

DESCRIPTION OF THE ISLAND

In the centre of the city is a small square fort, Providentia, which was also built by the Dutch, but like its larger sister Zelandia it has succumbed to the influences of time and neglect, and is now merely a picturesque ruin.

Outside the north gate of the city there is a large green space of about fifteen acres in extent, marked by its two poles and its temple-like house. This sward is of melancholy interest as the place of execution of many shipwrecked Europeans during the first China War.

Outside the east gate there extends a considerable suburb with orchards and market gardens. Beyond this are level fields of waving yellow rice, and in the far distance again rise the immense chain of mountains in the interior.

Beyond the great south gate one views a vast graveyard of many acres in extent, where white tombstones glisten drearily amongst the sandy desolation.

Near the small south gate, outside the city wall, there is a fine temple to the Goddess of Mercy, but, perhaps because the worship of this deity is falling into disrepute, the erection is rapidly decaying through neglect.

Taiwanfoo is at the best nothing more than a typical Chinese town. One would see its characteristics repeated, with but few essential changes, throughout China.

The climate of the Formosan capital is exceedingly fine —dry, clear, and bracing—except for an occasional 'northeaster,' when the air is filled with sand and dust, making the houses in a very dirty state, and rendering peregrination joyless while it lasts.

Pursuing our course northwards up the western coast, we now reach the port of Tamsui, or 'Fresh-water-town.' This port would seem to have a better future before it, as it has a more accessible harbour, and therefore greater facilities for trade. The anchorage, however, is insecure, being formed of shifting sand. The town lies between a double-peaked hill on the south-west, which has an elevation of about 1,700 feet, and the Tamsui range of mountains, which rise to the height of 2,800 feet and extend far into the interior.

A small river, issuing from a gorge, empties itself into the harbour. This river has its source near the city of Bangkah or Mangkia, one of the largest and most exclusive of the northern towns of the island.

Upon a hill on the right bank of the Tamsui River there is an old Dutch fort, part of which is now used as a consular residence, of which one can find no European account, and which itself bears no inscription of record of the past. It is in a fair state of preservation, though damp and deserted, and said by the natives to be haunted. It serves as a guide to the entrance to the harbour.

The rainfall is heavy in Tamsui and the whole of northern Formosa, thus rendering the air cold and humid.

The Bangkah people have executed one laborious engineering work, which is of great benefit to this district. The water supplied by the springs of their marshy district was found to be brackish and unwholesome. They therefore formed a scheme for bringing down a mountain stream to supply the populations of the plain. A suitable stream was discovered about eight miles in the interior from Bangkah, rushing down the mountain side in what was then, some sixty years ago, savage territory. The Chinese proceeded to destroy the savage hamlet in the neighbourhood, and drove the aborigines up into their fastnesses in the mountains. They then cut a tunnel into the foot of the mountain, sixteen yards long, eight feet broad, and about fourteen feet deep, gradually diverting the course of the stream into their channel. This work was by no means easy, as the labourers were frequently attacked by the deposed savages, and about sixty of their number were killed before its completion. The water, which is very sweet and fresh, is directed, in a prepared

DESCRIPTION OF THE ISLAND

channel of from three to four feet deep, into the village of Kieng-bay, about two hours' walk eastward of Bangkah. This village is built upon the two high banks of an affluent of the main river, and has therefore an aqueduct to conduct the water across, running from bank to bank about thirty feet above the river. This aqueduct is *three-sided*, formed of thick wooden planks battened together, with wood nailed *quadrilaterally* round it. The interior is rendered watertight by being lined with Chinese plaster, or chunaum. It is about five feet deep, by eight feet broad, and has forty-seven crutch-like supports.

A considerable amount of tea is grown on the Tamsui hills, and, though not of superfine quality, it is sufficiently good to give scope for far more enterprise than has been devoted to it. However, since my day, owing to the efforts of Mr. John Dodd, this industry has greatly improved, the tea being favourably known in the market as Formosa Oolong.

Tamsui also exports a large amount of coal.

To the north-east of Tamsui lies Kilung, which is the last port upon the northern coast. This was formerly a Spanish settlement, but it was subsequently captured and held by the Dutch until they were forced to evacuate the island. Its surroundings are far more beautiful and picturesque than the scenery of the western coast. The port itself is situated on the shores of a wide bay, between the capes of Foki and Petou, some twenty-two miles apart. In this bay, about two miles from the actual harbour, there uprises a tall black rock called Kilung Island.

The scenery behind the village is very charming; undulating, well-wooded hills gradually resolve themselves into the mountain range beyond. The varied outline of these heights tells of earthquake and of their volcanic origin. Yellow sandstone and masses of coraline limestone abound.

Kilung is a great coal-mining neighbourhood. The mines are situated in a bay known to Europeans as 'Coal Harbour.' In my time they were worked in Chinese manner, horizontally, producing a small bituminous mineral, which was exported in large quantities. European enterprise has, however, brought modern methods and machinery into use in the mines, with satisfactory results, and those interested have at length become alive to the important source of wealth which lies hidden in the coalfields of northern Formosa. There are now two railroads in this district, which greatly facilitate the distribution of the produce of the mines.

Slight earthquakes are of frequent occurrence throughout the island, as also are typhoons, in the south, at the breaking up of the monsoons.

There is but one fresh water lake of any size in Formosa. This lies among the high mountain ranges, some three days' journey from the city of Chiang-hoa, to the south-east. It is a beautiful expanse of water, which glitters like a lake of glass upon the green plain in the clear tropical atmosphere, causing the Chinese, who looked wonderingly down upon it from their mountains, to name it Polisia (glassy).

This lake was visited in 1873 by the Rev. W. Campbell, who gave it the name of Lake Candidius, in memory of that single-hearted Dutch pastor who began Protestan missionary work in the island about 1624. And as Lake Candidius it figures in all the recent maps of Formosa.

With regard to the fauna of Formosa, in the mountains are to be found the black climbing bear, the leopard armadillo, monkeys, the wild boar, and deer—the antlers of the latter may be purchased from the savages—the wild dog or coyote, gibbons and apes, badger and anteater, while weasels, flying squirrel, a species of leveret and musk rats are common everywhere. Mention must also be made of a peculiar kind of hog with dorsal bristles,

DESCRIPTION OF THE ISLAND

and the piebald pig. Snakes of many descriptions abound, mostly harmless, though the cobra de capello has been seen. There are numberless lizards, a poisonous water-snake, and a vividly marked and poisonous sea-snake.

There are also innumerable species of insects: flying beetles, centipedes, mosquitoes, mantis, and various grass-hoppers, etc., while residence in the Taiwanfoo district is rendered miserable during the winter months and sugar season by myriads of flies and fleas. It is, however, the paradise of the entomologist, on account of the magnificent butterflies and moths to be obtained.

The rivers contain an abundance of fish, with their attendant otters on the banks.

During the months of December and January the sea literally swarms with 'black fish,' a species of large grey mullet, and a fish the shape and size of a large chad, with a skin like a sole but the flavour of a turbot. These shoals are eagerly looked forward to by the natives, when the fish come down from the Japan seas to spawn; and the fisher-men's nets are often broken and the catamarans swamped with the amount of fish they take. Fin whales are seen along the coast, and sharks, said not to be man-eating, are common, the fins prepared being exported as a Chinese delicacy.

During the north-east monsoon, in the marshes round Takao and Taiwanfoo, Europeans can have splendid sport amongst the pheasants, snipe, and golden plover which are plentiful in the sugar and rice fields. In the marshes by the sea-shore all kinds of water-fowl abound. Out at sea they may be counted by the thousand, and the natives net them for sale in considerable numbers before their early morning flight seawards.

With respect to the geological features of Formosa I am not qualified to speak with authority. I, however, know that on the east coast some adventurous Chinese, at the risk of their lives, did a little gold-washing in the streams of the savage territory. Gold-washing also now goes on regularly in the north. The precious metal has also been found near Lung Kiao, and between Takao and Taiwanfoo. Auriferous quartz is known to exist in various other places, whilst lead and silver are also present in the island. In the north, coal, sulphur, and petroleum abound. In the high mountains of the interior, shale and slate are the principal feature, whilst at Kilung, in the north-east, within the influence of the warm Gulf Stream, and at Takao, in the south-west, coral reefs appear. Near the latter port, almost at the summit of Ape's Hill, 1,500 feet above the sea-level, there is to be seen a stratum of shells identical in species with those found on the coral reefs in the sea below.

As regards the flora of the island, there are innumerable rare and beautiful plants to be studied, and I believe that Mr. Veitch and other ardent botanists have enriched our conservatories with many beautiful orchids and ornamental plants transported from Formosa. There is still, however, much scope for the collector, as the most interesting half of the island, the mountainous portion, has not been botanised over, except in a meagre way by native collectors in the southern part, and in the north by one or two Europeans, who have made short excursions from Tamsui. The Rev. W. Campbell some years ago made, in the centre of the island, a collection which was, however, unluckily much injured by accidental immersion in a flooded stream while it was being taken coast-ward. This collection is now embodied, so far as it was available, in the herbarium of the British Museum.

Fruit is abundant. Large and beautiful pineapples grow wild in the lanes round the towns ; the Sai-lé loose-skinned oranges are delightful and wholesome ; mangoes, lungans, bananas, soft-squash or custard apples, pumeloes, persimmons, and pomegranates secure ideal fare for the vegetarian.

DESCRIPTION OF THE ISLAND

The commercial products of the island are various, and capable of almost unlimited extension. The first in value is rice. Formosan rice is both abundant and of very fine quality, and it has earned for the island the title of the 'granary of China.'. The export is entirely in native hands, and considerable quantities are shipped to the Pescadores.

Tea, which is found wild in the interior, is extensively cultivated near Tamsui, from which port a large export is carried on. The greater part of the Formosan tea goes to America; some is consumed by the Chinese in the Straits and the Dutch East Indies. The latter kind is scented.

Sugar is also largely grown. In my time, a considerable quantity of a fine white kind was exported to Japan and Australia, but this industry has greatly deteriorated of late years owing to neglect.

Indigo, turmeric, sesamum seed, hemp, and hard woods are also plentiful. Sulphur is found near Takao, and in large quantities near Tamsui and elsewhere, whilst there are numerous sulphur springs in the island, both hot and cold. There are petroleum wells at Toa-kho-ham, which could be turned to great account. The castor oil plant grows wild, and is cultivated. Camphor of the best kind is extracted from the Camphor Laurus tree (found in the high mountains of the interior), and forms an article of trade, especially with China.

This by no means exhausts the list of Formosan products. The possibilities of this still undeveloped country, both in vegetable and mineral wealth, may be imagined when one learns that during the year 1893 trade to the value of four and a half million pounds sterling passed through the ten or twelve European houses doing business in Formosa.

CHAPTER IV

HISTORY OF THE ISLAND

THE Chinese claim to have been the discoverers of Formosa, in A.D. 1430, the event being due to the accident of a shipwreck. But whether this was so or not, no great honour can be claimed, as the bold outline of the Formosan mountain ranges can be seen on a clear day from the highlands on the Chinese coast.

The Portuguese were the pioneers of Europe in the East, and there are records that they visited Formosa in 1590. But they do not appear to have made any permanent settlement there.

The Spaniards are said to have built two forts, one at Tamsui and the other at Kilung, in the north, the ruins of which still exist. There is, however, now no tradition amongst the natives of their occupation. The only trace I could find of them was when an old Sek-hoan, giving me a vocabulary of his nearly forgotten language, told me that his grandfather used to count in a different way; and, to my surprise, the man repeated a corruption of the Spanish numerals up to ten.

The Chinese annals also assert that in 1620 the Japanese attempted to form a colony in Formosa; but previous to this date considerable numbers of Chinese must have crossed the channel from the mainland and settled themselves among the aborigines, for when the Dutch arrived in 1624, and prepared to establish themselves in Formosa, they found there communities of Chinese in sufficient numbers to cause them annoyance.

DOCUMENTS IN LANGUAGE OF CIVILISED ABORIGINES, PRESERVED FROM TIME OF DUTCH OCCUPATION, 1650

HISTORY OF THE ISLAND

It was in the year 1624, shortly after achieving their independence, that the Dutch sent from Java a fleet, which, after an unsuccessful attack on the Portuguese at Macao, took possession of the Pescadores Islands. By threats and promises of the Chinese, the Dutch were induced to evacuate the Pescadores, and to pay their attention to the west coast of Formosa. They settled at the spot now occupied by the capital, Taiwanfoo, and proceeded to build their two great forts, Zelandia and Providentia. They appear to have used every effort to civilise the wild inhabitants of the plain. They introduced good laws and promoted useful industries, appointing officers to each tribe to administer the laws under the governor. Their missionaries, also, were having great success; churches and schools were multiplying, and thousands of converts were baptized. They reduced some of the languages to writing, and their labours, in the shape of vocabularies of now obsolete dialects, exist. The colonists were also beginning to intermarry with the natives. So beneficent was the Dutch rule that their memory is still beloved by the aborigines, and, even to this day, some of these people, though they have entirely forgotten their old language, and are scarcely to be distinguished from the Chinese amongst whom they dwell, yet retain a traditional regard for those estimable men. They cherish, as sacred heirlooms, documents which have been handed down from the times when the missionaries laboured amongst their ancestors, and they welcome any Europeans as being, in their eyes, relations of the Dutch. Unfortunately, however, at that time the Dutch were cultivating commercial relations with Japan; and the Netherlands East Indian Government, fearing to excite the anger of the emperor of that country by spreading Christianity, discouraged the efforts of their missionaries in Formosa.

A few years before this date, the Spanish and Portuguese missionaries had been converting whole districts in

Japan to Christianity. Intoxicated with their success, the Fathers began to quarrel amongst themselves, and to intrigue with the natives against the established government of the country. The emperor rightly determined to stop this movement. He carried out his determination in a fashion cruel indeed, but pretty prevalent at that period even amongst professedly Christian nations in Europe. The priests paid the penalty of their imprudence by banishment or death, which they met with the greatest fortitude and heroism. Thousands of their Japanese converts suffered martyrdom with the most horrible tortures rather than renounce their newly acquired faith. Christianity was proscribed throughout the empire, and all Europeans were forbidden to reside within its dominions, except on the condition that they should be confined to a small island called Desima, that they should only be permitted to send one or two vessels yearly to Japan, and that annually they should all perform the ceremony of trampling upon the Cross, to evince their detestation of Christianity.

The Dutch alone consented to these degrading terms; and under these prohibitions they continued to reside at Desima, carrying on a lucrative but declining trade with Japan until the year 1858, when the country was opened out to foreign commerce by the American fleet under Commodore Perry. During that long interval, I am glad to say, the descendants of the first native Christians in many cases continued steadfast to their religion, which they were compelled to practise in secret.

Thus it was the fear of losing Japanese trade which caused the Dutch East Indian Government to hinder the progress of Christianity in Formosa. They paid the penalty of their pusillanimity some thirty years later, when they were driven out of Taiwan by the Chinese.

In 1640, the Chinese native dynasty, Ming, which had enjoyed uninterrupted power for more than two hundred years, had fallen into a state of utter corruption and decay. The people, therefore, refused any longer to obey the powers that were, as, according to Chinese ideas handed down from Confucius and Mencius, when an emperor or dynasty evinces by its conduct that it has forsaken the principles of truth and justice, they consider that it has forfeited the mandate conferred by Heaven to rule the Celestial Empire: *ergo*, the people have a right to rebel, and to depose the existing government.

Upon this occasion the Chinese invoked the assistance of the Manchu Tartars. These allies responded willingly enough, but they were not content with overthrowing the Ming dynasty. When they had overrun and subdued sixteen of the eighteen provinces of the empire, they proceeded to instal themselves as a new dynasty, under the title of 'Ts'ing,' or 'Pure,' which has continued the reigning dynasty at Pekin to the present day.

The new powers found themselves sufficiently strong to compel the Chinese, under penalty of death in case of refusal, to adopt the Tartar fashion, and to shave the front of the hair, which they formerly wore long, and to braid the back part into a queue, or tail, hanging down behind. This is the form in which the Chinese still wear their hair—a mode which we term a pig-tail.

Though this fashion began as a mark of degradation and servitude, the Chinese have grown to be proud of it, as distinguishing them from the 'outer barbarians.'

In every political outbreak in China, however, the first thing the rebels do is to let their hair grow, in order thereby to show their detestation of the Manchu rule.

The inhabitants of the only two unsubdued provinces, Canton and Fuh-kien, continued to resist the invaders stubbornly for some years; and even when they were compelled to capitulate, numbers preferred to lose their heads rather than submit to the degradation of the tonsure. The Fuh-kien Chinese are even now distinguished from the rest of the empire by turbans, which they adopted to hide the disgrace of shaving their heads.

The pig-tail is most useful in catching thieves, and also in Chinese warfare, which generally consists of two parties meeting together for a short time, one party running away, and the pursuers promptly inflicting indiscriminate slaughter upon the pursued. Thus many a poor fellow has lost his life owing to the hairy appendage hanging behind him.

One of the bravest of my followers in Formosa on one occasion only saved his head by sacrificing his tail. He had been drawn for the Chinese militia during a rebellion, and in an engagement where, as is generally the case, the rebels were victorious, he was taken prisoner. His captor was dragging him away by his hair for immediate execution; when, availing himself of a favourable opportunity, he, with great presence of mind, snatched the rebel's knife out of his belt, slashed off his pig-tail, and escaped to fight or run away another day.

The last of the Chinese to hold out against the Tartar conquerors was Koshing or Koxinga, a notorious pirate of the time. This man collected an enormous fleet, with which he ravaged the whole of the southern coast of China. The Tartar emperor, however, acquired sufficient power to compel the coast population of the southern provinces to remove ten miles into the interior, leaving the country behind them a desert. This stratagem deprived Koxinga of supplies, and, being obliged to find some other field for his operations, he proceeded to turn his attention to Formosa, and attacked the Dutch settlement at Taiwanfoo.

It is curious that amongst the natives of the island oral traditions about Koxinga, or Teh-kok-seng as they call him, have survived to the present day. According to their tales, Koxinga saw in a dream Fort Zelandia and the surrounding country, and the dream proceeded to inform him that the goal of his ambition would be reached within a short space of time after his arriving at the place thus

HISTORY OF THE ISLAND 45

mysteriously revealed to him. No definite instructions were in this dream vouchsafed to him, though he imagined the island to lie in the direction of Batavia. He had, however, a further convenient vision, which gave him the necessary information. He therefore fitted out a fleet in three portions, and sent them to sea with sealed orders.

At this time there was a want of harmony between the Dutch government in Java and the governor of Formosa. The result was that reinforcements for the Formosan garrison were diverted to the coast of China. Koxinga blockaded the coast of Formosa, and found sympathisers amongst his countrymen, the Chinese who were settled in the island, whose numbers had been largely increased by refugees from the mainland of China. He contrived to cut off the communication between the two great forts, and compelled the surrender of the garrison in Fort Providentia. The Christian natives assisted the Dutch most loyally in their resistance; but after a siege of nine months, and the loss of eighteen hundred men, Fort Zelandia was obliged to surrender, and thus ended Dutch rule in Formosa, after the short period of twenty-eight years.

Koxinga treated the Dutch clergymen and schoolmasters, with their native converts, with peculiar severity, on account of the brave resistance they had made. He crucified great numbers, and nearly exterminated all.

Having done this, Koxinga conquered the whole west coast of the island, and settled down to rule as an independent monarch. His grandson, however—a weak man—was induced to visit the Emperor at Pekin; he was there ennobled [1] with the title of 'Sea-quelling Duke,' but detained; and Formosa, with the Pescadores, was thus added to the Celestial Empire.

In 1664 the English appeared in Formosa, and en-

---

[1] According to Dr. Wells Williams, the descendants of Koxinga and of Confucius are the only hereditary title-bearers amongst the Chinese. 'Middle Kingdom,' vol. i. p. 40.

deavoured to establish a trade with Koxinga's son, but this chieftain had little other idea of trade than as a means of helping himself to every curious commodity that the various ships brought, and levying heavy imposts upon their cargoes. It is true that a very advantageous treaty was entered into with him, but when Formosa became part of the Chinese Empire this treaty was of course ignored, and consequently the English ceased trading with the island.

In the last century Formosa was brought prominently before the notice of society in London by an impostor named George Psalmanazar, who professed to be a Japanese convert from the island, and who published in Latin a wonderful and fictitious account of its model government, flourishing towns, and civilised population. Amongst other marvels, he affirmed that in Formosa the sun shone directly down the chimneys. Dr. Johnson was a great admirer of Psalmanazar's intelligence, and had unbounded faith in his veracity. Upon one occasion when, in some club or coffee-house, a gentleman ventured to doubt the accuracy of some of the statements made by him, Dr. Johnson sternly rebuked him in words to this effect: 'Sir, you contradict George Psalmanazar; let me assure you, Sir, that you might just as well contradict a Bishop!'

The next occasion on which the English appear in Formosa was in 1842, when the transport 'Nerbudda' and the opium vessel 'Anne' were wrecked upon the west coast. The survivors of the crews were shut up in prison by the mandarins, and ultimately a hundred and eighty-seven of these unfortunate men were taken to a parade ground outside the city of Taiwanfoo, and executed.

When I first arrived in Taiwanfoo, the names of several of these prisoners were scribbled upon the walls of the granary wherein they were incarcerated, with calendars for checking the progress of time, such as schoolboys make to show how many days have to elapse before the holidays.

UNIV. OF
CALIFORNIA

GRANARY WHERE 187 BRITISH SUBJECTS, ex TRANSPORTS 'ANNIE' AND 'NERBUDDA' WERE IMPRISONED BEFORE EXECUTION, 1842—TAIWANFOO

HISTORY OF THE ISLAND 47

No adequate redress was demanded for these atrocities, and I may say that, after the Dutch evacuated Formosa, the chief experience which the Chinese officials and people had for many years of Europeans was that of plundering and ill-treating the crews of shipwrecked vessels.

By the treaty concluded between Great Britain and China at Tientsin in 1860, Formosa or Taiwan was at last thrown open to foreign trade, and the four ports, Tamsui and Kilung in the north, and Taiwanfoo and Takao in the south, were declared open ports; a British consul was appointed for the whole island, and a fixed tariff of all articles which could legally be imported and exported, on payment of the tariff duty, but without payment of further taxes, was drawn up and approved by both governments. Also about this time, with the consent of the ambassadors of the European Powers, the 'Maritime Customs' Service at all the Treaty Ports in China was formed, and placed under the supervision and control of Europeans in the employ and payment of the Chinese Government.

In 1871, some fifty-four Liu-Chiu sailors having been wrecked and murdered on the east coast of Formosa outside the Tao-tai's jurisdiction, the Japanese Government claimed redress from the Chinese, and, not receiving satisfaction, landed an army and occupied the district of Lungkiau, at the South Cape of Formosa, in 1874.

The difficulty, however, was arranged by Sir Thomas Wade, then our minister at Pekin, and the Japanese evacuated their position, having, by their presence and occupation, prepared the way for the Chinese to include that barbaric part of the island as a governmental district.

During the war between France and China in 1883-4, Formosa was blockaded by the French. Tamsui and Kilung were taken, and the Pescadores were also occupied. All these positions were, however, given up at the conclusion of the war, and, whilst the French effected very little in the north of Formosa, they suffered much loss from cholera in the Pescadores.

A prominent actor in the struggle with the French men-of-war who bombarded Kilung and Tamsui, was Liu-Ming-Chuan, who directed the Formosan defence, and was afterwards created the first Chinese governor of Formosa. This man was of singular enlightenment; and it is to be regretted that, through the corrupt supineness of those in authority at Pekin, he did not accomplish all that he had it in him to do for the good of Formosa and for the benefit of the Chinese Empire.

It is to Liu-Ming-Chuan that the island owes the division of territory which is recognised there now. In the year 1885 he divided the whole of Formosa and the Pescadores into four prefectures, subdividing these into eleven counties or districts and five sub-prefectures; two of the latter include all the eastern side of the island, while one of them covers the whole of the Pescadores group.

In 1895 Formosa and the Pescadores were occupied and annexed by the Japanese. The Chinese Government called in the help of the famous Black Flag warriors from the borders of Tonkin, under their redoubtable leader Liu-Yung-fu, who, on hearing that the Pekin Government had relinquished Formosa to the Japanese barbarians, obtained the authority of some of the officials and principal inhabitants, and proclaimed a 'republic.' It is to be doubted whether any of these patriots could imagine what form of government is implied by the term 'republic.' This romantic scheme, however, soon collapsed upon the appearance of the Japanese army. The general, Liu-Yung-fu, promptly escaped from the island in the disguise of a woman, with a baby in his arms. The capital was opened to the Japanese general, to the joy of the more respectable inhabitants, who had more to fear from their own mandarins and corrupt military protectors than from the new government of the 'dwarf slaves,' as they contemptuously chose to call the Japanese.

There is no possible doubt that, under a just and firm government, Formosa will be a most valuable acquisition to Japan, and in her success every civilised nation should rejoice. Much firmness and great tact will be required, as although the aborigines, both savage and semi-civilised, will cause little or no trouble, yet the Hak-kas, who have never submitted quietly even to the government of their own empire, will be amenable only to the sternest measures, and the large population of Fuh-kienese, whilst gladly accepting the protection of their conquerors in their commerce and agriculture, will in their hearts despise what they deem the rule of an inferior race, and will therefore be open to the influence of intrigue from the mainland.

As regards the European residents of Formosa, it is only too probable that, until the Chinese portion of the island is thoroughly subdued and pacified, both merchants and missionaries must suffer many inconveniences; but these should be borne with patience and sympathy, in view of the enormous difficulties to be overcome, and considering that ultimately, under the more enlightened Japanese rule, benefits must certainly be enjoyed which could never have been attained under the utterly corrupt, effete, and hopelessly anti-foreign régime of the Chinese.

CHAPTER V

RELIGIONS OF THE CHINESE INHABITANTS

THE Chinese of Formosa, like those upon the mainland of China, are in religion Confucianists, Buddhists, and Taoists. There can be no doubt that the China of to-day is the outcome of the mind of Confucius. Confucianism, however, can scarcely be termed a religion; it is rather a system of philosophical rules for the performance of social and political duties, giving small encouragement to any worship beyond that of ancestors.

Although both in the government and in the family the Chinaman has sadly degenerated from the high standard fixed by the sage, yet the superiority of the Chinese over all other Oriental nations, and, indeed, the fact of their very existence as an enormous united empire, composed as it is of so many provinces, populated by men speaking languages differing as much as French and German from English and Spanish—each man in favour of his own province and clan, and bitterly prejudiced against the others—is undoubtedly due to their possession of the teaching of Confucius in a written language which they can all understand. Confucianism, also, is the salt which has preserved the Chinese from sinking lower than they have done into the degrading superstitions of practical Buddhism and Taoism.

The chief end of Confucian philosophy is the inculcation of filial obedience, benevolence, righteousness, propriety, wisdom, and sincerity.

By filial piety, Confucius means not only obedience to

RELIGIONS OF CHINESE INHABITANTS 51

parents during their lifetime, but also worship of and service to them after their decease. He also commands obedience to the emperor as the father of the State, and to the officials as delegates of the emperor.

By wisdom, Confucius understands the knowledge of oneself, whilst the other virtues are of course intended to represent man's duty to his fellow-men.

With all this high and pure teaching, Confucius, in some instances, inculcates the most unrelenting revenge, and prevarication, polytheism, and fortune-telling are also countenanced by him. He does not recognise any relation on our part to a living Supreme Being; indeed he rather discourages the idea of a spiritual world, excepting only the spirits of parents.

Confucius says: 'Reverence the spirits, but keep them at a distance.' 'We do not know about this life; how can we know about a future one?'

He also bases his philosophy upon the supposition that man by nature is inherently good, and that by self-inspection and careful obedience to his rules one may attain the perfect ideal of an ancient sage. This ideal was the reward which he promised to his disciples, whilst the sages whom he held out as models were semi-mythical monarchs and ministers of state, who had drained the land of China after a great inundation, and had instructed the people in the useful arts and the rules of good government.

Now if man were indeed by nature good, and if this life were all, no teaching could be more suited to gain the end he desired than that of Confucius. We, however, all have daily experience that such is not the case; and men, either for want of comfort under misfortune and sorrow, or through a curiosity which seems implanted in their nature, must needs have belief in a future state, a world of spirits, and either one Supreme God or a multitude of supernatural deities.

Confucius, though he believed in the perfection of our nature, was not so foolish as to hold that 'force was no remedy.' On the contrary, he was of firm opinion that, while education was preferable, yet wholesome physical coercion was necessary to bring out the good qualities hidden beneath the evil practices.

The literati and the officials are by profession Confucianists, as a belief in his teaching is necessary to obtain office, whilst it is most useful in governing the people. Moreover, a knowledge of the classics shows a nice superiority over the unlettered multitude, who merely know enough of Confucius to teach them obedience, and to provide them also with a few good maxims to guide them in social and family life. The educated classes, however, in spite of their Confucian materialism, when in trouble, sickness, or distress, find in it but little support, and then they are glad to apply for comfort to Buddhist or Taoist priests, whom in their prosperity they affected to despise.

Buddhism, the religion founded by Sakyamuni or Gautama, the son of an Indian king, born B.C. 623, was officially introduced into China in A.D. 65, by the Emperor Ming Ti, who, hearing that, according to Confucius, 'sages existed in the west,' despatched ambassadors to India. In accordance with his invitation, Buddhist missionaries came to China, and under imperial sanction propagated their doctrine, which had already been surreptitiously introduced and had gained ground in the empire.

Buddhism is a system of good works and self-denial, by which its votaries may purify their life and attain perfection, and what they consider the summit of happiness —Nirvana, annihilation, or absorption into the Buddha.

As, however, perfect purity of life is not to be attained in this one existence by any human being, the theory of metempsychosis, or transmigration of souls, has perforce to be accepted; men, for their virtues or faults here, appear in a future life either as superior beings or inferior

RELIGIONS OF CHINESE INHABITANTS 53

animals. A regular debtor and creditor account is kept of good and evil deeds, and a man can atone for any sin by fasting, almsgiving, building a bridge, or making a road. Moreover, by such righteous deeds, he may accumulate a considerable balance in his favour. He may be 'too holy for this world,' and is at liberty to consider himself so.

A strict Buddhist is scrupulous not to kill animal life—even the vermin of his own body—for fear it might contain the soul of some relative; yet, at the same time, he may be utterly callous to the destruction of human life, excepting perhaps that of his own family or clansmen. For their death he will demand the most cruel revenge.

There is a Buddhist Heaven, and a Hell, or rather an interminable Purgatory. The hopes held out regarding the former, though material, are very pure and attractive, whilst the tortures of the latter are such as we see depicted in Continental churches.

The chief features of Buddhism in China and Formosa, at the present day, consist in a Pantheon of 'Gods many and Lords many'; a ritual in an unknown tongue; a celibate priesthood, which is slothful and often sensual; and a laity even more superstitious than the priesthood, although superior to that body in morals and intelligence, owing to the salutary influence of family life, and to the necessity of exercising their minds and bodies in gaining their daily food.

As with the Confucian system, so the doctrines of Buddhism, in spite of all the purity and inculcation of virtue which they contain, have proved inefficacious to satisfy the Chinese heart.

I do not underrate the superiority of Confucianism and Buddhism in comparison with many Oriental creeds. I am aware that numerous European philosophers, saturated with Christian ideas, and Orientals educated in our government and missionary colleges, profess to have discovered in the sacred books of their religions, principles and ideas as transcendental and as beautiful as those contained in our own Holy Scriptures.

Personally, after many years' acquaintance with educated Confucianists and Buddhists, who were thoroughly well read in their own sacred classics, yet totally unacquainted with any country or literature save their own, I have never found that they have been able to apprehend the sublime principles and ideas supposed by European philosophers (reading through Christian spectacles) to exist in these ancient books.

I myself have carefully studied the works of the Chinese sages, Confucius and Mencius, and I must affirm that the book of Proverbs contains more wisdom, human and divine, than do all their writings, or the commentaries of their disciples.

Taoism was established by Laotze in the sixth century before Christ. This religion is supposed to consist in the worship of Pure Reason and Virtue. The teaching of Laotze, as contained in the canon attributed to him, recommends retirement and contemplation as the most effectual means of purifying the spiritual part of the nature, annihilating the passions, and of finally returning to the bosom of Tao, or Pure Reason.

Undoubtedly, Taoism in the abstract contains, in spite of many absurdities, some very sublime and pure principles. Indeed some European philosophers affirm that 'Tao' is the Greek 'Logos,' and it is curious to note that this character 'Tao' in Chinese expresses 'the Word,' 'the Way,' and 'the Right.'

I cannot of course enter into this subject comprehensively, but there is reason to believe that the Greeks obtained their higher philosophy from the East, probably from Indians, and these Indians, I suggest, might have absorbed their enlightened ideas from the ten tribes of Israel who were scattered throughout Central Asia in the eighth century B.C. All the purest eastern religions

RELIGIONS OF CHINESE INHABITANTS 55

sprang up after this date, and at a time when communication was constant between the countries in which these different systems had birth, and those in which the Israelites were transplanted.

Unfortunately, whatever Laotze may have intended, at the present day Taoism has degenerated into the grossest superstition and imposture. The priests, not being celibate, are perhaps superior in morals to the Buddhists; but the practice of the religion ranges through geomancy, necromancy, the planchette, and hypnotism, with a larger Pantheon than that of Buddhism, and includes the worship of rocks, trees, snakes, while it encourages the self-inflicted tortures of 'passing through the fire,' and walking upon bridges of knives.

The real religion, however, of China and of the Formosan Chinese is undoubtedly that of the worship of ancestors. This existed long before the days of Confucius, and, whilst discouraging other forms of spirit worship, he encouraged this.

Moreover the government, in the 'Sacred Edict,' which was composed by a great emperor of the present dynasty and ordered to be read by the mandarins in public at each new and full moon, warns the people not to waste their money upon the foolish and useless superstitions of Buddhism and Taoism, but to observe the teachings of the sages to worship the 'two divinities in the house,' *i.e* the parents, dead or living.

This causes some curious results. The three hundred or four hundred millions of Chinese are divided into about four hundred clans or surnames, each claiming one original ancestor, and a motto, generally describing the physical position of the birthplace of the clan.

Although the members of the same clan have in course of centuries been scattered all over the eighteen provinces of China, and now speak mutually unintelligible languages, yet they all are considered blood relations, and intermarriage with the same surname is condemned as incestuous. This is something like an English 'Smith' not being allowed to marry a German 'Schmidt.' Some of these clans exclusively inhabit large tracts of country, and in Fuh-kien the clan Lim occupies tens of square miles, wherein dwell tens of thousands of clansmen. It being, therefore, impossible for them to find wives of another surname, they are obliged to intermarry, and to suffer in consequence the reproach of being called 'the incestuous Lims.'

There are often long and fierce vendettas between different clans; but so long as they do not interfere with government, the mandarins wink at these, as they keep the people from turning their attention to the corruption and oppression of the officials, besides providing a rich harvest in the shape of litigation.

Now the Chinese believe that their ancestors are in Hades, and that they possess influence either for the protection or the injury of their descendants. They also believe that these ancestors, or their spirits, require food, clothing, money, etc., in their disembodied state. These needs are supplied by offerings of animals, rice, spirits, tobacco, etc., and of furniture, clothing, money, etc., made of paper. The eatables are presented before the shrine containing the spirit of the ancestor, and there eaten by the offerer, who is considered only to partake of the material substance, while the ethereal essence of the sacrifice has been consumed by the spirit. The paper articles are burned, and so are supposed to pass into the spirit world.

In all districts there is an ancestral temple for each branch of a clan, and in this the tablets of all ancestors of that branch are kept. The elders appoint a committee yearly to collect subscriptions for the expenses of a daily offering to the spirits; and in each house tablets to the memory of the deceased parents are kept, and daily worshipped by the male members of the household.

Unless the deceased are well cared for, misfortune is sure to overtake the family, and, as only males are worthy to keep up the worship and service, the most fervent prayers of a Chinaman are for sons in abundance. With this I have not been able to understand how, even though he may be a bad man in this life, he need fear déstitution in the spirit world.

In the seventh moon, or autumn time, a feast of 'All Souls' is held throughout the Chinese Empire. Grand sacrifices of eatables are offered to deceased ancestors. Enormous sums of money are spent upon this, and Buddhist priests realise a fine profit by the sale of paper articles, recitations of prayers for the dead, etc.

Devout Buddhists, also, atone for many sins and accumulate merit by liberal gifts for the benefit of unfortunate souls who have died without male posterity, and who are therefore supposed to be starving and cold in Hades.

At this time, in order to stimulate the liberality of the people, grand theatricals are held, representing the descent of some ancient personage into Hell for the redemption of his relative, and portraying with dreadful realism the torments of the lost; men are seen changed into dogs, pigs, etc., boiling in molten metal, sawn asunder, or brayed in a mortar.

These scenes have but little effect on the fears of the people; the eatables are all consumed by the sacrificers or distributed to the poor, and it is therefore a season of general mirth and jollity.

Undoubtedly the maxims of filial piety given by Confucius have had a good effect upon the Chinese character, and I sincerely believe that the mere outward compliance with the divine command has preserved the Chinese in their own country as a great nation for so many thousands of years.

I must own, however, that this virtue is largely practised because the government enforce the *patria potestas* as a means of ensuring obedience. Parricide and rebellion against the emperor are equally punishable with the cruellest death. Every father has power of life and death over his children ; and filial disobedience is punished in the courts of justice by severe flogging.

While the status of the parent is so well secured, the position of the female children is deplorable, and infanticide is common throughout the empire, in spite of Buddhistic humanity.

All classes of Chinese, upon certain occasions, patronise Buddhism and Taoism, whilst they are proud of Confucianism.

Now I maintain that, although Confucius, Sakyamuni, and Laotze were wonderful men, sages possessing a great superiority over their fellow-countrymen, and actuated with a sincere desire to do them good ; yea, though I hope they may be counted amongst those 'prophets and kings who desired to see and hear the things which we see and hear, and could not '; yet I fear that they were all guilty of worshipping the creature more than the Creator, and that they confined their teaching to their own select disciples, rather encouraging the common people to continue in their ignorant superstitions. I do not hesitate to say that in China—and in Formosa most certainly—the result has been a state of things to a certain extent analogous to that described by St. Paul in the letter to the Romans.

Doubtless I lay myself open to be fiercely assailed by many learned men for venturing such a statement. Should they contradict me, I would reply that they must be unacquainted with the social and official life of the Chinese.

With reference to the practice of infanticide, the following anecdote may interest my readers.

When a small boy, I had, of course, read accounts of how the Chinese drowned their girl babies, of the towers in Pekin, and of the carts which went round every morning

RELIGIONS OF CHINESE INHABITANTS 59

to collect the dead bodies; but again I had read that this was a gross exaggeration—that the Chinese loved their children, and that only in extreme cases did they drown them to save them from a life of shame.

During my residence at Foochow, although I mixed as much as possible with the Chinese in order to learn their dialect; yet, as the Customs officials lived in a hulk on the river, I had not the best opportunities of becoming acquainted with the true inwardness of their social habits and customs. When I was appointed to take charge of the Customs House at Taiwanfoo, however, I had a house on shore at Anping, the seaport of the capital. Around me here there dwelt a community of respectable, well-to-do fishermen, with whom, as with most people in the town, I became intimately acquainted. Just opposite to the Custom House, over the way, lived one of these fishermen. His family consisted of himself, his wife, and two infant sons; his widowed sister-in-law with her two daughters and a son; and—most important member of all—his mother, who was between seventy and eighty years of age, nearly blind, and a perfect virago, as are most Chinese old women.

Now many friends had asked me if I could get any one to make a model of the Chinese fishing boat or catamaran, which I have described in a previous chapter. I therefore proposed to my acquaintance the fisherman that he and I should try to make one, so that if we succeeded he would be enabled, when he could not get to sea, to make these models, and realise a profit by selling them to the European captains who frequented the port. The man assented to my plan, and accordingly, in my leisure hours, I used to go to his house and work at the catamaran.

I was there as usual one afternoon, and he was showing me how to bend the bamboos and to fasten them with rattan canes. His womenkind were seated around us, making nets, clothes, or embroidering shoes for their own small feet, whilst the children played without in the sunshine, and the old grandmother squatted upon the bed, smoking a long bamboo pipe, and at intervals scolding and abusing every one of the family.

During a lull in the venerable lady's tirade, there came suddenly from a house near to us a shrill cry of ' Ma-beh ! Ma-beh ! '

Now in English ' Ma-beh ' would mean ' Grandmother desires me.' I wondered idly, but held my peace. Meanwhile the cries went on, and the wife lifted her head from her task, and said, amused :

' What is the matter with Ma-beh now ? '

' What *is* Ma-beh ? ' I then inquired.

' Oh, don't you know Ma-beh ? ' the woman replied. ' She is Pok-a's big daughter over the way there.'

' But why do they call her Ma-beh ? ' I persisted.

The women exchanged glances, and began to giggle. At last the widow answered me.

' Well, you know, just after Ma-beh was born, the midwife was going to nip her neck, but the grandmother cried out that she desired the baby, so they spared her life, and that is why she is called Ma-beh.'

' Why, you surely do not kill your children here ? ' was my shocked query. ' I thought it was only the very poorest who ever killed a child. Ma-beh's father is a thriving man ; he neither smokes opium, gambles, nor drinks.'

The widow sobered down. Her smile died away.

' Oh, we all do it about here,' she replied. ' We don't kill the boys, of course ; but girls are a lot of trouble, and very little good. I *nipped* two, and only saved these two here. You see, if we have one girl after another, and they are not very pretty, we can't get husbands for them, so they are left on our hands. We don't like to sell them for slaves, or to lead a bad life, and so '—she sighed—' we choke them before they know where they are, and they don't feel anything.'

'Then you people are worse than cats!' I answered wrathfully. 'In *our* country they seem to think more lovingly of girls than of boys. I was the only boy of a family of eight, yet I think my father petted my little sister more than he did me.'

The old woman grunted from her point of vantage upon the bed. She laid down her pipe, and replied contemptuously:

'You red-haired barbarians don't know what's right. Girls are no use anyway! Look!' and she pointed a trembling finger at the widow, 'there's my son, the best fisherman in Anping. He has been taken away from me: he used to earn money and bring me anything I wanted. He has left behind him his useless widow and those two girls there; what can they do but eat rice?'

As time went on, I became acquainted with all sorts and conditions of Chinese in Formosa; and, after making searching inquiry, I found that female infanticide was universally practised in cases of a succession of girls in a family—and this not only among the poorer but also among the well-to-do classes. The people informed me that they had brought the practice over from the mainland; and I discovered that the aborigines, both civilised and savage, look with horror upon the Chinese for their inhumanity in this respect.

It was in my friend the fisherman's family also that, a short time afterwards, whilst still engaged upon the catamaran model, I had an opportunity of observing what filial obedience, according to the rules of Confucius, means amongst the Chinese.

The old grandmother was sitting as usual, smoking her pipe, which was long and thick as a walking-stick, formed of bamboo, with a brass-bound bowl. The fisherman's son, a fine boy of about five years old, was playing naked on the floor. His mother brought him a pair of trousers, and told him to put them on, asking him whether 'he was not ashamed to appear like a beast before the foreigner?' But the boy threw the garment away from him in a pet, and called his mother (as is too usual with Chinese male children) an opprobrious name. She, being in a bit of a temper, slapped him on the head, whereat he roared lustily. The grandmother, roused by the boy's cry, took her pipe, and beat her daughter-in-law about the head until the blood streamed down her face, accompanying the blows with the filthiest language.

I called on the man to interfere, which he at last reluctantly did, merely stepping between his wife and mother; but the old woman, being, as I have said, nearly blind, and having very small feet, tripped over a stool, and fell to the ground. She immediately set up the most awful howl, which could be heard all over the neighbourhood, calling out that her son was unfilial and had beaten her, so must be taken to the mandarin for punishment. The neighbours crowded in, and when the old woman had got on her feet, after bestowing a few blows upon her son, she accused him of having assaulted her, knocked her down, and of taking the part of his hussy of a wife against his own mother. She vowed that she would have justice, and she called upon the people to take her son to the mandarin that he might be punished according to law.

The neighbours were very excited and indignant, and several men proceeded to lay hold of my friend. The situation was now getting serious, and the noise had attracted the two European subordinates of the Custom House over the way. I requested them to fetch their revolvers, and, when they returned with the arms, I addressed the crowd, and told them the facts of the case, saying that I would take the man to the military commander of the town, and would dispense with their services.

This did not seem to please the Chinese, but I and my companions got the son away in spite of them, and conveyed him to the yamen, or court of justice, a great mob following us, and condemning in very strong terms the wicked conduct of my friend.

In the meantime the old woman, accompanied by a number of sympathising old hags, had gone ahead to the court, and when we arrived there, we found her upon her knees, knocking her head on the ground before the mandarin, crying loudly for justice, while her friends echoed her demands. Fortunately, however, I was on friendly terms with the commandant; I therefore explained the whole circumstances of the case, and the official contented himself with giving, through the interpreter, a long oration upon the necessity of obeying one's parents, whether of the family or of the State.

This seemed to satisfy the crowd, and my friend was let off with the slight penalty of presenting a pair of candles, with an apology to his mother.

By this time the walk to the yamen and the exertion of knocking her head upon the ground had exhausted the old lady, and her temper had somewhat cooled. She also doubtless recollected that her son was her only support, and that had he, according to law, received one or two hundred blows with the bamboo, it would probably have laid him up for a week or two, thus rendering him unable to earn money. Moreover, he certainly had no money wherewith to bribe the executioner to use his knack to lay on the blows with great sound and scarcely any ill effect, as is frequently contrived.

CHAPTER VI

THE ABORIGINES AND THEIR RELIGIONS

WHEN, in the year 1624, the Dutch arrived at what is now called Taiwanfoo, they found the whole of the western coast and the plains inhabited by numerous tribes of savages, whose manners and customs seem to have been identical with those of the aborigines who inhabit the mountains at the present day.

These tribes spoke many different dialects, but all seem to have had an affinity with that Malay-Polynesian form of speech which, in its multitudinous varieties, is spoken in Luzon, Celebes, Borneo, Java, and indeed everywhere from Madagascar to New Zealand.

During the early years of the Dutch occupation, their missionaries seem to have been indefatigable in their work amongst the natives. They laboured unselfishly to improve both the mental and spiritual condition of the natives, and, as I have mentioned in a previous chapter, their memory is still revered amongst the aborigines.

When, after thirty-seven years' occupation of the island, the Dutch were driven out by the Chinese, the tribes who refused to renounce Christianity were slaughtered. The remainder either submitted (and now shave their heads) or returned to the hills, and some even crossed over to the east coast.

Those who submitted to the Chinese rule adopted the language, dress, and religious customs of their conquerors, with the exception of the women, who still retain their ancient coiffure.

PEPO-HOAN CIVILISED ABORIGINES

THE ABORIGINES AND THEIR RELIGIONS 65

These submissive tribes are called by the Chinese Pepo-hoans, *i.e.* 'barbarians of the plain,' or 'Sek-hoan,' 'cooked barbarians,' in contradistinction to the savage aborigines of the mountains, who are termed 'Ch'i-hoans,' or 'raw barbarians.' It is instructive to notice, in parenthesis, that in the Chinese estimation this world contains only one race of 'men,' one empire, one human language, and one true civilisation.

The 'men' are of course the Chinese, 'the black-haired race'; their empire is 'all under Heaven,' whilst the emperor is the 'Son of Heaven.'

China is the 'middle kingdom'; indeed, they honestly believe it to be the hub of the universe.

Chinese is the sole language worthy of a man, and there is no true system of civilisation outside Confucianism.

All other nations are but inferior developments of the human species; their languages are but jargons, and their civilisation is of little account.

At any rate, we are all Hoans, or 'barbarians.' English have the peculiar honour of being called 'Ang-mo-hoan,' or 'red-haired barbarians,' and I am happy to say that we are the most respected and the least disliked of all European nations.

But to return to the semi-civilised tribes of the plains of Formosa:—

The Pepo-hoans for the most part speak Chinese, and those dwelling on the borders of the savage territory act as interpreters and middlemen in times of peace between these old-time foes.

They practically adopt the Chinese dress and tonsure, but their features distinctly show that they were originally of the Malayo-Polynesian stock.

They seldom make an unprovoked attack, being a simple-minded and quiet people, and the Chinese do not scruple to possess themselves of their lands, under pretence of renting them; the complaints for redress to the officials

F

being too often unattended to, it being utterly incomprehensible to a Chinese that 'barbarians' have any rights at all.

They are frequently molested also by the wild savages, who look upon the acquisition of human heads with pigtails as a proof of valour. At present, therefore, these borderers pass a somewhat uneasy life.

They are distinctly superior to the Chinese in morals, although perhaps their views upon the obligations of the marriage state may be somewhat lax. In religion they usually adopt the Chinese observances, retaining, however, various customs of their own.

The Sek-hoan, in point of civilisation, are equal to the lower orders of Chinese, but are simpler and less cunning.

They subsist chiefly by agriculture, but, though tolerably good farmers, they are not equal in this respect to the Chinese. They are very fond of hunting. Fortunately they are not much addicted to opium, although they are fond of wine and spirits; in both these points they resemble the rest of the aborigines of the island. They distil a sort of whisky from rice or sweet potatoes, but this is so weak that they are seldom intoxicated.

In appearance they are of a somewhat distinctive type, being taller, slighter, and fairer than their brethren of other tribes. They have large dark eyes, wide mouths, and long, projecting upper teeth.

The west coast and all the alluvial plain from north to south is inhabited by immigrants from the Chinese province of Fuh-kien, and these speak variations of the language called by Europeans the Amoy dialect of the Chinese. This language is totally unintelligible to the natives of any other province in the empire, except to those in the prefecture of Chao-chiu in the north of Canton, or Kwang Tung. These emigrants are called Hok-los. The Hok-lo women, excepting slaves, all have those small or compressed feet which the Chinese euphoniously term 'golden lilies.'

In the villages between the lower ranges of the moun-

FORMOSAN CHINESE ('MAN'), HOK-LO

THE ABORIGINES AND THEIR RELIGIONS 67

tains and at the South Cape, indeed everywhere on the borders of the savage territory, we find another and totally distinct race, called the Hak-kas, or 'strangers,' in their own language, and termed by the Hok-los, 'Kheh-lang.' These people are a peculiar race, speaking a dialect of the mandarin or court Chinese.

Some hundreds of years ago, their ancestors left their original home in the north of China, and spread themselves south until they occupied a considerable portion of the Canton province, to the disgust of the native Puntis. Nearly seventy years ago the west coast of China was in a state of anarchy through the feuds between the Hak-kas and the Puntis, or native Cantonese. Ultimately the government came to the aid of the natives, and the help of European adventurers was enlisted. Tens of thousands of Hak-kas were slaughtered; numbers emigrated to the Malay Archipelago, and hundreds of families crossed over to Formosa. These passed through the country of the Hok-los, penetrated into the lower ranges of hills, and either squatted in the unoccupied valleys or drove the savages further into the mountains.

The people are most enterprising agriculturists and good artisans, but they are also exceedingly turbulent and quarrelsome. The mandarins had little control over them, and, when not occupied in their legitimate pursuits of agriculture, or the manufacture of farming implements and arms, they are continually fighting, both with the Pepo-hoan and Hok-los (the Amoy Chinese), and occasionally, by way of a change, they get up a clan feud amongst themselves.

They are also gradually encroaching upon the savages. In times of peace, they take women from the savage tribes as wives, and these, becoming semi-civilised, introduce many luxuries and wants amongst the tribes, which inevitably have an enervating effect on their simple and hardy habits.

The Hak-ka women preserve their feet in a natural

state, and altogether enjoy much more freedom than usually falls to the lot of Chinese females. As a consequence they almost rival the men in energy and enterprise.

We now come to the Ch'i-hoan, or 'raw savages' of the high mountains. These people remained untouched by the semi-civilisation of the Chinese occupiers, and they had never been visited in their haunts until 1865, when I succeeded in gaining access to those near Mount Morrison, whilst Mr. Dodd, a merchant of Tamsui, visited the tribes in the north of the island. Of my excursions into their territories, and of what befell me there, I will tell later.

The Chinese of the west coast seriously believed that these men had tails, that they were little better than monkeys, and that they were cannibals. I need scarcely say that the belief as to their dorsal appendages is incorrect; as to their cannibalism, it is a fact that they are enthusiastic head-hunters, esteeming it a praiseworthy feat for a warrior to bring home the head of his enemy. Upon such occasions his family and tribesmen feast and rejoice with him on his success. They mix the brains of the dead man with some spirits, and drink the concoction to increase their strength, and to make them brave in the future.

With this exception I must deny that the savages of Formosa are cannibals; and even for the above gruesome practice the Chinese are not in a position to despise them, as amongst that highly civilised race it is a common custom, upon the execution of a notorious rebel or hardened malefactor, for the executioner to abstract the liver of his victim, fry it, cut it up into small pieces, eat a portion himself, and sell the rest to the bystanders who desire to be imbued with the hardiness and courage of the man who has been beheaded. During the persecution of 1868, an unfortunate Christian convert was torn to pieces by a Chinese mob near Taiwanfoo, and his liver was treated in the manner I have described.

These aborigines of the hills live in villages. Their houses are built of stone, roofed with slate, and have a remarkably clean, home-like appearance. Those living in some districts contrive their houses of bamboo, grass, and mud.

They are, with a few exceptions, friendly to foreigners, particularly appreciating a discreet present of soap, beads, red cloth, steel implements, and small mirrors. They have the greatest antipathy to the Chinese, but the exceptional occasions when they have been hostile to Europeans have generally been due to some indiscretion upon the part of their visitors.

They have to a high degree that extra sense which enables them to track a foe by signs which would be totally invisible to the ordinary civilised eye. They have been known to 'shadow' for many miles parties of strangers of whom they were suspicious, surrounding them very effectively when the most favourable opportunity occurred.

All the mountain aborigines are bold and skilful hunters and fishermen; the young men can run down a deer, and they have a special breed of dogs for this purpose.

In all the tribes that I have visited, the men never seem to think of doing anything but hunting, fishing, fighting, and constructing and ornamenting their arms.

The woman carry all the burdens, cook, labour in the fields, and weave cloth, this same cloth being formed of fine hemp, with which are interwoven threads of various coloured European cloth, forming very pretty patterns.

Upon all hunting expeditions, women accompany the men, for the purpose of carrying back the heavy loads of meat, which are usually dried over fires of green wood at the hunting ground.

The costume of the men consists usually of a short sleeved jacket and a very short kilt. When dressed in all their finery for a head-hunting expedition or for a drinking party, they are gorgeous.

The jacket often consists of a leopard's skin or of the variegated native cloth. Many bead necklaces are hung round the neck, whilst the arms and ankles are adorned with numerous bangles, or the arms are circled with large wild-boar tusks, hung either with tassels of red cloth or human hair.

As weapons, they carry a long knife, with a case for a short stabbing knife and tobacco pipe, a long matchlock, and a spear, whilst the bow and arrows are used for some kinds of game ; but this primitive weapon is going out of fashion amongst the savages in all parts of the island, although I have seen the Chinese of Lung-kiau, in the south of Formosa, carry a bow and a quiver of arrows on setting forth upon a journey.

Whilst visiting the Banga tribe, I viewed a party of savages who had come to see their neighbours, and their heads were adorned with wreaths of flowers, interspersed with small oranges, which formed a very striking coronet.

Some of the Bangas, again, wear a small flag fastened behind the head and shoulders.

In all the tribes, north and south Formosan, that I have visited, the lobes of the ears of both men and women are perforated, and extended for some length, with a round, ornamental stud of shell or metal inserted.

The food of the savage tribes usually consists of millet, mountain and glutinous rice, sweet potatoes, and taro ; with dried venison, wild boar, and bear's flesh.

They are all good fishermen ; and, besides using the rod, they poison the water with the root of the lo-tin, a poisonous creeper.

They drink, besides Chinese spirits, a kind of wine made from millet, the grain of which is formed into a sort of curd, and when required it is mixed with water. At their meals they imbibe cold water, also a little warm water mixed with chili pepper.

THE ABORIGINES AND THEIR RELIGIONS 71

As a matter of course, they all smoke, and chew betel nut. The teeth are blackened with a plant, and a custom exists, in some parts, of knocking out a tooth when arriving at the age of puberty.

The hands of the women are generally tattooed, whilst some tribes have also peculiar marks upon different parts of their body.

Great fasts are held after a sickness or when any of the tribe have been killed. At such times they will be silent, and will only eat sufficient food to maintain life.

They have an intense dread of smallpox, keeping a strict blockade when the disease is known to exist amongst the Pepo-hoans or Chinese of their neighbourhood. Should a savage have the misfortune to be attacked by this fell disease, he rushes away into the jungle, and either recovers or dies there.

The Chinese, who are exceedingly careless about contagion, think this dread a sign of barbarism.

These savages are capable of enduring much fatigue, and of great spasmodic exertion, but they are averse to any steady labour.

When on a head-hunting expedition, they will go away for days together, travelling long distances, subsisting only upon a few balls of glutinous rice and the grubs which they obtain from certain trees, and drinking only the water which they find in the streams.

Upon these occasions they draw their belts so tightly as to appear nearly to cut themselves in two ; this they say prevents them from feeling the pangs of hunger.

When, however, they return from a successful bear, deer, or wild pig hunt, they gorge themselves with flesh, and with an intoxicating liquor which they produce by fermenting millet. They then stay idly at home until an empty larder and hunger force them abroad again.

They spend their leisure time in making and decorating their weapons, their tobacco pipes, and personal ornaments. Their gun-barrels, knives, indeed all their metallic articles, are procured from the Chinese, with whom they barter deer horns, skins of various kinds, venison and bear's flesh, tobacco, hemp, native cloth, and charcoal. The Chinese in return supply them with gunpowder, salt, sugar, European cloth of bright colours, beads, and a fiery spirit made from rice or sweet potatoes, which is called by Europeans 'samshoo.'

The women do all the cultivation of their fields of millet, mountain rice, hemp, and tobacco. They are also very skilful in making fine net bags, and in weaving cloth from a fine kind of hemp, interwoven with different coloured threads which they draw from European woollens.

But although they are kept in such a subordinate position, I have always found that they contrive to have their full share of control and management of the house and family.

If the lady agitators will permit me to whisper so great a heresy, I have invariably found that, in every eastern country I have visited, though the fair sex is apparently kept in more subjection than in Europe, yet they manage to get their own way, and contrive to keep their men in a proper state of terror. I will go further than this statement; I will dare to affirm that the less fuss they make about their rights in public, the more certain they are to receive their full share of them in their legitimate sphere, the home and the family.

These Formosan savage women have a peculiar honour. They are the priestesses of their tribes. The religion of the aborigines consists in the ecstasies of these priestesses, and in the offering of a little of the food and spirituous liquors to the spirits before meals, sprinkling a pinch to the four points of the compass. They also observe the flight of birds, and a kind of totemism, each tribe being supposed to be under the tutelage of some bird, beast, or reptile. The Ban-tau-lang keep a large snake which they believe ensures prosperity to the tribe. All the savages are much hampered by superstitions about good and bad luck—thus it is unlucky to step on a gun or to carry a spear a certain way, to encounter birds, etc.

Upon public occasions, the priestesses execute certain mysterious ceremonies of adoration to the one Supreme Deity, in whom they believe; and having excited themselves until they fall exhausted in a trance, these women, upon waking, foretell the success or failure of the projected hunting and fighting expeditions.

In their groping after truth these savages seem to have a glimmer of light, which is probably the faint tradition of the Dutch missionaries' teaching. For example, they have an idea of the first man and woman. They believe in one Supreme Deity, and in an after-state of retribution for evil, and reward for good. They attribute sickness and misfortune to the ill offices of certain maleficent demons, whom the priestesses are employed to exorcise.

They are fond of music, listening with evident pleasure to the efforts of the foreigners, either instrumental or vocal, and they will return the compliment by executing one of their pathetic chants, in a minor key, accompanying their efforts with a weird war dance, making music upon a bamboo jew's harp, or a flageolet breathed into from one nostril.

Divorce is allowed for incompatibility of temper; and in devotion to parents these people rival their Chinese neighbours.

With regard to their language: the aborigines are divided into many tribes, speaking different languages, and although their origin is unknown, it seems conclusive that they must in the beginning have arrived in the island from widely different countries.

My experience of them extended chiefly to the tribes of the centre and the south of the island, and these resemble in features, habits, and languages, the Tagalas of the Philippines.

Some tribes, on the other hand, have a language which reminds one of the Mexican or Aztec; the majority of their words ending in 'tl,' thus—

>Lukutl—a deer.
>Kwangoritl—the neck.
>Hutl-hutl—beads, etc.

Tradition describes the Ami-a (Ami or Amigo?) tribe, scattered along the east coast of Formosa, as descended from a shipwrecked crew of white men, whose lives were spared, and who were allowed to settle and to intermarry with the tribe, on condition that their descendants should be in subjection for ever.

This theory, too, is probable, from an examination of their build and physique, which still retain European characteristics.

The tribes of the north, again, are said to be of Japanese or Loochooan origin.

All these speculations are highly probable, as, within the last thirty years, Loochooan junks have been wrecked on the east coast, and their crews murdered by the savages, whilst in 1867 I was able to rescue twenty or thirty men, women, and children, natives of the Philippines, who had been blown off the land, and had drifted helplessly in their canoes until they arrived at the southernmost point of Formosa.

The population of the plain is estimated to be about three million Chinese, with perhaps half a million Sekhoans. There is absolutely no method of ascertaining the numbers of the savages. These all reckon by the number of fighting men, of which the smaller tribes possess from thirty to one hundred, and the large tribes one or two thousand.

Altogether, excepting for their periodical drinking bouts, I have always found the Formosan savages modest

THE ABORIGINES AND THEIR RELIGIONS 75

and kind. Having visited and held communication with some twenty tribes of aborigines dwelling in the mountains between Chang-hwa and the South Cape, I have had every opportunity to form an opinion; and I believe that, had the Dutch held Formosa till the present day, the whole island would have been civilised and Christianised.

The Chinese, with their inordinate ideas of superiority, treat both the Pepos (civilised aborigines) and the Ch'i-hoans (the savages) as children or wild beasts; consequently they are hated in return.

With the exception of the Koa-luts, who inhabit the extreme point of the South Cape, the savage tribes seem to be prepossessed in favour of Europeans, whilst all the Pepo-hoans welcome them as friends.

Before leaving Formosa, I made acquaintance with the Sek-hoans of the more northern districts, Chang-hoa and Ka-gi, and I also visited the whole of the Chinese portion of the island, from Kilung to the South Cape. I am happy to say that my relations with both the Chinese and the aborigines were always most friendly, except when the mandarins interfered, and that in all the villages of the Pepo-hoans where I visited, the Presbyterian missionaries were welcomed, with the result that these people have been to a great extent evangelised.

CHAPTER VII

THE PROGRESS OF CHRISTIANITY IN FORMOSA. THE GREAT STORM

CHRISTIANITY, when I arrived in Formosa, had been represented for some years by the Spanish Dominicans from Manila, who in 1859 established a mission amongst the Chinese near Takao, and also carried on successful work amongst the Pepo-hoans at a village some twenty miles inland, at the foot of the high mountain range, on the borders of savage territory.

Well do I remember the genial and liberal-minded Father who was head of their mission. When I was appointed to the Customs service at Takao, and had settled down to my new duties, I felt somewhat aimless and dreary in my leisure hours. I viewed the long expanse of the shallow lagoon with the reviving instinct of the fisherman, and I thought lovingly of a certain Esquimaux kajak, or sealskin canoe, which I had parted with to a comrade before leaving Foochow. I broached the subject to that comrade in a letter, and he responded by forwarding the wished-for boat. From that time my chief enjoyment was in paddling about upon the placid blue waters, sometimes fishing, sometimes merely luxuriating dreamily; and again, seized with an exploring freak, I would paddle up some side stream, between narrow banks where the bamboo and banyan waved their green foliage, penetrating into the interior as far as time permitted.

It was upon one of these explorations that I came upon a village of Chinese, amongst whom the Dominicans

THE PROGRESS OF CHRISTIANITY 77

had established their head-quarters, and were pursuing their half-paternal proselytising efforts, having beside an outpost among the Pepo-hoans, as I have before stated, at the foot of the mountains, some twenty miles further in the interior. I had some knowledge of Spanish, and when a benign-faced man in priest's attire greeted me as I moored my boat, I responded joyfully, and our acquaintance progressed as rapidly as was natural in a land where one's life is of light value, and where, in a sense, every European is as a brother to be cherished, since to-morrow his place may know him no more.

That conversation was the first of many. The Padres were very kind to me, and my sealskin canoe often lay at rest by the bank where the substantial mission-house stood, and many a long, earnest discussion we had, which would have been impossible had not my friend been a broadminded man, a Christian even more than a Dominican, a greater lover of truth than of creed. I recollect one instance of this. We had been speaking of the grand self-denial of those who leave their native country, their dear ones, and all the comforts of civilisation to become the pioneers of the Gospel in savage lands like Formosa. The Padre was silent for a moment, then he said:

'*Bueno, hombre!* That for your English missionaries may be a fact. They indeed renounce much. They have many tender bonds binding them to earthly love and to their native land. But for us Catholics in holy orders this does not exist to such a great degree. Take us as we are—Spaniards, Portuguese, Frenchmen, Italians—to what do we bid farewell? Some squalid provincial village, where every one is poor, poor, poor, as you English cannot comprehend poverty; we exchange our thin sour wine and dry black bread for at any rate no worse diet; the climate here is not much hotter than in some parts of Spain and Italy. And loved ones—a wife? children?—we have renounced all such earthly ties by the vows of our order, whether we go or stay. Wherefore, my friend, we must not whine, nor dare to claim compassion for imaginary renunciations.'

Thus would this good man argue against himself, in order to do justice to men with whose teaching he could not on many points agree.

It was by the Padre's assistance that I was first enabled to get into communication with the savages, although the Fathers themselves had never visited them. The Sek-hoan converts were on intimate terms with the savage aborigines, and they gladly introduced me to some of their head men.

The Roman Catholics have made some progress amongst the Chinese, but their chief success has been with the civilised aborigines.

In 1864 the English Presbyterian Mission determined to attempt the conversion of Formosa. They therefore sent over the Rev. Carstairs Douglas, a most accomplished Chinese scholar; and Dr. Maxwell, a medical missionary, who had left his post as house-surgeon to the Birmingham Infirmary in order to preach the Gospel. These gentlemen commenced operations at Takao and Taiwanfoo.

At first they were well received by the people, and the apparently miraculous cures effected by Dr. Maxwell by the use of quinine, the operation for cataract and lithotomy, soon drew numbers of sick people from all parts of the island.

But this success excited the animosity and opposition of the native doctors, who spread the usual false reports that the foreigners were killing Chinese and extracting their brains and eyes for the purpose of making opium, They thus raised a popular tumult, which the mandarins in no way discouraged.

The result was that the missionaries were attacked by the mob, their meeting-house was destroyed, and they themselves were obliged to leave the capital and return to Takao.

THE PROGRESS OF CHRISTIANITY 79

In 1865 Dr. Maxwell came up for a visit to Taiwanfoo, and I was able to take him into the interior, amongst the savages, and also to introduce him to the Sek-hoan communities of the plain, with those of the lower ranges, at Baksa, near Taiwanfoo. These all received him gladly, and he made some converts amongst them.

In 1867 the Rev. Hugh and Mrs. Ritchie joined Dr. Maxwell, and the mission amongst the Chinese inhabitants flourished considerably.

During the camphor troubles, native Christians, both Catholic and Protestant, suffered much persecution owing to their connection with Europeans. Their chapels were destroyed, their cattle maimed, their fields laid waste, and many converts were beaten. In one instance, as I have mentioned before, a poor Christian was brutally murdered.

Happily, upon the settlement of the troubles, the mission prospered more than ever amongst the Chinese, whilst some of my old Sek-hoan friends in the camphor district of the north, who came to visit me at Taiwanfoo, and were taken to the mission hospital, were so delighted with what they saw of the treatment of the sick patients and at the earnest preaching, that, on their return home, they sent an invitation for the missionaries to go and visit them.

Dr. Maxwell and Mr. Ritchie accepted their invitation, and the result has been that Christianity has spread amongst the civilised aborigines throughout the whole island, even to the villages upon the east coast. Men, women, and children have learnt to read the Scriptures in Chinese through the medium of Roman characters ; and hundreds of converts have been gained, who have built their own chapels, have contributed largely to the support of native catechists, and who lead a consistent Christian life.

Thus the record of missionary enterprise in Formosa is a hopeful augury for their future efforts.

It is auspicious to notice that in the late war with Japan, when the defenders of the island, the redoubtable Black Flags, had evinced their valour by running away into the hills, and a terror-stricken fugitive in woman's attire, with a mock baby to complete the disguise, was all that was left of the president of the brief republic, the great Brigadier-General Liu-Yung-fu ; when the Japanese army halted within a day's march of the capital, to prepare for their attack upon it, and the people of the city were crazed with terror—it was these same brave missionaries who, at the request of the populace, went out to the invaders' camp to treat with them, carrying their lives in their hands.

And to their unselfish temerity it is due that the Japanese conquerors entered the city peaceably, thus sparing many thousands of lives and much valuable property.

May their great and good work in the island increase and prosper exceedingly under the new rule!

It may interest my readers if I recount a terrible experience I had, which illustrates very forcibly the illogical methods in which the Chinese Formosan practises his religion.

It occurred in the days of my connection with the camphor trade of the island, and after the settlement of the first disturbance. Our firm had a considerable quantity of camphor awaiting shipment at a small port, called Tai-kah, some seventy miles north of Taiwanfoo. The consul thought it of importance that, as soon as possible, we should ship the camphor, in order to test the sincerity of the Tao-tai's promises that its export after payment of all legal dues should be freely permitted.

The native Chinese, however, who knew their own officials better than we did, correctly suspected that directly the moral effect of the presence of our men-of-war was removed the Tao-tai would repent, and would not relinquish his monopoly so easily. They rightly feared the consequences to themselves and their families of assisting the foreigners against the mandarins. It was therefore almost impossible to secure any craft to bring the camphor away to Taiwanfoo.

I accordingly went up overland to Tai-kah, and after much difficulty I succeeded in hiring a small boat of about ten tons, which fortunately had water-tight compartments, according to Chinese fashion. It had a nondescript crew of four men, with a captain who was an old opium-smoker.

However, I shipped my camphor on board, and one fine Monday morning I embarked, accompanied by my Chinese clerk and servant, a well-to-do camphor dealer, and the young son of a savage chief, who had never before seen the sea, and whom I was taking down to see Taiwanfoo.

The harbour dues were paid; a port clearance was issued; the wind was fair, and I hoped to be in Taiwanfoo the next day.

Alas! the customary difficulties with Orientals occurred. Our crew had to take leave of their friends, to spend their advances, and to do a little gambling. The result was that the afternoon came before they put in an appearance; and in the meantime the wind had increased, and there was every sign of a gale from the north-east.

However, the old skipper assured me that we could get down to a place called Go-ch'e before dark, where we could put in, in the event of the weather getting worse. I was in a hurry, so consented to our putting to sea.

Now from Go-ch'e to Taiwanfoo there is no shelter for a vessel; sandbanks stretch out for miles from the coast towards the Pescadores, and should one be capsized there, if one were so fortunate as to escape death from the sea, it would only be to fall a victim at the hands of the pitiless pirates and wreckers who plied their ghastly business along the coast.

The wind freshened, and we had to reef down; the

tide also was against us, and we made but slow progress with the old craft. Darkness came on, to still further dispirit us. We had not reached Go-ch'e; things looked extremely gloomy in prospect, and I would have given something to have been on shore. The captain, however, was confident that he could recognise the lights of the village.

Time went on; the wind and the sea had greatly increased, we had taken in sail to a single bamboo, and our captain began to sigh, for the lights still did not appear. Later on he muttered a prayer, and said that we had missed the port.

Then a wild-eyed sailor rushed aft, cursing the day he had ever seen the boat or the foreigner who had engaged her; whereupon the entire crew seemed to lose heart, and they all began to call loudly upon their gods to help them.

We drove before the gale for an hour or two. I was dozing off, when bump went the boat; a big sea dashed right over her; away went our solitary mast overboard, and we were washed out of her. However, we all presently found ourselves on board again, and we realised that the vessel had been washed over the tail of a bank into deeper water. This must have been about midnight. Fortunately the water-tight compartments kept the boat afloat, but the weight of the camphor and of ourselves sank her to such an extent that we were up to our shoulders in water.

All through that interminable night our little craft drifted about, unmanageable, in the trough of the seas, whilst every now and then, as she slewed round, a big sea would wash over her, first on one side and then on the other, leaving us scarcely an interval to recover our breath.

The grey day broke at last. The gale was furious; the waves seethed with cruel white teeth around us, whilst the

THE GREAT STORM

spindrift blew in sheets from the tops of the seas. The wild howling of the wind was deafening; one could, as it were, scarcely hear oneself think! The elements held a wild orgie.

The sailors, however, finding that the boat kept well afloat, and seeing that we had drifted off the banks and far to sea in the channel, seemed to regain a little hope. As the wooden anchor and cable were still on board, they proceeded to rig up a sea anchor, to bring the boat head-to-sea, and thus to relieve us from the overwhelming broadside seas. To accomplish this, they took a heavy bag of rice, which fortunately remained in the hold, and having collected money from the purse of every one on board, as an offering to the Goddess of the Sea, they put it in the bag, made all fast to the anchor, which they threw overboard, and then veered out the cable to the bare end. This contrivance relieved us considerably.

When we rose on the top of the sea, one of the sailors cried out that he could see the Pescadores not far off; and sure enough we soon all perceived an island, which was eventually recognised by the crew as that dedicated to Ma-tso-po, the Goddess of the Sea, or the Queen of Heaven. Upon this island is a temple of this goddess, which is visited by the vessels trading between Formosa and the mainland, and here offerings are made by the sailors in order to secure a prosperous voyage.

Ma-tso-po is supposed to have been a maiden born in an island on the coast of Fuh-kien, who, as a reward for the purity of her life, was endued with supernatural powers. During a violent storm, her brothers were at sea in a junk, and they were about to founder, when the maiden appeared on board suddenly, and by her occult authority quelled the tempest and steered the vessel safely to shore. Ma-tso-po is therefore worshipped as the patroness of sailors, and is also called the ' Holy Mother of Heaven Above.'

Our crew began to recover their spirits somewhat;

they exclaimed that we surely should never be allowed to perish in sight of the sacred island. They began to cry:

'O Ma-tso-po! O Holy Mother, here are we, thy poor children! Have mercy upon us! Let us not perish! Think of our wives and our children! Always have we been liberal to thee! If thou wilt only let us once more reach the shore in safety, we will offer many candles at thy shrine, and give thee as many pigs as thy soul can desire!'

The camphor dealer, who, in a sheltered corner, had been invoking a certain Buddhist god, whose temple was near to his house, now turned his attention also to Ma-tso-po, and vied with the sailors in making liberal promises to her.

Still, however, the gale raged; every now and then a huge sea dashed over us, threatening to swamp us. Suddenly one of the sailors rushed forward; extending his arms, and gazing out across the seething waters in a wild ecstasy, he cried:

'Here she comes! Here she comes! Behold the Holy Mother! Pull away, brethren, pull away! We shall reach the shore directly. Ma-tso-po herself has come to succour us!'

As all our oars had been washed away, and we were drifting helplessly about, we saw that the man was raving.

There was a breathless pause, whilst he gazed away across the waters at the invisible. Then again extending his arms, he cried:

'Behold her! See, my brothers, she is holding out her gracious hands to me. Ma-tso-po, I come to meet thee!'

He dashed wildly overboard. The angry waves closed over him, and we never saw him again.

All this time we had been drifting to the south, and we soon lost sight of the island; whereupon the crew

CALIFORNIA

THE GREAT STORM
From a Drawing by the Author

THE GREAT STORM

sank down in despair, giving up all hope of Ma-tso-po's assistance.

'There is no hope,' they wailed. 'We are lost men! We are all doomed to perish!'

The camphor dealer then entreated them to join him in trying *his* god, Lo-t'ien-ya, or the Old Lord of Heaven. They all cried loudly, tears streaming from their eyes, whilst the camphor dealer led their prayers thus:

'O, Lo-t'ien-ya! Lo-t'ien-ya! Dost thou not know me? Rememberest thou not? Hast thou forgotten the devout man whose house adjoins thy sacred temple? But last year did I not give twenty-five dollars of my hard-earned savings to repair thine abode? I have always been a good man. I have never done a bad thing in my life. Wherefore art thou thus punishing thy devoted slave? Consider, too, the fate of all these poor fellows with me. Aid us, oh, Lo-t'ien-ya, to get ashore, and nothing will I deny thee!'

The weeping and frantic tearing of hair was shocking to witness. Moreover, in spite of all their entreaties, the storm did not lull in the least. The waves at intervals stopped all language, and occupied us in a struggle to keep our breath.

Again the camphor dealer invoked his god.

'Art thou asleep, oh, Lo-t'ien-ya? Art thou away? What doest thou, thou god so slow of hearing? Dost thou forget all I have done for thee? If I ever get ashore alive, I will give my money to the other temple!'

My servant also was joining in the cries. The only unconcerned person in the boat was the young savage. He had never been to sea before, and did not appear to realise the gravity of our situation. He was laughing gaily at the impassioned gestures and wild utterances of the Chinese, which he did not understand, and drinking the salt water.

I felt nearly crazy, listening to the incoherent words of

the men, for as no favourable answer was vouchsafed to his prayers, the camphor dealer anathematised Lo-t'ien-ya in the vilest language, and began to invoke a Taoist god, using the same petition and promises that he had made to the Buddhist deity. All was in vain, and the man fell back exhausted. At that moment my servant laid his hand upon me, and said :

'Master, can you not aid us in our distress? Surely our gods are deaf that they do not hear us. Dr. Maxwell and your foreign missionaries are continually talking and preaching about Ya-so (Jesus). They say that He could work miracles, and do wonderful things. Perhaps He would listen and help us, if you would but say a prayer to Him for us.'

The boy's beseeching words filled me with a great shame. The truth really was, if I must confess it, that I had not given much heed to praying whilst I was in safety on shore, and somehow there seemed a sense of cowardice in beginning when I was in danger.

However, I am glad to say that I was guided to listen to the boy's request, and to the others, who joined him. I offered up, from my heart, a prayer in Chinese aloud to God, entreating Him to help us, for Christ's sake, and to bring us home in safety.

I felt indescribably better after this, and my servant also seemed encouraged. The camphor dealer and the crew were quite helpless, not seeming, in their apathy of despair, to care whether we lived or died; indeed I had great trouble to prevent them from jumping overboard.

The weather improved very little all that night, but we found ourselves all alive the next morning, when happily the gale moderated somewhat, seeming to have spent its strength.

About noon the sky cleared, the sun came out; the storm was over, leaving nothing but a heavy sea, and to our surprise, the tops of the highest mountains in the

THE GREAT STORM

interior, near Takao, appeared on the horizon. A slight draught of wind came from the westward, blowing right in towards the land.

I then tried to get the crew to exert themselves to throw the camphor overboard, in order to lighten the boat, and so to get our bodies above the surface of the water. They, however, refused to do anything. They whimpered that the gods refused to hear them, and that we were all bound to die; therefore we might just as well die quietly as try to work! I told them that I had prayed to my God, and that He had not refused to help me; that I was determined not to die if I could help it, neither did I intend to let them die.

I looked around for some persuasive weapon to emphasise my words. The rudder was washing astern, hanging by a lanyard, and in it was a short hardwood tiller. My resolve was made. I had my knife upon me, and my revolver with waterproof metallic cartridges; therefore I was not afraid of what the crew might do to me. I just took the tiller, and belaboured them all with it until they were bruised all over, and only too glad to do anything I told them.

Though our mast was gone, the stump remained, and part of the cotton sail, with a few bamboos. We lashed the bamboo to the stump, and rigged up a sail. We threw the camphor overboard, and bailed out the boat as well as we could; so we were now comparatively warm and comfortable.

Of course we had had no fresh water all the time, nor food; but, with the exception of the savage, we had all been too excited to think about eating or drinking. Now, however, the neglected claims of nature began to assert themselves.

In the fore compartment was an albino rabbit which my servant was bringing home as a curiosity. This was cut up, and served us with meat and drink for our meal, after which I used a bottle of chlorodyne which I chanced to have in my pocket. A few drops of this, mixed with a handful of sea-water, quenched our thirst, and did us no harm.

On Friday afternoon our terrible experience ended, and I am thankful to say that God brought us safely to the little port of Tang-kang, about ten miles south of Takao. Here the crew of some junks supplied us with rice, tea, and tobacco, and took us on shore in their boats to the local Mandarin. This official attended to our wants, and sent me, with my servant and the young savage, in sedan chairs to Takao.

After they had eaten well, and received their pay, the Chinese crew came to me, and, kneeling, thanked me for the way in which I had treated them. I impressed upon them that it was my God who had saved them. They, however, faithfully performed the vows which they had made in their peril, whilst I provided for the widowed mother of the man who jumped overboard.

In conclusion, I can earnestly affirm that I shall be thankful to my life's end for the experience I gained during those four miserable nights and days on board that cargo boat.

CHAPTER VIII

CORRUPTION AND RAPACITY OF CHINESE OFFICIALS

AT this moment, when the unwieldy empire of China is tottering to its base, when there is evidently a gathering of eagles around this very sick man, each eager to be the first to secure a large portion of spoil, a few remarks upon my experience of the official system of the Chinese mandarin, and of his peculiar method of upholding law and order and of encouraging legitimate business, may not be without interest.

Until a few years before its occupation by the Japanese, in 1896, Formosa, together with the Pescadores Islands, was governed by a Tao-tai, or intendant of circuit, who resided at the capital of the island, Taiwanfoo. The Tao-tai was directly subordinate to the viceroy of the two Chinese provinces Fuh-kien and Cheh-kiang, but he had the power of life and death, and also possessed the special privilege of communicating directly with the Emperor at Pekin. He was the highest magistrate, and was bound to make an annual inspection of the departments. It was believed that he was paid only 1,600 taels (not £600) by his imperial master, but his emoluments from many sources were very large; those drawn from the taxes on camphor especially reaching a fabulous amount.

The next in civil authority was the Tai-wan-Fu, or prefect, and then the Hiens, or district magistrates.

The Hiens had charge of the seven or eight hien, or districts, into which the part of the island under Chinese jurisdiction was divided. As I have before stated, the Chinese could only claim dominion over the plain on the west coast, and over one or two of the ranges of hills: the mountains in the interior, and the South Cape, being still in the possession of tribes of aborigines and savages, all of whom were of totally different races and languages to the Chinese.

The viceroy, who resided on the mainland, at Foochow, was bound by an often disregarded law to visit the island once every three years. These formal visits were lucrative to that high functionary, though anything but agreeable to the subordinates whom he visited; for, if they did not welcome him with handsome presents in their hands, they were liable to be shelved for the first trivial offence.

To recoup themselves for this compulsory generosity, the mandarins in their turn inflicted additional taxes upon the people; and thus at the expense of all classes the great servant of the emperor fulfilled his duty, and complaisantly returned with a well-filled purse.

The Tao-tai and the commander-in-chief received annually an ample amount of money for the suitable maintenance of land and naval forces, for the protection of the island from foreign aggression and from internal disturbances. The greater proportion of this sum was, however, pocketed by these officials, and the army and fleet languished so greatly as to be practically non-existent.

A visit of inspection by such a high official as the viceroy would therefore have been extremely inconvenient, and, if faithfully carried out (there *are* a few Chinese officials of probity and sternness), would probably have had serious consequences for the mandarins of Formosa. To avoid these dangers it had for many years been the custom for all officials, high and low, to contribute, from the wealth which they extorted from their unfortunate subjects, a sufficient sum of money to make it worth while for the viceroy (who was probably every bit as grasping as themselves) to

CORRUPTION OF CHINESE OFFICIALS 91

stay at home in China, and to forward from Foochow to the emperor a favourable report of the island.

During all the time I was in Formosa, his excellency did not put in an appearance, although we had one amusing false alarm.

Some three years before I left the island, a despatch came from China, officially notifying that the viceroy was determined to do his duty, and that he would visit Formosa shortly on a tour of inspection.

There was immediately a great stir throughout the country. Peasants and labourers were taken from their toil, and impressed into the service of the government; they were put into uniform, and matchlocks, spears, shields, and warlike weapons were placed in their hands.

The fleet at Taiwanfoo consisted chiefly of old junks which had not been in the water for more than thirty years. During this lengthened period the sea had receded, and the land had formed to the extent of more than a mile; the consequence being that these ancient vessels were high and dry; their masts, sails, and gear had rotted away from the long exposure to the sun and rain; the paint had peeled from their sides, and, in some cases, the very planking had been stolen for firewood.

Now, however, the greatest activity was evinced in the work of refitting these old wrecks: carpenters, sail-makers, and painters were busily employed, and a liberal allowance of paint and putty soon made the vessels look quite smart.

The difficulty then was to get them down to the nearest water, to enable them to lie afloat during the brief visit of the viceroy.

Captains and crews were engaged, and appointed to the several vessels. One or two of the junks were being transported on huge rollers to the nearest creek, when, before they reached their destination, a further despatch came from the viceroy to say that he had relinquished his intention of coming over.

The junks were just left where they were, to relapse into their former sorry condition; the workmen were discharged, and the peasants and labourers were permitted to quit the army and return to their ordinary peaceful occupations.

As to the officials, they were only too happy to be at liberty to misgovern with impunity, and to be free to turn their attention to extorting as much money from the common people as would liberally compensate them for the bribe which they had been obliged to send to Foochow.

One of the recognised methods of providing for an aged parent or sick relative in China is to pay a sum of money to the military mandarins as a bribe, in order that his name may be entered on the rolls of the militia, so that he may, in consequence, receive monthly three measures of rice and a small monetary allowance.

I have heard this transaction spoken of just as we should speak of purchasing an annuity.

The result of the misgovernment and oppression by the officials was that the resources of one of the most fertile islands in the world were either undeveloped or wasted; and instead of being a source of profit to the imperial government, Formosa was a drain upon its revenue.

Rebellions broke out every ten or twenty years, and were generally put down by the simple process of buying over the leaders, and then pitilessly exterminating their deluded followers. On the sea-coast, pirates and wreckers abounded, to the terror of honest fishermen and traders, who received no protection from their so-called 'paternal' government.

On land, gangs of robbers and bitter clan feuds rendered the highways continually impassable, whilst the savage aborigines made frequent incursions for bloodshed and plunder.

At rare intervals some general, desirous of gaining a

reputation at Pekin, and of testing the fighting quality of his troops, armed with European rifles, would organise an expedition into the mountains to subdue a savage tribe, and to extend the emperor's dominion.

Usually, however, these valiant onslaughts were fruitless and disastrous, the Chinese soldiers being either defeated from ambush or decimated by the deadly fever of the jungle.

On one or two occasions a Chinese commander did indeed induce a savage tribe, by liberal gifts, to consent to 'the tonsure,' thus owning themselves vassals of the 'Son of Heaven' at Pekin.

The general upon this sent out for a supply of razors, and proudly announced his great victory over the barbarians. When the shaving had been completed, he returned with all speed to a life of ease in the capital, Taiwanfoo, accompanied by the remains of his army.

Alas for the dominion of the illustrious 'Son of Heaven'! As soon as the gifts were consumed and their hair had grown, the savages, in almost every instance, repented them of their bargain and of their new civilisation; and, throwing off their allegiance, they returned to their familiar wild habits and customs.

Another anomaly was this :—The Tao-tai of Formosa, by virtue of being obliged to find timber for the keeping up of the imaginary fleet, claimed all the trees in the island as his private monopoly. Consequently, as camphor is produced from a tree, and had to pass through the Tao-tai's country for exportation, he also claimed a monopoly of that article, although by treaty all monopolies had been abolished, and although camphor had been provided for in the tariff as a legal subject for export, after payment of duties.

While the governor dared not, therefore, openly oppose the European who desired to purchase this article in the market, yet he did not scruple to harass, by every means in his power, any person who dared to trade in it except through his own agents.

When the Customs Service was established in Formosa, the Tao-tai and other officials viewed this important innovation with great alarm. They judged rightly that their former large gains and impositions on cargo would be greatly reduced ; that foreigners, upon payment of tariff duties, would be permitted to buy and sell freely in the markets, and that their arbitrary exactions, especially in respect of the camphor monopoly, would be taken out of their hands. They therefore determined that, if they could not resist the decree openly, they would contrive to make Formosa so hot for Europeans that they would be glad to retire, leaving the mandarins and their country to their former blissful state of monopoly and extortion. Their complete immunity from punishment for their wholesale execution of British subjects, and for their numerous outrages upon shipwrecked crews, no doubt emboldened both the officials and people to take this course.

Of their vexatious persecution of European merchants, and of the uneasy life the wily Tao-tai and his subordinates caused me to lead for years, by reason of this determination, I shall narrate further in my chapters on the Camphor War. Suffice it now to give one little illustration of their composed, quiet, and effective method of disposing of any man who had the misfortune to displease them.

When Lieutenant Gurdon took the Anping forts in 1868, the Hiap-tai, or brigadier in charge of the garrison, committed suicide, and the new Tao-tai appointed a successor from Canton, a man who was very favourable to Europeans. One of our gunboats, the 'Bustard,' having been forced over the bar into Anping Creek at spring tides, she was obliged to remain there for several weeks, and, during this enforced imprisonment, the brigadier was very kind in sending fresh provisions to the crew ; he also accepted invitations to visit the gun-boat, to dine,

CORRUPTION OF CHINESE OFFICIALS 95

and to witness the musical entertainments got up by the men to relieve the monotony of their compulsory idleness.

Well do I remember this genial Chinaman. He was of fair size, about six feet in his official boots, blessed with a keen sense of humour, and easily diverted. He had, I believe, at one time been a pirate, had afterwards served in Gordon's army on the mainland, and could speak a very fair jumble of pigeon English.

I can picture him now, on the deck of the gun-boat, after having partaken of the good fare provided by the commander, my old friend, Cecil Johnson, watching the sailors dancing a hornpipe, with delighted interest; and at length, when the music and the excitement grew irresistible, it was unspeakably funny to see this ordinarily stolid mandarin pick up his dignified silken robe and foot it with the rest of them!

Unfortunately the political atmosphere darkened. The action of our consul was disowned by the British Government, and the old Tao-tai was reinstated in Formosa. He secretly sent an accusation to Pekin, charging the brigadier with being friendly with the Europeans, and of rendering assistance to the man who had inflicted such a disgrace upon his predecessor in the Anping forts.

One morning, just before daylight, I was returning by sea from Takao, and my man was poling our shallow boat up the narrow canal which runs through the sandy plain between Anping and the suburbs of Taiwanfoo. Suddenly, through the grey dawn, we heard a greeting from the banks.

'Ho-á'!' responded my boatman.

'Hast heard the news?' came back the voice to us.

'No, what news?' he demanded. 'We are but now back from the sea.'

'The Hiap-tai has just been beheaded for being friends with the barbarians. Even now he lies out there,' the man pointed, passing on his way, and leaving us filled with horror at his news.

Later in the day the fact became public property, and I learnt, on most competent authority, the details of the case.

The Tao-tai invited the unsuspecting brigadier to meet the prefect, the sub-prefect, and all the chief notabilities at a feast in his Yamen, or official residence. On his arrival he was received with the greatest cordiality. He was the favoured guest of the evening. They all sat eating, drinking, and conversing until midnight, when the brigadier politely asked permission to make his adieus.

The smiling faces around him profoundly deprecated such haste. He resumed his seat.

Another convivial hour passed. The brigadier said he must really go. His family would be anxious.

The imperturbable faces around him smiled on.

'By no means,' they replied. 'We are enjoying ourselves too much to part yet. Why hurry?'

So passed yet another hour. Then the brigadier said he really *must* go.

The face of the Tao-tai, at the head of the table, set like ice, with the smile frozen upon it. He shouted loudly once, twice, for his attendants, who rushed in and stripped the poor brigadier of his official dress. The emperor's warrant was waved before his bewildered eyes, and he was led to the execution ground and beheaded.

His wife and family waited for his return with gradually increasing anxiety. Time passed on, until the following afternoon, when a dark rumour of that fell night's work reached them, and they had to flee for their lives to China.

Needless to say, this action of the Tao-tai struck terror into the hearts of any officials inclined to favour Europeans.

There is, throughout the Celestial Emperor's dominions,

CORRUPTION OF CHINESE OFFICIALS

a very effectual system of secret espionage. Each official, large or small, is 'shadowed.' No man is safe from spies who may misconstrue his simplest action.

Moreover, in all the Yamens, archives are jealously kept, in which are recorded the civil and criminal cases of the district, adjudicated upon or left unsettled. These have been handed down for generations, from official to official, and the system is highly useful to the mandarins, as upon any provocation—such, for instance, as a man unguardedly displaying a too comfortable degree of prosperity, or depending too much on his connection with Europeans—they can refer to these books of doom, and trump up some criminal charge, or unsettled civil suit, which will give them an opportunity of relieving him of a goodly portion of his superfluous wealth, besides affording them the satisfaction of annoying the objectionable barbarians.

The Rev. W. Campbell, F.R.G.S., of Taiwanfoo, in an article in the 'Scottish Geographical Magazine,' thus comments upon the departure of the mandarinate from Formosa :—

'Now it is no part of our duty to speak evil of dignities or of anybody else, but twenty-five years' observation leads to the conclusion that there are tremendous difficulties in the way of regarding Chinese officialdom with anything like feelings of confidence and respect. No doubt some members of the class are capable (from the native point of view), unselfish, diligent, and really helpful to the people. Generally speaking, however, this countless host, from the viceroy down to the lowest yamen runner, goes on the fundamentally pernicious principle that the country was made for the mandarins, and not the mandarins for the country.'

CHAPTER IX

MY FIRST VISIT TO THE SAVAGE TRIBES OF THE INTERIOR. THE END OF GENERAL BURGEVINE

AFTER I had been some months domiciled in my watery home on the 'Ternate,' the old Dutch frigate in Takao harbour, and when my pleasant acquaintance with the worthy Dominican Fathers had ripened into friendship, I confided to them my great desire to explore those parts of the interior of the island where as yet the foot of white man had not trodden, and my curiosity to see some of the wholly uncivilised inhabitants of the mountains. The Padres very kindly assisted me in my desire by giving me a letter of introduction to their mission station at the foot of the hills, on the outermost fringe of Pepohoan civilisation.

I forthwith obtained a short leave of absence, and prepared to start upon my pilgrimage. A Hamburg three-masted schooner, the 'Japan,' was discharging cargo in the harbour, and the chief officer, upon hearing my project, eagerly volunteered to accompany me. The compradore of the firm of Jardine gave us an introduction to a Chinaman on our route; and on a Friday afternoon we turned our backs on Takao, and our faces to the distant mountain ranges.

Armed with revolvers and double-barrelled fowling-pieces, we took but little luggage with us—just a blanket each, strapped on our backs, and a number of bright coloured beads, small mirrors, flint and steel, needles, and lengths of crimson cloth to propitiate the savages.

SAVAGE TRIBES OF THE INTERIOR 99

We stayed for a short time at Ling-a-liau, the mission station, to receive the introductory letter, and the 'Godspeed' of my kind Dominican friends.

We then commenced our march towards the district city of Pi-t'au or Hong-soa, through a country well cultivated by the industrious Chinese with rice, hemp, sugar, and sweet potatoes; generally flat, but at intervals broken by low sandy ridges producing nothing but the Pandanus, or screw pine. These elevations mark the different coast-lines, as the land has gradually encroached upon the sea by the silting up of the rivers and streams from the high mountains.

Both of us were altogether unaccustomed to pedestrianism, and quite out of training through confinement on board ship; so when at sundown we reached Pi-t'au we were thoroughly tired out, and glad to obtain the rest and refreshment which the letter of my friend, the compradore, procured for us at the house of his countryman, a prosperous sugar merchant.

We were afoot early on the following morning, bidding farewell to our host, who ridiculed the idea of two Europeans ever hoping to penetrate through the Hak-ka and Hok-lo country to the land of the Ch'i-hoan, or savage barbarian. However, we set our faces firmly, and tramped on towards the hills.

The first part of our journey was similar to that of the previous afternoon, but we soon came to a wide sandy plain, the dry bed of the Tang-kang, or southern Tamsui River, several miles in extent. Here the travelling was very fatiguing; the sun was oppressive in its power, and the air was filled with dust.

The hot hours passed until mid-day; we were almost choked with dust and thirst, until, at a wayside refreshment hovel, we contrived to concoct a primitive species of cocktail, composed of samshu (rice whisky), ducks' eggs, and coarse brown sugar, which we drank out of dirty earthenware rice bowls. Uninviting as this mixture sounds, we were then very glad of it, and tramped on with renewed energy.

In the early afternoon we reached the market town of A-kau, on the extreme border of the Hok-lo country. Here we were hospitably entertained by a connection of our Pi-t'au host, who warned us of the dangers we should incur in passing through the territory of the warlike and turbulent Hak-kas. We found the weekly market in full swing, and upon our appearance amongst the crowd in the marketplace we were at once surrounded by an inquisitive and vociferous throng. My intimacy with the 'white' or intelligible language—that is, the Hok-lo dialect—enabled us to both answer and ask all kinds of questions.

Where were we going—we red-haired barbarians? When we explained our earnest purpose, to get through to the savages, we were greeted with shouts of laughter.

'Did we really think that we could do that and live? It was impossible! No white man had ever done such a thing! The savages had tails, and ate men; no "man" would go near them.'

We met all their chaff and incredulity with firmness. In truth, the nearer I got to the goal of my ambition, the more feverishly anxious I was to succeed. We would go on at all costs.

There were among the crowd some Hak-ka women, who had come from a distance to the market, bearing grass and sundry home manufactures upon sticks resting on their shoulders. They had made their little purchases, and were preparing to return. I had never met any of these people before, but had heard that they came from the Canton province, and spoke a language akin to the court dialect; so trying Pekinese mixed with a smattering of Cantonese acquired from the tea-men at Fu-chau, I made an experiment which succeeded in pleasing the women. As they all could speak Hok-lo, we had no difficulty in understanding each other. When they found we were really serious in our

PEPO-HOAN AND CHINESE GROUP FORMOSA

determination, they laughingly suggested that we should accompany them, as our roads lay together. I gladly consented to this, for I fully recognised the protective value of their companionship.

So we trudged on, a merry party in the deepening twilight. The women bantered us on our project; they tried to scare us with terrible tales of the dangers ahead. Then, too, they were full of curiosity as to the ways of the 'red-haired barbarians,' and their questions were unending. We parted a little before dark. While glad to have had the novelty of our company as far as they went, they refused to guide us to the Padres' Pepo-hoan village, as they had a feud with those people.

At last, after many mistakes, to our great satisfaction we safely reached the little Dominican outpost at Bankimtsng, where we received a warm welcome from the hospitable Padres.

They regaled us with the best food they had to offer, principally pork and rice. They brought out excellent wine and spirits, and good cigars, for our comfort and repose.

To our chagrin, upon our laying our project before them, they impressed upon us the utter hopelessness of such a scheme. We could not get through to the savages alive, and any such attempt would be superlatively foolhardy. The country on the lower slopes of the mountains was very unsettled; there were constant feuds in progress, while one was never sure when the savages might swoop down from above upon a head-hunting expedition. We must abandon our plan. My disappointment was extreme. To have come so far, to be so near the savages, and to return without seeing them after all!

The worthy Padres sympathised with my mortification. They called in a wise old Pepo-hoan to assist at our conference, but he confirmed their cautions to us. It was not possible. After a while he proposed a scheme, to which, in default of anything better, we were glad to agree.

This old Pepo-hoan had had many dealings with the savages when in brief spells of peace they descended to a sort of debatable land between two gorges, and bartered with the Pepo-hoans for Chinese luxuries, tobacco, red cloth, bright beads, samshu, etc., offering in return, skins of wild animals, velvety deer horns, tobacco, charcoal, and a native cloth woven by their women, of grass intermixed with threads of bright cloth.

He knew several of the savage chiefs well, and, if we would make it worth his while, he would start off at once and tell his Ka-le-hoan [1] friends of our desire to see them; and perchance he could induce them, under cover of night, to come down to the mission to visit us.

It was Saturday night, and our leave expired on Monday evening. There would be many miles to go; he would try to be back on Sunday about midnight, if we could wait so long.

Well, it was a chance; so we agreed, and the old Pepo-hoan with a companion started off, whilst we tested the comfort of one of the Padres' beds.

Sunday passed restfully and pleasantly. We chatted with our hosts, smoked, interviewed many of the Pepo-hoan villagers, and wandered as near as we dared to the beautifully wooded slopes of the mountains. I was all impatience. Would the old Pepo be as good as his word? Would evil befall him?

The evening seemed interminable. At last, as the hours dragged on, we slowly gave up hope, and went to bed.

I seemed but to have slept a moment, when I was awakened by a confused hubbub of voices; torches flared before my bewildered eyes. There were the Padres, the old Pepo-hoan, with half the village behind him, and, as they parted to make a passage way, there emerged two figures who had surely stepped bodily from the pages of Marryat or Fenimore Cooper— two stately, dusky, black-

[1] In the south the savages are called Ka-le-hoan, or 'puppets.'

teethed savages, in all their glory of paint and skins and feathers.

I pulled on a few garments, and hastened to give them greeting. I had accomplished my heart's desire. The Pepo-hoan was our interpreter. How we talked and laughed! They turned out to be very good-humoured, intelligent fellows. I told them of the Chinese conviction that they had tails; I was made to examine them to prove that they possessed no such appendages. They were convulsed with laughter at the idea, and in return for our scrutiny made us show them our white bodies.

I brought out our gifts for them, which gave them much delight. In return, they presented me with some armlets formed of wild boar's tusks, and gave us each a native pipe. We smoked and chatted enthusiastically until the first streaks of dawn warned our visitors to be up and away to reach their own country before the daylight might reveal them to their lurking foes. So with many an expression of friendliness and goodwill we bade our dusky guests adieu.

Then, after a substantial breakfast, we ourselves made our thanks and farewells to the good Padres, and, with a Christian Chinese letter-carrier belonging to the mission, we started to retrace our steps.

All went well until we were stopped by a band of Hak-kas, who viewed the incursion of two white men with frowning suspicion, and our Chinese Christian guide was terror-stricken. I addressed them in the Hok-lo tongue, and afterwards added a few words in their own Hak-ka dialect, assuming a friendly and unconcerned manner. This propitiated them somewhat, and we parted amicably. Such good fortune did not attend my old friend Elles, who, in passing through their country some years later, was accosted by such another band of Hak-kas, and he, not knowing their language, was nearly done to death at their hands.

Dusty, thirsty, and exhausted, we at last reached Pi-t'au, where our Chinaman acquaintance regaled us with some indifferent champagne, and we pressed on again.

We reached Ling-a-liau and the hospitable roof of the Padres about eleven o'clock at night. They were delighted to see us back safe and sound. We partook of a substantial meal, after which they sent us down the lagoon in their own boat to Takao, which we reached about two or three in the morning, deadly tired, stiff, and dirty, but triumphant.

For many a long day after that our adventures were discussed and exclaimed over. Our presents were examined curiously as proof of our good faith, and we were treated as heroes to have dared so much to see the savages.

My companion on this little adventure—a right good fellow—had a sad fate at last.

When I had left the Customs service, and was in the firm of McPhail Brothers, this same man was appointed captain of their coasting schooner—a fine smart boat. He was taking treasure to Amoy, when he was caught in a typhoon, and went down with all hands, except one. A miserable Manilaman, half dead with fright and starvation, was found clinging to some wreckage far out at sea; but of my friend, a European passenger, and the rest of the crew there was no trace.

About the time of the New Year of 1865, I accompanied Mr. Maxwell, the Commissioner of Customs, from Takao to the capital of the island, Taiwanfoo, to establish a branch of the Customs service there; and to my surprise and gratification I shortly afterwards found myself appointed to the charge of the Customs at Anping, the port of that city.

One chief cause of satisfaction to me in this promotion was that in my improved status I had better opportunities of mingling in Chinese society, and thus of enlarging

UNIV. OF
CALIFORNIA

ANPING (PORT OF TAIWANFOO) VIEW OF OLD DUTCH FORT 1650

my knowledge of the character of this interesting people, and of perfecting my studies of their language and their classics.

At Anping the official residence was on shore—another advantage; and I lost no opportunity of cultivating the acquaintance of the people, of every rank and station.

On my installation at Anping there was much to do, and all the organization to arrange. Mr. Maxwell stayed long enough to choose my future official residence—a small house which had been used as a Chinese club; after which he was forced to hurry back to Takao.

He, however, left with me a man in whom he reposed great confidence, to advise and assist me in establishing my new station.

This man, a Manchu by race, and a Sze-yeh or government secretary by official rank, inspired confidence and respect by his striking personality. Tall, dignified, composed, with most polished manners, deeply learned in the sacred classics of China, and with a handsome face, he seemed the embodiment of all that a cultivated servant of the emperor should be.

Besides this imposing person, I had with me my Chinese instructor from Fu-chau, who was also a Manchu, an American tidewaiter to board the vessels on their arrival, and several coolies to act as the crew of our boarding catamaran.

We soon got the little club-house clean and ready for my occupation. We then found it necessary to form a small canal from the creek to the Custom House, up which boats could bring import and export cargo, and to erect sheds for examination.

The organising of this piece of work the illustrious Manchu made his special business. He drew up plans, engaged the contractor for the dyking and building, and chose a gang of labourers from among the indigent Chinese fishermen who lived near. His zeal was of great assistance; and when in a week or so he had to return to Takao, I bade him *bon voyage* regretfully.

Time passed on until the monthly pay-day arrived. I summoned all the labourers into the office, and proceeded to pay every man his due. They got very good wages for their work—some five dollars, and some ten dollars a month; but as I placed the money in each outstretched palm, I noticed anything but satisfied expressions upon their faces. There arose a vague hum of discontent and grumbling. I could not catch any distinct utterances of complaint, but so much was evident to me, and I could not comprehend their reason for dissatisfaction.

'What is wrong?' I inquired frankly.

They, squatting on their hams, Chinese fashion, looked up at the tiled roof, and down on the floor, everywhere but at my inquiring face.

'Come!' I persisted, 'I am a just man. I would deal rightly with every one. Why are you not satisfied? What is the matter?'

'Oh, nothing, nothing,' they replied.

Still the murmurs went on. I could make out a few phrases in the confusion.

'Just look at this!' growled one to another. 'Not enough to keep us in rice for a month! And we have wives and children!'

In despair I called in the assistance of my Chinese teacher, but he professed to be ignorant of their meaning, not understanding the local dialect well.

'Come, tell me,' I tried again, 'what is wrong? Are you not satisfied with your money? It is good pay.'

At last one man, bolder than the rest, broke out:

'Good pay, you call it, do you? When one-half of it has to go to that Manchu man who engaged us!'

'Yes,' then ventured another, 'and two-thirds of mine!'

'And of mine,' said they all.

So indeed it proved to be. The immaculate Manchu,

SAVAGE TRIBES OF THE INTERIOR 107

apparently so superior and so trustworthy, had not scrupled to bargain with these poor labourers to himself receive half their pay.

I questioned the contractor; it was the same story. I was highly indignant. Yet I was troubled as to the best course to pursue.

The Manchu was implicitly trusted by Mr. Maxwell: he was almost above suspicion, whilst I was young, and a new-comer.

Moreover, even if I told Mr. Maxwell everything, such was the evasive and cowardly nature of the Chinese that the men would very probably deny their statements made to me, and profess gratitude for the upright and just Manchu.

At last my resolve was made. The truth, and justice, at all costs.

'Look here, my men,' I said, 'I will tell the great man (Mr. Maxwell), and I will see you righted. But you must stand by me and tell the truth to him, as you have told it now to me.'

'Oh, yes, yes, of course we will,' they replied.

Then I turned to my Chinese teacher, making him listen to their story (which he could sufficiently understand), that he might confirm it to Mr. Maxwell. He was by race a Manchu also, and it was instructive to observe how very dense he grew when requested to pay careful attention to the men's statements.

However, I condemned him from his own sacred classics. I impressed upon him the sinfulness of complicity in unrighteousness, until I gradually worked him into a state of indifference to the claims of clanship, and I was sure of his confirmation, however reluctantly given.

When Mr. Maxwell next visited the station I laid the whole matter before him, and his indignation was extreme. The Manchu was severely censured, and the workmen henceforth had the whole of their wages for their own benefit. The Manchu's dignified presence was still to be seen in Takao, and he always treated me with impressive courtesy; but as I shortly afterwards left the Customs service, he fortunately had no opportunity of expressing his affection for me in practical Chinese fashion.

It was a few months after this, when I had settled down in my new position, that the following incident occurred.

One morning during the south-west monsoon (at which season the anchorage is unapproachable, except for a chance day or so in the course of the month) my American assistant and I were agreeably surprised by the appearance of a large fore-and-aft schooner, flying the American flag.

My assistant boarded the vessel in the revenue catamaran, and speedily returned, bringing with him three gentlemen, who were respectively introduced to me as Mr. Preston, the owner of the vessel; Captain Page, the master; and a passenger. The schooner, we were informed, was the 'General Sherman,' and she had cleared from Shanghai for Taiwanfoo in ballast.

We welcomed our visitors gladly. It was a relief to have our monotony broken by the advent of three strangers. We were eager to have news of the outer world, as for two long months our society had been restricted to the Anping fisherfolk.

The owner and captain made general inquiries of us as to the possibility of obtaining a charter to load sugar in Formosa, for North China or Japan; but, on being informed that during the south-west monsoon trade was confined to Takao, they decided to go there, and cleared the vessel for that port.

The passenger, we observed, was a small, dark man, somewhat of a Welsh type, with keen black eyes. He appeared of a reserved disposition, volunteering no in-

THE END OF GENERAL BURGEVINE 109

formation regarding himself, and merely asking a few indifferent questions as to the Chinese officials and the people of the island.

Our visitors lunched with us, and we spent a pleasant afternoon together; after which the Americans returned to their schooner, having invited us—weather permitting—to lunch with them next day, before their departure for Takao.

The elements proved kind, and we were able to take advantage of the invitation, enjoying in consequence a thoroughly American entertainment of the best kind, which was a welcome change from our customary fare of tough buffalo, skinny fowls, or curried frogs.

Tiffin over, the captain asked us to excuse him whilst he superintended the preparations for getting under weigh, and the owner retired to his cabin under the plea of writing letters. The mysterious passenger still held aloof from us, leaning over the rails, with thoughts apparently far away, whilst I and my companion settled ourselves on the stern gratings over the wheel chains, and solaced ourselves with some of our host's excellent cigars.

Upon the gratings lay an open sketch-book; and we, as idle men will do, innocently examined more closely its cleverly drawn contents.

Within its pages were sketches and plans of forts, interspersed with water-colour paintings of scenery on the Yang-tze. Beneath several of the sketches was scribbled the signature, 'Burgevine,' in pencil. We looked at each other with dawning intelligence. The conclusion was obvious. The mysterious and taciturn passenger could be no other than the famous—or rather the notorious—General Burgevine, the American adventurer who had preceded General Gordon in command of the Ever Victorious Army.

This accidental discovery placed us in a very embarrassing position. Burgevine, we knew, had quarrelled with

Li-Fu-tai (Li-Hung-Chang) and had gone over to the Taiping rebels. He was, therefore, a dangerous enemy to the Chinese Imperial Government, whilst we, as the Chinese saying is, were 'eating the emperor's rice.'

After a perplexed consultation, we came to the conclusion that, as we had made the discovery under the seal of hospitality, and as, after all, our surmises had no further confirmation than a chance sketch-book, we were justified in reconciling our consciences with our racial sympathies.

We therefore determined to make no use of the discovery we had so innocently happened upon, but we decided to quit the vessel as quickly as possible; so, after a hasty leave-taking, we dropped into our waiting catamaran, and were paddled back to the Custom House; whilst the 'General Sherman' weighed anchor for Takao, where she would arrive that night or the following morning.

The same evening I received a letter per courier, from the Acting Commissioner of Customs, Takao, informing me that news had come from Amoy to the effect that General Burgevine had secretly left Shanghai for Amoy to join the rebels at their last stronghold, Chang-Chau-fu, in Fuh-kien (near Amoy), and further, that the vessel in which he had sailed had cleared for Taiwanfoo.

As the 'General Sherman' would have reached Takao before I could reply, we were relieved from any responsibility.

We learned later that, upon the schooner's arrival there that evening, the Chinese local authorities had requested the Commissioner of Customs to search the vessel and to arrest Burgevine; but there being no American consul in Formosa, and the mandarins having no force with which to support the Commissioner, the captain and owner of the 'General Sherman' were able to defy the authorities, and Burgevine was unmolested.

The schooner, however, hastened to leave for Amoy, where it appeared an American negro servant was waiting

THE END OF GENERAL BURGEVINE

to receive Burgevine, to convey him with all speed to Chang-Chau-fu, where the Tai-ping rebels were impatiently awaiting him, relying upon his presence to revive their failing cause. This servant, however, had treacherously sold his master to the mandarins. After landing the general at Amoy during the night, he quietly conveyed him into the hands of the imperial authorities.

The Chinese officials decided not to run the risk of losing such a precious prize by handing him over to the American consul-general; they therefore determined to send Burgevine overland, under strong guard, to Pekin. He was accordingly put into a sedan-chair, and carried to the northern provinces. Before reaching Pekin, however, by an extremely convenient coincidence, either the chair coolies stumbled or the ferry-boat in which the chair was being carried capsized: the exact details are shrouded in mystery. Certain it is that, after a wild and romantic career, General Burgevine met his fate by drowning; wherefore the Chinese Government was saved any further anxiety or trouble on his account.

It is interesting to follow briefly the subsequent fortunes of the 'General Sherman'; the hapless fate of the owner, master, and vessel is worth recording as a matter of history in the Far East.

After landing General Burgevine, the skipper succeeded in obtaining a charter in Amoy to return to Formosa for the purpose of loading sugar. Taking advantage of a spell of fine weather, the schooner came from Takao to Anping to fill up; but while she was lying in the roads a typhoon came on, and she was forced to put to sea, where, with her sails blown away, and dismasted, she drifted helplessly round the South Cape and along the east coast of the island. The captain and crew were obliged to sit despairingly still, with two equally appalling alternatives in prospect, either to be dashed to pieces on the rocks, or to fall a prey to the tender mercies of the savages.

Eventually, however, the storm abated somewhat, and Captain Page was able to navigate his ship round the North Cape, by the Formosa channel to Takao, and from thence he left Formosa with his ship for the last time.

The end was dramatic. There were, in those days, wild travellers' tales of the wealth of gold and jewels to be found in the native tombs in Korea, a country practically unknown to Europeans at that time. The owner of the 'General Sherman' fitted her out for a filibustering expedition to Korea, fired with the desire to handle a portion of this mysterious treasure; but the Koreans arose and massacred all hands, and destroyed the ship.

So, by some strange fate, the three men whom we had entertained at Anping all came to a tragical end.

CHAPTER X

COWARDICE AND PLUCK. VISIT TO THE SAVAGE VILLAGES. MY LIFE AT TAIWANFOO

A FEW months after I took over the charge of the Customs at Anping, some German and Danish vessels had received special government passes permitting them to enter a port to the north of Po-te-ts'ui, for the purpose of loading salt.

Reports shortly afterwards reached the Commissioner of Customs that other vessels were smuggling this article. Mr. Maxwell thereupon ordered me to proceed to the port, to examine all the vessels lying there, and to inspect their passes.

I accordingly set out from Anping one morning in a native fishing boat, with a small crew, of whom a queer little Chinaman, named Chiau-a, was the head.

We beat about for many hours, trying to make our way up the coast, but the wind increased in strength, and the tide was adverse; we therefore made but little progress. Chiau-a advised that we should run inshore for several miles, where there was a channel between the sand banks, through which our boat could be poled or tracked up to the port for which we were bound.

Several of the crew objected to this plan, as this portion of the coast was a notorious haunt of pirates, who lurked there, waiting for small craft; but it was finally agreed to take Chiau-a's advice, and we therefore bore away for the mouth of the channel.

On arriving we found, to the dismay of our crew, that two suspicious-looking junks were already at anchor there,

I

their sides covered with rattan shields. However, my Chinese servant endeavoured to encourage the crew by reminding them that the master had plenty of guns, and that they had no need to fear, for if they were pirates they would not dare to attack a European.

On this we entered the narrow channel; the sailors jumped overboard, and with a tow-line proceeded to track the boat along, head to wind.

We had not progressed a quarter of a mile when a gun was fired, and tom-toms began to beat on the junks in our rear.

Our terrified men all climbed aboard, leaving the boat to drift aground. Luckily she swung round on her heel, with her head pointing towards the entrance.

The crew began to beat their hands and cry, whining:

'We are all dead men! They are pirates after all! They will rob us of all our clothes and leave us naked. *Why* did we come?'

I was not experienced in such adventures then, and my heart fluttered a good deal at the idea of pirates; but even at such a moment it amused me that the sailors should be in so great a panic at the prospect of losing half a dozen pairs of ragged cotton breeches.

They scurried below like rats to their holes, whilst my servant and I on deck could see the junks' crews hoisting sail and heaving up anchor. I hastily jumped down below, and thrashed the fellows with a stick until they were forced to come on deck. Then I said:

'You rascals! My guns and my clothes are worth more than a hundred dollars, and I don't intend to lose them so easily. Come, hoist the sail, and we shall get away before the pirates can catch us.'

They managed, tremblingly, to hoist the sail half-mast up, and we flew back out of the creek with the wind behind us.

On seeing that there was a chance of escape, the sailors

began to laugh and to shout abuse to the junks. Then suddenly the boat grounded, and as suddenly their laughter changed to tears. Driven overboard by the stick, they contrived to get the boat afloat again, and we passed the junks before they could get under weigh. I bestowed a salute upon them with my rifle, and down dropped their sails.

My crew absolutely refused to go any further, and insisted on returning to Anping; we therefore put out to sea, and ran swiftly before the breeze, with full sail, out of sight of the low land.

In gibing the sail a rope caught my cork helmet and sent it flying overboard. To my surprise Chiau-a, who had shown himself such an arrant coward, sprang into the waves after it, and before we could bring the boat to the wind he was half a mile astern.

We dodged about for an hour before we could pick the man up, but he was eventually pulled on board none the worse, and smiling with glee that he had saved my helmet, which was worth about ten shillings.

It was in the autumn of the same year, 1865, and while I was still in the Customs service, that I visited Sin-kang, a village about nine or ten miles from Taiwanfoo. Here I found the remains of an ancient Pepo-hoan village, dating from the time of the Dutch occupation in the seventeenth century. Sin-kang had been used by these beneficent settlers as a principal mission station, and the present village contains the descendants of the aboriginal inhabitants. These Pepo-hoans, however, dress like the Chinese, and have forgotten their old language.

The chief of this village was a Pepo-hoan, who was a small mandarin, having gained some military rank as a reward for his services in China during the Taiping rebellion. He had brought back from the mainland a singular trophy, in the shape of a small-footed Chinese wife, whom he had captured by his sword and bow.

I became very friendly with this man, and in the course

of our conversations he told me that the majority of his tribe had migrated into the interior, and that they had settled in villages which were scattered even as far as the east coast.

I acquainted him with my interest in the aborigines of the island, and he promised that if I felt inclined to visit the savages of the high mountain ranges, he would give me an introduction to his people in the lower hills, who, he assured me, would welcome any 'red-haired relation,' and who would pass me on to those of their tribe who were upon terms of friendship with some of the savage tribes.

I was delighted to avail myself of this opportunity, and having obtained the necessary leave of absence I arranged for a fortnight's expedition into the interior.

Dr. Maxwell, my friend, who was a medical missionary of the English Presbyterian Church, had just been driven out of Taiwanfoo by the ignorant and prejudiced inhabitants, and had been confined to the port of Takao. When he heard of my projected expedition he expressed a wish to accompany me, as he thought it possible that the simple aborigines might show themselves more amenable to the Gospel than the conceited Chinese had proved to be. Dr. Maxwell's companionship was most acceptable to me, not only because of his personal good qualities, but also because I was aware of the wonderful cures he had accomplished on the fever-stricken and ophthalmic Chinese —cures which would undoubtedly appear miraculous to the simple Pepo-hoan and the barbarous Ch'i-hoan.

Our intentions caused no little excitement, for with the exception of my previous interview with the savages, which I had been able to accomplish with the assistance of the Spanish missionaries during my residence at Takao, no European had ever communicated with the unsubdued aborigines of the south of Formosa, and none of their villages had yet been entered by the white man.

One afternoon in November, 1865, we quitted Taiwanfoo with our servants and three Chinese coolies carry-

VISIT TO THE SAVAGE VILLAGES 117

ing provisions, medicines, etc. We spent the night at Sin-kang, at the abode of my friend the military mandarin, who was very hospitable. He appeared to regret having encouraged me to make the excursion; he tried to dissuade me from going further, for, he explained, although our mutual 'kindred' would do everything in their power to entertain us and to assist us, yet the savages themselves were utterly barbarous, and only anxious to secure the heads of all strangers. However, when he found us unmoved by all his doctrines of expediency, he furnished us with a guide and accompanied us part of the route.

Soon after leaving Sin-kang we entered the lower ranges of hills, and turned our backs upon Chinese impertinence and civilisation. Early in the afternoon we reached our preliminary destination, Kong-a-na, about fifteen miles from Sin-kang.

I had already spent a night at this place, and we received a most hearty welcome from the T'ong-su, the headman of the tribe, responsible to the Chinese Government. We found him a fine specimen of his race, frank and simple, and without the sophisticated notions of his clansman, our friend the chief of Sin-kang, who had unavoidably been to a certain extent corrupted by Chinese influence.

Here in Kong-a-na the people were proud of calling themselves 'Hoans,' or 'barbarians,' and the old people retained a knowledge of the language spoken by their forefathers. They reverenced the memory of the good Dutch settlers, loving all white men, and claiming kindred with them for their sake. It was really very touching to hear them, the old women especially, saying, 'You white men are our kindred. You do not belong to those wicked shaven men, the Chinese. Yet what kind of people do you call yourselves? Ah! for hundreds of years you have kept away from us, and now, when our sight is dim, and we are at the point to die, our old eyes are blessed with a sight of our "red-haired relations"'!

Nothing could exceed the kindness shown to us by these simple people; appreciation extended to us chiefly because of the traditions handed down amongst them of the beneficent Dutch rule, and the wise brotherliness of those old-time missionaries.

Dr. Maxwell was happily able to make them some return, by effecting quick relief in cases of ague, fever, and ophthalmia.

Bad weather and the kindly importunities of our entertainers obliged us to stay two days in Kong-a-na; but early on the third day our host, with his sons and several clansmen, accompanied us to another branch of the tribe, who had settled on the outskirts of Chinese jurisdiction, and were in communication with some of the independent savage tribes.

A portion of this day's journey was through a wild and barren tract of country, but in the afternoon we arrived at a Hak-ka town, called Lam-tsng, situated at the western foot of the last chain of mountains, which rise to a height of about 4,000 feet, and which separate, as the Chinese express it, 'the dominion of men from the mountains of barbarism.'

We were here most hospitably entertained by a flourishing Chinese doctor and druggist, who felt amply recompensed by our gift of a portion of the wonderful quinine.

After a good meal and a rest, we commenced our ascent of the mountain range, where, on attaining the summit, we were rewarded by a most ravishing prospect.

All the lower ranges, under Chinese rule, had long been denuded of trees for the sake of firewood, but before us, looking down, lay a fair and fertile valley, through which ran a rapid rocky river; whilst, beyond, the mountains rose, covered with luxuriant jungle. Beyond, again, the peak of Mount Morrison (nearly 13,000 feet) fitly crowned this dense green verdure, and an additional charm was imparted to the great peak's beauty by a slight covering of pure snow, which glistened in the sun, confirming our

MOUNT MORRISON FORMOSA

UNIV. OF
CALIFORNIA.

VISIT TO THE SAVAGE VILLAGES

Chinese coolies' opinion of the wisdom of their ancestors, who first named the peak the 'Jadestone Mountain.'

Just before dark we arrived at Keng-chio-k'a, the last village of Pepo-hoans who pay respect to Chinese authority. The people here are chiefly engaged in protecting themselves from the oppressions of the Hak-ka Chinese, and from the head-hunting incursions of tribes of savages.

Our friend, the old T'ong-su, was received by them with great respect; and when, in response to their inquiries, he announced that he had brought them some 'red-haired kindred,' we were welcomed heartily. They slaughtered pigs and fowls for the suitable entertainment of ourselves and our escort.

These people spoke Chinese but imperfectly, and chiefly used their aboriginal language. They also intermarried with the friendly savage tribes, and they were more in sympathy with these barbarians than with the Hak-kas.

It was at our evening meal with them that we first saw their custom of dipping the finger into the cup of samshu, or potato whisky, and sprinkling a few drops towards the four points of the compass before drinking, as an offering to the spirits; also before eating they scattered morsels of food in the same way, and for the same purpose.

After supper our Pepo-hoan friends entertained us with native songs, whilst Dr. Maxwell's skill was entreated for cases of fever and other ailments.

When we unfolded our project to them, our hosts begged us not to venture amongst the savages, prognosticating doleful results for ourselves; but the old headman of Kong-a-na reassured them, saying that even the great Chinese mandarins were afraid of the 'red-haired hoan.' They therefore agreed that the next morning they would furnish us with a guide and an escort to accompany us to a place called Lau-lung, which was situated on the further slope of the first wooded range, in the valley at the foot of Mount Morrison, in the central range of the island.

The Keng-chio-k'a people suffered much from the attacks of two savage tribes, the Bangas and Bantaulangs, who were in the habit of lying in wait in the jungle bordering their rice fields during the harvest time.

Only a few weeks before our arrival the Bangas had murdered several of their women.

At the same time, these two savage tribes were friendly with the Pepo-hoan village called La-ku-li, some seven miles south of Lau-lung, and they were also confederate with three other tribes, the Pai-chien, Bilang, and Gani, in order to protect themselves against the Sibukun, a powerful tribe of nearly one thousand fighting men, who lived upon the eastern slope of the island. The Pai-chien, Bilangs, and Ganis, in their turn, were friendly with Keng-chio-k'a and Lau-lung Pepo-hoans, as they depended on these villages for their supply of guns, knives, powder, lead, and salt.

Early on the morrow our guide appeared, with one or two companions. He was an old Pepo-hoan who had spent his whole life in hunting and in fighting with savages or Hak-kas.

He had never seen a white man before, and he was immensely proud of introducing us to the Lau-lungs. He assured us that our 'relations' would be glad to welcome us.

Our Chinese coolies at this point declined to accompany us any further; but we speedily engaged other burden-bearers, whilst our servants, after the manner of Chinese boys, were rather glad to accompany their masters, for the sake of seeing something new.

Our Kong-a-na friends now bade us adieu, with many good wishes for our safe return to civilisation.

We crossed the broad valley and the river, which, as it was the dry season, was confined to a narrow channel. Arriving at the foot of the mountains on the further side of the valley, our guide gave us the first intimation that

CALIFORNIA

NEW GROUND BROKEN BY RAIN—CENTRAL MOUNTAIN RANGE p. 121

VISIT TO THE SAVAGE VILLAGES

we had left behind us our simple friends, by suggesting the advisability of putting our arms in order, whilst he and his followers loaded their matchlocks and lighted their fusees.

I had with me a Colt's revolver, a double-barrelled fowling-piece, and a seven-shooter Spencer rifle; all of which astounded the old man when he discovered how many shots the whole amounted to, and how the guns worked without any apparent fire.

He assured us, however, that no number of guns would avail us upon the route which we were now to march, a route usually haunted by his enemies, the Bangas and Bantaulangs, who could perceive us whilst they themselves remained invisible amongst the undergrowth. He enjoined the strictest silence, and forbade the use of tobacco except when he gave permission.

We now entered a narrow gorge, formed by the dry bed of a mountain stream, filled with huge boulders, hemmed in on either side by hills covered with the densest jungle. At one point of our march we passed between cliffs two or three hundred feet high, where our guide hurried us through at the risk of our necks, it being a favourite place of ambush for the foes of his tribe, several of his relatives having been murdered there.

After several toilsome hours of ascent, we reached the summit of the range, and saw below us a beautiful valley. Here our guide informed us that we had passed all danger, and that we were now in a friendly country.

The old man then persuaded us to sit down and tell him all about ourselves. He particularly desired to know why we, being his 'relations,' were yet so different in appearance and habits to the Pepo-hoans. He also entreated me to fire off all my guns, and expressed a wish that we would come to help his people to exterminate both the Chinese and the savages.

After a brief rest we descended into the valley, and

arrived about 3 P.M. at Lau-lung, a hamlet of substantial farm-houses.

Our guide shouted triumphantly to the people:

'Hoé, hoé! come out and see some of our red-haired relations, our relations of long ago, the men of whom our forefathers have told us!'

Upon this the T'ong-su, or headman, hastened out, followed by all his people, and after some explanations from our old guide, he turned to us and welcomed us heartily. He installed our hot and dusty selves and our travel-worn servants in comfortable rooms, whence, after refreshing ablutions, we were summoned to a goodly feast of venison, pork, and rice, with delicious trout from the neighbouring river. Here we found three savages of the Gani tribe, who had arrived that day; and, shortly after we had finished our meal, the chief of the Sibukun, with six attendants, appeared from the eastern side of the island. These important guests had not visited Lau-lung for two years. They brought with them bear and deer skins, sinews, and bezoar for barter. The men were fully armed with matchlocks, knives, spears, and bows and arrows; and they were gaily dressed in leopard-skin jackets, red cloth, bracelets of wild boars' tusks, with much elaborate adornment of beads and feathers.

Unfortunately the Gani and Sibukun tribes were at deadly feud; therefore our host demanded and temporarily impounded the arms of both parties.

A pig was killed, cut up, and boiled in a large caldron, and an *al fresco* feast was set forth, accompanied by several buckets of samshu. The savage guests seated themselves amicably, and prepared to do justice to the Pepo-hoan hospitality.

The Sibukun chief was a noted warrior, having taken as many as twenty to thirty heads in his time, whilst the Gani chiefs, though in the minority, were all redoubtable fighting men.

These rivals began the feast in a friendly spirit, chatting amiably; but, alas! the influence of the samshu did not make for peace; and, as they came more and more under its spell, their superficial courtesy fell from them, even as it has occasionally been known to do amongst highly civilised folk under like circumstances.

Each party began to boast of its superior prowess and of its mighty doings. Alternate fits of conviviality and warlike enthusiasm ensued, ending in a debauch which 'made night hideous,' and effectually murdered our sleep.

Just before daylight the remaining wakeful ones subsided into the sleep of intoxication, and they all presented a sorry spectacle, prostrate upon the ground, around a big fire, with their finery scattered in the dust.

The disturbances of the past night prevented us from putting in a very early appearance, and, when we at last encountered our host, he apologised to us for the discomfort we had undergone.

The Gani men had already left the village, whilst the Sibukuns seemed to be in a very dazed and subdued condition after their night's orgie. This condition was of distinct advantage to the Pepo-hoans in their subsequent bargainings with them, as it enabled them to obtain the merchandise, which their muddle-headed guests had brought, on advantageous terms.

It is to be feared that the Pepo-hoans have absorbed only too readily the lessons taught them by Chinese civilisation; and, with their new-found worldly wisdom, they treat the savages as their conquerors have treated them.

This day being Sunday we decided to have a complete rest. We visited some of the neighbouring farms, and Dr. Maxwell endeavoured to inculcate some elementary notions of Christianity, speaking to the people in Chinese, a language which all the Pepo-hoans understand. Whilst thus caring for their souls he was also able to relieve many sick bodies by the administration of simple remedies.

Later in the day we received an embassy from the chief of the Pai-chien tribe. This chief had been a notable man in his time, but he was now crippled with rheumatism, and could only give his tribe the benefit of his advice. He had heard of our arrival on the savage frontier, and sent out his adopted son to give us a friendly invitation to visit his village. The young man was to our surprise a Chinese, whom the chief had saved from some massacre in his boyhood, and who had now become a complete savage.

The following morning we prepared to start for the Pai-chiens, accompanied by our old guide and an escort of young men from Lau-lung; but an unexpected check occurred.

The Sibukuns were making ready to return home when news arrived that the Gani men had started on the war-path, and were determined to waylay their old enemies upon their route.

Now the Lau-lung men were responsible for the safety of their Sibukun guests, and they had more to dread from them than from the Ganis; they therefore hastily formed a party to accompany their visitors until they were out of danger, and we remained until this was accomplished.

Upon the return of the Lau-lung men from this errand we set out for the Pai-chiens, who were at that season occupying a hunting station situated in a most inaccessible spot in the mountains.

The Pai-chien tribe, we found, was decreasing at a rapid rate, owing to the feuds with the Sibukuns. They could only maintain their ancient reputation for valour by making raids amongst the Hak-ka Chinese.

We received a hearty greeting from the principal men of the tribe. Dr. Maxwell had already sent a bottle of medicine to the chief, and on our arrival we found that the remedy had produced so beneficent an effect that we were welcomed as very great friends. They feasted us with the best fare they had to offer, in the shape of dried venison and boiled millet ; and we talked long and amicably, whilst the old chief's son, Awang, was of great use to us from his knowledge of Chinese. He was thus able to interpret between us, and to give us information concerning the various tribes and their habits and customs.

We passed the night with our savage friends ; but as their hunting lodges consisted of nothing but thatched roofs over holes in the rocks, at an elevation of 6,000 feet, we were miserably cold under our blankets and deerskins.

They themselves lay on the ground around a large fire, with nothing but a piece of cloth round their loins. Their spears were stuck in the ground, and their firearms lay ready at their sides, as they lived in continual apprehension of an attack from their enemies.

When Dr. Maxwell and I rose in the early morning we were charmed with our surroundings. The situation was most romantic ; at our feet ran a mountain stream, with deep clear pools, into which fell cascades of sparkling water. The opportunity was tempting ; we determined to enjoy a good swim in the pools. No sooner said than done, and we were disporting ourselves in the water, revelling in its fresh coolness, when we were disturbed by much laughter.

To our dismay we discovered that we were being watched by all the women and children, who were amused and astonished at our white skin. This brought our bathe to a hasty conclusion.

We returned to the old chief, and after partaking of breakfast we were conducted to the Pai-chien village proper, which was composed of circular huts, with walls of reeds and thatched roofs.

Our escort showed us a house which was occupied by the unmarried men of the tribe. Here the walls were ornamented with the skulls of their enemies of other tribes, and the pig-tails of the Chinese whom they had slain. Amongst this gruesome record I counted eighteen Chinese queues.

After another entertainment here our old guide suggested that we should visit the Bilang tribe. We reached their village after two hours of wearisome climbing, and here again we found the old chief was utterly prostrate from rheumatism. He was delighted to see us, as he had already been told of Dr. Maxwell's remedy for the Pai-chien chief's complaint.

This old man had a very pretty little daughter, of whom he seemed exceedingly fond, and upon whose dress he bestowed unusual care. Fortunately we had with us some few articles of adornment, which we presented, and which were greatly appreciated. We were soon upon terms of friendship with the Bilangs.

Our visit, however, was fated to be of but short duration, for we had not been with them an hour when our old guide and the Lau-lung men rushed in, crying in consternation that the Bangas were on their way to pay a visit to their friends the Bilangs, and therefore we must leave at once, as they dared stay no longer.

We therefore reluctantly made our adieux to our hosts, accompanying them with a bottle of medicine for the aged chief, and again started on our pilgrimage.

'The best laid schemes of mice and men gang aft agley!' As fate would have it, we had not been tramping for more than half an hour in the thick jungle and high grass when we stumbled upon the Banga party, which consisted of four men and three women, all beautifully attired, from a savage's point of view, and armed to the teeth.

Dr. Maxwell and I were in front, and the savages were

VISIT TO THE SAVAGE VILLAGES 127

so much astonished at our appearance that they stood still striking their mouths with their hands to express their amazement.

I called out to them in a conciliatory manner, in Chinese, 'Ch'in-lang!' (kinsmen).

The Banga leader, a fine frank-looking man, smiled, and repeated the word. The women had some knowledge of the Celestial tongue, from being employed as go-between in their bartering with the Chinese, and they came forward to question us.

Our guide and the Lau-lung men scowled upon them as enemies, and retired to a distance, whilst Dr. Maxwell and I squatted down to have a chat with our new-found acquaintances.

We lighted our pipes, and I exhibited my guns to them, fired them off to further impress them, and let them examine my white skin; so we soon made friends.

The leader informed us that his name was 'Chau-po,' and asked us what we were doing with his enemies, the Lau-lung men.

We told him that they had been kind to us; and we assured him that they were equally 'relations,' and not Chinese.

I presented Chau-po with some fine powder for priming, with some other little gifts; and he several times asked our names, repeating them afterwards, thus, 'Pukkering,' 'Ma-i-seng' (Dr. Maxwell).

When it became time to part, and we were bidding each other good-bye, our old guide stole up to us and whispered:

'Ask the chief when he is going back home, and what way, so that we can keep clear of him.'

I unsuspectingly asked him, and, having gained the desired information, each party passed upon its way.

We put up that night at the solitary hut of a Bilang man, and the next day we returned to Lau-lung, experiencing a slight shock of earthquake *en route*.

We slept the night at Lau-lung, pursuing our way next day to Keng-chio-k'a, where we bade our old guide farewell, making him happy with various presents and a small monetary remuneration.

The night before we left the village we observed that there seemed to be a great secret consultation amongst the Lau-lung people, and in the morning our guide informed us that his eldest son and some of the young men of the tribe had gone off on a hunting expedition amongst the mountains.

To our regret, we learned afterwards that, availing themselves of the knowledge I had innocently gained from Chau-po, the party had waylaid the Bangas on their return home, and had slain several of the savages.

Dr. Maxwell and I reached Taiwanfoo without further adventure, after a very enjoyable excursion, which was somewhat saddened by the knowledge that we had unwittingly been the cause of the death of the people who had met us in such a friendly spirit.

It is, however, just to the Pepo-hoans to remember that they were taking the only means in their power to protect themselves from the raids of savages whose sole object in making warfare was the accumulation of human heads, and who were therefore necessarily regarded as akin to wild beasts, both by the civilised aborigines and also by the Chinese, who were anxious to cultivate the land and to develop the country. Our own countrymen in the last century suffered the same kind of harassment from the Red Indians in America.

The monotony being broken occasionally by these excursions, I spent a busy life at the Customs in Taiwanfoo, gratified by the continued kindly interest of Mr. Maxwell—interest which, I have every reason for believing, would have found practical expression in my speedy promotion, had not that gentleman died in the August of 1865, at Amoy.

MY LIFE AT TAIWANFOO

His successor was a man of a very different type; and after waiting, with all the patience I could muster, from August until Christmas, I sent in my resignation. This was most promptly accepted.

I had already received a very favourable offer from Messrs. McPhail, British merchants of Taiwanfoo, with which I therefore closed, glad once more to be in the service of my own countrymen.

CHAPTER XI

ADVENTURES IN THE VICINITY OF TAIWANFOO

I ENTERED the service of Messrs. McPhail Brothers after the Chinese New Year (February 1866).

The firm, trading under the Chinese style, 'T'ien-li' ('Heavenly profits'), was the principal European house in South Formosa; our credit was first-rate, as we were supported by some of the principal British and American firms in Hong Kong and Amoy.

We considered ourselves fortunate in possessing the services of a Chinese compradore who was above suspicion, a man of prepossessing appearance, on excellent terms with the Chinese authorities, and possessing a domestic establishment which reflected credit on his employers.

At that time we Europeans had not incurred the open dislike of the mandarins, and Mr. McPhail, besides acting as British consul for some months, was appointed consul for France and the Netherlands.

My successor in the Customs at Anping, Mr. Gue, was an old acquaintance and friend, and we employed the leisure time during the south-west monsoon, when no vessels dare approach the coast, in exploring the country around Taiwanfoo on horseback. At that time the highways were infested by bands of daring robbers, who defied the mandarins with impunity, and considered all travellers and unprotected merchandise as their lawful prey.

This caused us an amusing adventure on one occasion.

Gue and I arranged an expedition to the district city of Ka-gi, about thirty-five miles to the north of Taiwanfoo, whence we hoped to be able to reach the savages, as the mountain ranges are within a comparatively short distance of that city. We were accompanied by our servants and a couple of coolies to carry our bedding, change of raiment, provisions, etc. As our journey took us through the robber-infested districts, we were armed with our revolvers, a rifle, and a double-barrelled fowling-piece.

Leaving Taiwanfoo by the north gate, after passing through a marshy and uncultivated country, we came to the market town of Hm-kang-boé. Here we were informed that the traffic was stopped on account of the exactions and outrages committed by the inhabitants of two villages some seven or eight miles to the north.

I must tell my readers that between Hm-kang-boé and Ka-gi is a most fertile plain, highly cultivated with rice, sugar, indigo, turmeric, ground nuts, etc., and producing many kinds of fruit, such as oranges, shaddock, mangoes, lung-ngans, etc., etc. Indeed, every prospect pleased, and only man was vile—very vile indeed, as the villagers were almost always engaged in clan fights or as highway robbers. Every village was surrounded by an impregnable stockade of very high living bamboos, and had only two gates for ingress and egress.

Our boys and coolies were inclined to leave us; but as we rode ahead out of Hm-kang-boé, they, fearful of being left behind, followed us, accompanied by several people in the town, who took advantage of our escort to go to Ka-gi with merchandise.

The mid-day heat was intense, and we were clad in the airiest of costumes, Chinese pyjamas and sleeping jackets; whilst, as protection for our heads, Gue wore a large bamboo Chinese hat like a gigantic mushroom, and my head was swathed in a black silk Formosa turban. At a distance we could not be distinguished from the natives of the country.

We picked our cautious way along the high road which

ran for miles across the solitary plain. I call it a high road for courtesy; in reality it was but a single line of rough granite slabs, laid down more or less imperfectly on the top of a mud bank which sloped down to the paddy fields on either side.

In the distance, on one side of our path, were visible the high clumps of bamboos denoting a village, but no sign of life was to be seen in the fields. Our guides and coolies began to murmur that we were approaching one of the worst nests of highway robbers, and that they would be sure to be stripped of all their clothing. As this consisted merely of a very short pair of cotton trousers each, we did not feel very anxious about their prospective losses; so telling them that we would compensate them with half a dozen pairs each if necessary, we pushed on. Presently, however, our attention was called to the gate of the village, out of which poured a string of men, armed with spears and matchlocks which glistened in the burning rays of the sun. These men took positions on each side of the road in the fields, leaning against the banks and awaiting our approach.

We watched their manœuvres with keen interest. The Chinese who had joined us at Hm-kang-boé threw down their burdens and refused to go further. Our coolies and servants, after enduring from us some abuse and encouragement, followed us to within about two hundred yards of the armed men, when they too lay down, and began to cry.

The robbers one by one arose and appeared to be coming to meet us. Gue and I, revolver in hand, rode ahead, and just when we came up to the rascals we threw off our hat and turban, showing to the astonished robbers our light hair and unshaven heads. With a British yell, we fired our revolvers, and galloped into the middle of them, crying, 'The red-haired barbarians are coming!' On this, there was a general *sauve qui peut*, and the brave

BAMBOOS FORMOSA

ADVENTURES AT TAIWANFOO 133

banditti scattered back into their village, crying, ' Run, run ! Ayo ! ayo ! they are not men ! they are red-haired barbarians. They may be bears or they may be tigers ! Run !' The road was clear.

The most ridiculous part of the affair was that our ponies, though docile enough, had not undergone a military training, and their riders were both sailors. At the report of the revolvers, and in the general confusion, they became frantic, and spilled us both in the fields, where, had not the robbers been panic-struck, we should have been at their mercy. We, however, soon remounted, and rejoined our servants, coolies, and companions, who for some time were helpless from laughter and joy.

We had no further trouble from robbers, and arrived safely at Ka-gi, where we enjoyed a couple of days in the city and vicinity, but were unable to visit the savage country, though we did succeed in getting two or three specimens of one tribe to come out to a village in the lower ranges.

On our return journey we had another little adventure, which served to show us the true inwardness of a high-class Chinese gentleman's establishment, and gave us an opportunity of experiencing genuine hospitality. We had made a late start from Ka-gi, and had undergone the stifling heat of the ride across the monotonous exposed plain, when towards sunset our coolies, who had taken us out of the regular route to avoid the dreaded robbers, pointed out a village, and said, ' We will go there, and stay the night. It is the residence of a Siutsai (a Chinese B.A.), a mighty man of great family. He will be glad to see a barbarian ; you can talk mandarin to him, and he will kill a sucking pig for you, and we shall all have a fine time of it.' We resigned ourselves into the coolies' hands, and, after entering the village, we arrived tired and thirsty and hungry at the portal of a fine Chinese mansion.

Whilst we sat on our ponies, staring irresolutely at

the closed gates with their three entrances, of which the centre one was for the honoured guest, the people gathered round us from the village street, and commented audibly upon our unwonted appearance.

Presently from one of the side gates some two or three of the long-robed literati class emerged, and spoke to us.

'Would we come within? Would we see the Toalo?'

I replied politely in mandarin. It would delight us to see the Toalo (or squire).

Then, after a pause, the big centre gate swung slowly open, and we passed into the great courtyard. Here our gaze fell upon pleasant flowers, green rockeries, with their cool fountains spraying in the sultry air, whilst we were soon surrounded by a number of curious retainers of many and varied rank; for this Toalo was a very great man indeed, his ancestors having come to the island with Koxinga, which is equivalent in Chinese eyes to our boast of 'coming over with the Conqueror.'

As we ascended the steps of the mansion, the venerable mandarin himself met us upon the steps, and greeted us with great cordiality.

We went through the usual etiquette: 'Your honourable name?—age?—place of birth?' etc. We must enter his abode; we must dine and rest with him. 'Pi-ki-ling?' Ah, yes, he had heard of Pi-ki-ling (from our coolies, I expect), who could even speak the language of men (Chinese). We must make him happy by entering. All that he had was at our service.

We politely demurred. We represented that we were scarcely in suitable trim to accept his hospitality. Some food, some water, and afterwards a quiet corner in which to sleep was all that we dared desire.

'By no means,' he responded. 'You are my honoured guests. Pray enter and refresh yourselves.'

It was an amusing predicament. Our attire was

picturesque, but scarcely conventional, and our garments all bore testimony to a long, hot day's ride, in their numerous traces of sand and mud.

Gue and I consulted hastily, and arrived at the philosophical conclusion that this was an occasion when mind must rise superior to clothes. We thanked our host, begging him to do with us as he would.

We were thereupon escorted by obsequious attendants to a spacious bedroom, sumptuously furnished, with a massive, handsomely carved, four-post bedstead, where slippers, hot water, and towels were provided; and after plentiful ablutions, a good brush, and a change of clothes, we emerged much refreshed.

We rejoined our host in the large hall, where, whilst we sipped tea and smoked, we conversed amiably.

Out of compliment to the Toalo, as a learned man, I first spoke in mandarin or court Chinese, but gradually both he and I relapsed into the more informal local dialect, and I found him a highly intelligent man.

What seemed to perplex him about Europeans, or 'barbarians,' as he (quite innocently) termed us, was our amazing energy. Why should we trouble ourselves so much, and take so much pains about anything on earth? To the phlegmatic, literary Chinaman this seemed an incomprehensible trait in our character. Was anything worth such fuss and bother? What was the good of going to see savages? It was the dreary old pessimistic query, *Cui bono?* in far Formosa.

We talked of many things, but never of the ladies of the household, for to a Chinese this would be considered a great insult.

The womenkind were all invisible, but from low whisperings from behind the paper screens of the walls, the suspicion of bated breath when our talk was interesting, and a subdued rustling of silken garments at exciting moments, I gathered that the fair ones were not very far away. Indeed, I fancied more than once that I discerned the scrutiny of some bright eye through the defects in the frail paper windows.

Before very long there came the summons to the dinner. Imagine several square tables, whereat ourselves were assigned the places of honour; and, in their proper places, the literati, the relations, and most honoured retainers of the household. There was somewhat of the feudal spirit about all the arrangements. As to the viands, we had a fine fat sucking pig, the equivalent to our baron of beef or saddle of mutton, and sharks' fins, etc., with many other delicacies, washed down with Shau-hsing wines and rice spirit. The feast lasted long. After it we adjourned again to the hall, where, sitting at our ease, with our pipes and tea, we talked of many strange things.

Of the geography of our country these Chinamen knew absolutely nothing. We were barbarians. We came from some poor village of our particular tribe outside civilisation, civilisation being solely within the dominion of the Celestial Emperor. All the rest of the world—if there were any poor remainder—was benighted, and but the home of 'barbarians,' not 'men.'

Still, they were politely curious about us. Had we intellectual minds, we barbarians? What could we do?

I unfolded to them the mysteries of steam as a propeller. I told them of our machinery. They were not much impressed. Some of them had even seen and travelled on a steamer. Yes, but that was not much; to invent those material things, was that worthy of a man's intellect? Such novelties were merely mechanical.

I told them somewhat of the stars, of our scientific conclusions. This appealed more to them. Then I quoted to them passages from their own sacred classics. They approved of me.

At length we obtained leave to retire, as we were weary from our travels. The mandarin bade us most courteous adieus. He should not be up in time to see us off in the morning, but his servants were ours. He would provide us with a guide to show us the best route. We must make him happy by returning some day.

Later, as I lay wakeful on my bed, I heard, through the thin paper partitions, my host and his cronies considering their strange visitors.

'Strange creatures, these barbarians,' grunted the mandarin, as he puffed at his opium pipe.

'Aye, they are, indeed,' acquiesced another.

A long pause, whilst they sucked their pipes reflectively.

'That Pi-ki-ling, he's a strange barbarian. Where did he learn to speak the language of men?'

'Aye, but he's clever—for a barbarian. He is almost a man.'

'Nonsense! he has not the eyes of a man. They are round, like the rest of the animals', not turned up at the corners, like we men have them. *He*'s no man, I tell you.'

There was a grunt from the man addressed. The argument was conclusive.

'Well, perhaps his mother might have been a man, anyhow!' he volunteered.

'May be, may be; but he is a clever barbarian,' settled my host, and the discussion ended.

In the morning we found a good breakfast of rice porridge, with fish and meat, prepared for us; after which we quitted the roof of the hospitable mandarin, and, with our guide, made our way back to Taiwanfoo.

The Toalo had done us the honour to approve of our good English leather saddles; so we sent him a fine one, with many courteous messages of thanks for his pleasant hospitality.

It was during this south-west monsoon that one day, after a heavy typhoon in which three German vessels, which had taken the opportunity of a few fine calm days to load sugar at Anping, were driven on shore, three ship's boats appeared in the creek off Fort Zelandia. It appeared that their occupants were the captain, his wife, officers, and crew of the Dutch barque 'Pomona,' of Sourabaya, bound from Chefoo to Swatow with bean cake, cotton, etc.

In beating down the Formosan channel they had encountered the typhoon, and had been driven on the sand banks to the north of Taiwanfoo, off Po-te-ts'ui, that noted den of pirates and wreckers. Directly the vessel stranded, the Chinese had come off by hundreds in their catamarans to complete the wreck, and the crew had just managed to escape with their lives, and loss of everything else.

After receiving the unfortunates, and providing them with food, clothing, and shelter, the captain consulted with Mr. McPhail, as acting Dutch consul. He said that he had left the barque in good order with all standing, and proposed to sell her by auction. This was done, and our compradore bought her for five hundred dollars, which sum the captain received, and left with his crew by the first vessel for Amoy.

The sum paid for the vessel and cargo was indeed small, but we knew that we had slight chance of recouping ourselves for even that trifle, after a vessel had got into the hands of the Po-te-ts'ui men.

Mr. McPhail had a notice of the sale translated into Chinese, to which he affixed the seal of the Netherlands Government, and, our compradore being on good terms with the Tao-tai's private secretary, we obtained a formidable document, stamped with the seal of the chief magistrate of the island, notifying all persons that 'T'ien-li' had bought the vessel, and warning all Chinese to recognise the sale, under the direst penalties for disobedience.

Now the question was, how could we make use of all this power?

ADVENTURES AT TAIWANFOO 139

The weather had moderated; so I was instructed to go to the wreck, stick the two notices on the fore-mast, and warn the wreckers to leave the vessel. I was only too glad to have a relief from the general monotony of Formosa life. Mr. Gue offered to lend us the Customs catamaran, and Mr. McSwiney, the Customs boarding officer, a descendant of the ancient kings of Ireland, from Kerry, and a brave relict of Alma and Inkerman, offered to accompany me, with a rifle, paste-pot, refreshment, etc. The old coxswain of the Customs catamaran, with his three sons, objected to the adventurous trip; but as I had got him into the service, and had saved his wages from being absorbed by Mr. Maxwell's Manchu secretary, he was fond of me, as were his sons.

Old Hok-a said, 'Ai-yo, Pi-ki-ling, you dare die; you are always wanting this kind of thing. Never mind, we will all go; but these Po-te-ts'ui rascals will rob us of all our clothes.'

The weather having lulled somewhat, we started, sitting in a tub lashed on the catamaran, armed with our rifles, revolvers, proclamations, and a pot of paste. We hoped, with faint hope, to interview the wreckers, to convince them of the error of their ways and of the sacred rights of property.

With an adverse wind, we arrived in sight of the wreck in the afternoon. Her mizzen-mast was gone, but the fore and main were intact. As we approached, however, we saw the main-mast, with yards, etc., drop over the side, and being towed towards the land.

As we drew near to the stranded barque, we perceived that she was surrounded by crowds of catamarans, amongst which there were several larger boats, fishing smacks, laden with all the necessary implements for breaking up and demolishing the unfortunate vessel, and forges for repairing the tools used in the process.

Up the sides of the barque, and all over her decks,

swarmed Chinamen, like so many busy ants, chattering, gesticulating, screaming at each other, whilst they plied their work of destruction.

When they discovered our proximity there was even greater excitement.

'What are you doing there?' I demanded in Chinese.

'What has it to do with you?' their spokesman responded impudently. 'We know you. Yes, yes! you are "Teng-lang-oé" ("Chinese Talk"—my sobriquet in Taiwan). You one wonderful barbarian. You just go back home. What you here for at all?'

I waved the Tao-tai's document before them.

'See this,' I replied. 'You are not to touch the ship. It is sold to the T'ien-li Hang (firm) for five hundred dollars. Come out of it!'

To emphasise my words I fired off my rifle in the air. Most of those on board jumped overboard and took refuge in the catamarans. The hubbub increased, and their faces grew dark and threatening. They evidently disliked my argument.

'Look here, you barbarians, be wise,' they advised. 'You just leave us alone. If you touch one of us with those guns of yours, we'll kill you both. Night's coming on. Just you go back home, and don't interfere with us.'

For reply I got alongside, jumped on board, and held the Tao-tai's authority before their shifty eyes.

'Don't know it! Can't read it! Tao-tai? What's the Tao-tai to do with us, anyway?'

They stubbornly refused to understand it.

Then I got my pot of paste and pasted up the despised document on the fore-mast, as high as I could reach.

'Now,' I repeated, 'this ship is sold to T'ien-li, and you rob it at your peril.'

'All right, Teng-lang-oé,' they replied conciliatingly. 'Now just you go back home. It's getting late, and it's very cold. Where are you going to eat and to sleep, anyway? It's very miserable sitting in that catamaran. We really cannot offer you any hospitality now; but just you come up to our village later on, and we'll sell you the chains and the sails, the chronometers, the brass, and the copper cheap. You're a wise barbarian, almost a man! You know our Chinese rules and customs, and you can judge when it is wise to say good-bye.'

Unfortunately I did know, and I also recollected that the better part of valour was discretion; so with more earnest reminders to them of the retribution that would follow their evil-doing, we pushed off into the open sea to return to Anping.

When we were a little distance off they attracted our attention with triumphant howls and shouts of derisive laughter.

'Come by-and-by to our village, and allow us to entertain you.'

Old Hok-a called our attention, and we turned our heads just in time to see the fore-mast, with the despised proclamation still upon it, waver, fall, and disappear overboard. They had cut it down.

The old man said, 'Ai-yo! Pi-ki-ling, heaven looks after you; if not we should all be dead men.'

Old Hok-a was quite right, but I did not appreciate the fact at that time.

The sequel was worked out a few weeks later, when the wreckers sent down to Taiwanfoo and invited me to visit their village. They received me with humorous friendliness, and I made some very good bargains with them amongst the despoiled chains, copper, and gear of the Dutch barque, and our compradore was well repaid by his purchase.

CHAPTER XII

SECOND TRIP INTO THE INTERIOR

TOWARDS the end of the same year, 1866, our firm interviewed some Chinese, who brought specimens of tea and cassia bark, stating that these articles were to be found growing in abundance in the savage territory near La-ku-li. We held a consultation, and it was ultimately arranged that I should make a few weeks' trip into the interior, to examine the country and to verify the correctness of these statements, with a view to trade.

Our Chinese 'shroff,' or manager, enlisted the services of a fellow-countryman who had dealings with the savages at La-ku-li ; whilst my old friend, the T'ong-su of Kong-a-na, gave me several introductions and guides to lead me to the Pepo-hoans, who inhabit the hills and valleys stretching between Taiwanfoo and La-ku-li.

Thus one morning in December I started off on my pilgrimage, accompanied by a Chinese clerk and servant, with coolies to carry our baggage, which consisted chiefly of presents for the various savage chiefs.

We halted at a Chinese market town, Kwan-te-bio, where two sons of the Kong-a-na headman were established in business. They welcomed us as friends, and sent some of their people along with us as guides.

The same evening we reached Bak-sa, a settlement of the civilised aborigines, who received us hospitably, although they had never before seen a white man. They accepted us at once as 'kinsmen,' and we slept that night at Bak-sa.

LAND SUBSIDENCE, ACTION OF SUBTERRANEAN TORRENT BETWEEN KWAN-TE-BIO AND BAK-SA

SECOND TRIP INTO THE INTERIOR 143

The following morning we prepared to continue our journey, but our Chinese coolies' valour had ebbed away; they refused to go further from civilisation. The Bak-sa people, however, soon provided me with some of their men in place of our recreant Chinese, and they also told off an escort for us, as the remainder of our route to La-ku-li was frequently made dangerous by bands of savages.

La-ku-li is situated upon the same river as Lau-lung, and our route thither was very similar in character to the country lying between Keng-chio-k'a and Lau-lung, through which we passed in my previous narrative.

Some three miles from La-ku-li, upon the summit of a high ridge, we were met by a hunting party of Pepo-hoans, who, when they had somewhat recovered from their surprise at the sight of a European in their Formosan wilds, took charge of our party, and led us to our destination.

Here I was received by Lo-liat, the Chinaman whom our 'shroff' had engaged as agent to procure specimens of the tea and cassia bark. This Lo-liat was a man of a stamp frequently to be met with upon the borders of savage territory. Reckless, unscrupulous, a confirmed opium-smoker, he carried his life in his hand, making a precarious livelihood by trading with, and lending money to, the simple-minded 'hoans,' both civilised and savage.

It chanced that the day after our arrival at La-ku-li, an old Ban-tau-lang woman came to barter some deer horns, etc., with Lo-liat.

A few attractive presents soon made us good friends. She entreated me to go and visit her tribe, who lived on the western slopes of Mount Morrison, promising me a cordial welcome from her brother, who was a great warrior of their tribe. This old woman, named Pu-li-sang, was no novice to the ways of civilisation, as she had, years ago, been married to a Chinese, and also had lived for some time with the Bangas, a tribe who formed part of the confederation whose object is to resist the encroachments of the great eastern tribe, the Sibukun.

This confederation consists of the Bangas, the Bilang, the Pai-chien, the Ban-tau-lang, and a few other tribes.

The unfortunate Ban-tau-lang, being situated near to the Sibukun, are compelled to bear the brunt of the quarrel, and they are consequently yearly diminishing in numbers.

Lo-liat informed me that the only safe method of visiting the Banga tribe would be in the company of a certain famous Pepo-hoan hunter.

This man of warfare had a romantic history. He had lost both his parents and family in some wild massacre by the Bangas. He therefore devoted his life to revenge them. He proved such a scourge to the tribe that they were glad to make peace with him, and they had given him a daughter of their chief for a wife.

I went to see this man, and found him to be the owner of a large farm and of numerous buffaloes. He expressed much pleasure at a visit from a European. I presented him with some powder, and unfolded my plans to him. He readily promised me his assistance with the Bangas, and we settled upon a day for visiting them, sending Pu-li-sang, the Ban-tau-lang woman, forward to inform the chief of our projected visit.

There were two Chinese in La-ku-li, who had recently crossed to Formosa from the mainland, and had drifted aimlessly up to this village in search of a livelihood. Keng-le, a youth of eighteen, hailing from An-k'oe (to the north of Amoy), was of a decidedly enterprising nature. The other, named Hoan-a, was a sort of harmless 'ne'er-do-weel.' These two unattached adventurers besought me to permit them to join our party, offering to be our luggage carriers.

Lo-liat also, who, during a residence of many years, had never ventured to quit La-ku-li, now took his courage

A PEPO-HOAN FISHING PARTY WITH BOWS AND ARROWS

SECOND TRIP INTO THE INTERIOR

in both hands, and valorously determined to embrace this opportunity of seeing a savage village.

I reviewed my stock of beads, looking-glasses, flint and steel, red cloth and bangles, which I had stored for presents, and when Pu-li-sang returned to us, bringing a favourable reply from her savage friends, we one morning sallied forth.

Our little party consisted of the Pepo-hoan hunter and Pu-li-sang as our guides, my clerk, Ah-san, and Lo-liat, the two volunteer bearers, Keng-le and Hoan-a, and myself.

After crossing the large river which flows down from Lau-lung, past La-ku-li, we immediately began to ascend a very steep range of hills, densely covered with jungle growth. The immense trees and thick undergrowth totally excluded the rays of the sun, and as a result it was not merely cool, but very cold. We were about three hours in reaching the summit of the ridge, the path in many places being almost perpendicular.

Half-way up the ascent Lo-liat and Ah-san, the clerk, lay down, and we could not induce them to move for some time. The hunter and Pu-li-sang, however, came to the rescue with such harrowing tales of unfriendly hunting-parties and fearful murders perpetrated upon this spot, that, in spite of a deadly want of opium, and with evaporating courage, they were fain to push on with us to the top of the ridge.

When we had succeeded in rousing their failing energies, alack! the two luggage bearers also gave in; but Pu-li-sang, with ineffable feminine contempt, took from them the greater part of their load, swung it on her back, and fixing it by a strap over her head quietly stalked away in front.

Upon our upward route we passed gigantic camphor trees and many specimens of the indigenous tea plant; we also came across a good deal of the cassia bark.

When we reached the top of the ridge Pu-li-sang

pointed across a wide valley to the opposite mountains, saying that the Banga village was there, and informing us that we must light a fire and discharge a gun to give notice of our approach. When we had duly made these signals there came the answering report of a gun, and a trail of uprising smoke was to be seen in the direction Pu-li-sang had indicated. The woman then gravely told us that we must now wait until she had been in to see whether we could visit the village, as it was necessary to know that no unlucky omen had appeared to veto our reception.

We found that at this point the narrow path was thickly planted with bamboo spikes hardened by fire, which proved that the Bangas were at war with some tribe or other. These spikes, though rendered harmless by stout boots, were highly dangerous to the barefooted natives.

Whilst waiting there for Pu-li-sang's return the spirits of Ah-san and Lo-liat again drooped. They lamented their foolhardiness in offering to accompany me. They stated that Europeans, being so inferior, might be so unwise as not to value their lives, and indeed it was possible for the same reason that the savages might not hurt the 'barbarians,' as they termed them 'kinsmen'; but Chinese, being 'men,' should be more prudent, and that if they had behaved according to their superior enlightenment they would then have been safely at home at Taiwanfoo, not enduring all these risks and discomforts in the company of barbarians.

Happily at length Pu-li-sang returned to us. The omens were propitious; all was favourable for our visit to her friends. We therefore resumed our march, and in about two hours we reached the Banga village.

This was situated on the brow of a steep and rocky hill commanding a good view of the surrounding country. The houses were built of small slates laid flat-wise, and

SECOND TRIP INTO THE INTERIOR 147

lined with large slabs, and the doors were about four feet high.

The natives, influenced no doubt by curiosity, were standing outside their houses, but they made no great demonstration beyond smiling at us and striking their mouths with their hands, which is their expression of surprise.

We were marched to the hut of the chief, and here we were denuded of all our arms and valuables, our host assuring us that he would be responsible for everything.

We spent the interval until dusk in being examined and questioned by men, women, and children, holding a sort of informal reception, and while this was in progress we had but little peace.

No lamps were used by the savages, but a large fire in the centre of the hut, with several grass torches, served to give an uncertain light. Suddenly from the outside darkness a tall figure rushed into the circle crying delightedly, 'Puck-a-ring! Puck-a-ring! Ma-i-seng!'

This unexpected greeting startled me; and my apprehension was not lessened when the new-comer seized hold of me, repeating my name in great excitement.

To my astonishment I found that this exuberant friend was none other than the amiable savage, Chau-po, whose acquaintance I had so romantically made a year before, when Dr. Maxwell and I were returning from our expedition to the Bilang tribe, and whom we had so unwittingly betrayed into the hands of his enemies. He had escaped from the Lau-lung men after receiving a severe wound in his side; and he had been carried home with great difficulty by his comrade, who alone came out scatheless from the Lau-lung attack.

Chau-po, I found, was one of the best men amongst the Bangas, and a notorious head-taker.

I felt for a moment that it was inevitable that he should

L 2

regard me as being implicated in his misfortune; but to my surprise and relief Chau-po was most cordial. He was genuinely delighted to see me again, and told me by signs that we were brothers.

The night was spent in singing the plaintive songs which are common in the mountains, the tunes of which are familiar to both Chinamen and Pepo-hoan.

I discovered that the unmarried men and boys slept in a shed raised from the ground. This building was regarded as a kind of temple, in which the vanquished heads were hung and feasts were held. The presence of the heads of their enemies was supposed to give courage to the youths.

At the period of our visit the Bangas were not in a very flourishing condition as to food; we therefore had to be content with boiled millet and sweet potatoes, with a little dried venison.

The custom was for each savage to entertain the visitor in turn, and I was very gratified to see the genuine hospitality with which every man gave what he possessed, though I must own that I occasionally found this generosity somewhat embarrassing, as for example at one hut a honeycomb in which the larvæ predominated was produced for my delectation! As my companions seemed to consider this condition rather an advantage than otherwise, I felt politeness demanded the sacrifice of my prejudices. I accepted the comb when it came to my share and munched it down with a paste made of taro.

Thus we spent two days in smoking and chatting, whilst the boys and girls of the tribe hunted the surrounding woods for cassia bark, which they succeeded in bringing me.

We had some perplexity in the distribution of our presents to please every one. Fortunately a very small thing delights the child-nature of the savage, and a little

ABORIGINES NORTH FORMOSA

SECOND TRIP INTO THE INTERIOR 149

powder or a bright button often turned a discontented look into a smile.

My Chinese companions soon grew weary of such barbarous life, and sighed for civilisation again. The games of the small children particularly frightened them.

The first playthings put into the hands of a savage boy are a wooden knife and gun or a bow and arrow. With these toys they play at lying in ambush and taking heads. In this amiable game, upon the victim falling, the aggressor would rush out of his ambush and pretend to cut off th head of his prey, holding it up with a proud look.

My clerk, Ah-san, upon seeing this mimetic comedy, expressed so much horror, with such a terrified face, that some of the more mischievous boys delighted to summon him, and, pointing to his head, to make signs of beheading him, just to increase his peace of mind.

This prophetic teasing, together with a story they had heard from the Pepo-hoan hunter, caused both Lo-liat and Ah-san to be anxious to return.

The story ran that the Bangas were taught how to build their slate houses by a 'man' (*i.e.* a Chinese), who was promised good pay in the shape of deer-skins, etc. However—so went the story—when the work was finished, the savages neatly cleared off their score by removing the Chinaman's head.

I suspected this was but a yarn: the Chinamen believed and trembled.

After a stay of three days, we bade a hearty farewell to our friends the Bangas, and made our way back to La-ku-li, with some bark, accompanied by an escort of savages.

I remained some days at La-ku-li for the purpose of collecting bark. Whilst there, I had an opportunity of noticing the superstitions of the Pepos (civilised aborigines) of this district, superstitions which, I believe, were almost identical with those of the savages in the neighbourhood.

I was one day invited to accompany some of the men on a hunting excursion. All was ready; we had still to wait for lucky omens. These necessary omens are represented by the flights and cries of certain birds.

Upon two successive mornings we set off, encouraged by favourable omens; but, after tramping for hours over the mountains, through river and jungle, birds were observed and heard under such conditions that our leader must perforce return. He gravely impressed upon us that we should not only get no sport, but that, by neglecting the warnings of the tutelary birds, we should probably come to grief, by meeting unfriendly savages. After this, we actually had one day with nothing to stop us, excepting —no sport! All this disgusted me, and I declined in future to go out with Pepo-hoan hunters.

I witnessed a kind of religious ceremony performed by the women of La-ku-li, which is dying out among the Pepos who live near the Chinese.

A large reaping tub was brought out into the open, and planks were placed upon the top to form a rude stage. On either side of this were fixed two upright bamboos, with a cross rail fastened to both.

A wise woman appeared, adorned with beads and attired in a kind of surplice of the hempen cloth which is manufactured by the Pepo-hoans, with bells sewn on the border.

She was surrounded by a circle of girls and old women, who, with hands joined, went round and round the tub, chanting a monotonous dirge. The woman upon the stage danced, at first slowly, but gradually increasing her pace, the song meantime growing louder and faster.

She at length appeared to wax frantic in the midst of the whirl; she fell down and lay in a trance. She was thereupon carried into an adjacent house, and her awakening was breathlessly awaited, as, when she regained her senses, she was supposed to show by her utterances, what

SECOND TRIP INTO THE INTERIOR 151

was the most favourable time to carry on field work during the coming season.

The females seem to be the privileged priestesses of the Pepo-hoan religion ; and the younger women are, I believe, initiated at a certain age into the mysteries of this occult ceremony.

The Ban-tau-lang woman, Pu-li-sang, informed me that her people were very desirous of seeing a white man, and as a further inducement to me, she held out the hope that the best man of the tribe, a brother of her own, named Li-gai, would take me to the summit of Mount Morrison, which was used as a common hunting ground by the tribes of the east coast as well as by the Ban-tau-lang.

The prospect was tempting ; the La-ku-li people endeavoured to dissuade me,' but I was eager to see this redoubtable tribe, and I determined to accept their invitation to pay them a visit.

I took with me only the two Chinese bearers, Keng-le and Hoan-a, Pu-li-sang engaging to carry the baggage if they failed.

Our route lay through the Banga settlement, and, as I knew them, though kind and hospitable, to be most importunate beggars for everything, even to the buttons on a person's trousers, I had to distribute the presents I was taking amongst our party, for the purpose of their better concealment.

We set out one morning, and the journey, which took us so long to accomplish before, we now executed in four hours, marching boldly into the Banga village about noon, *sans cérémonie.*

The tribe received us graciously, but we had to guard our presents carefully from their inquisitive eyes.

We told them of our proposed visit, but they would give us no encouragement in our scheme.

They informed us that some of the Ban-tau-lang had recently been killed by the Sibukun, the great tribe on the eastern slopes of Mount Morrison. A general fast was being held in consequence, and we should probably not be received. Pu-li-sang herself agreed that it would be wiser to stay until further news came out.

We therefore waited developments, amusing ourselves during the three or four days which intervened in exploring the country around, in being feasted at each of the savage establishments in turn, and in being each night entertained by a concert which lasted until daylight.

When the dawn appeared, the women and children, escorted by two or three males fully armed, went off to the small plots of cultivated ground, to plant sweet potatoes.

During this stay I endeavoured to procure some curiosities from the Bangas, and I thus discovered that they, in common with other tribes, had a kind of 'taboo.'

For instance, if I desired to barter for a pretty pipe or belt, the owner would refuse, saying it was 'hiang,' meaning that it was 'tabooed,' and so could not be parted with. I ultimately found this word somewhat convenient to myself, when the Bangas became too importunate, particularly when they begged the buttons from my very scanty clothing.

This diplomatic reply satisfied them for a time; but seeing from my face that I was making an excuse, they realised that I was merely turning the tables on them, and that we red-haired kinsmen had no such custom among ourselves.

Whilst I was with the Bangas they were at war with the Hak-kas of a village called Sin-ui-tsng, and also with the Lau-lung people. I was wet through one night when returning from an excursion, and my good friend Chau-po lent me a complete suit of Chinese clothes, including a turban, whilst my own garments dried; and when I was arrayed in the Celestial costume, he volunteered the gruesome information that all the articles had belonged to Chinese or Pepo-hoan whom he had slain.

It seemed a curious anomaly—when one witnessed the fondness of the savages for their children, the happiness which apparently existed between husband and wife, and brothers and sisters, and the kindly humane disposition evinced amongst themselves—to remember their universal delight in the death of their enemies.

Chau-po assured me that his wife and children received him with the greatest joy and feasting when he returned from taking the heads of his enemies.

After making many inquiries, I was forced to the conclusion that the Formosan savages were cannibals to a certain extent, in that they mixed the brains of their enemies with wine, and drank the disgusting mixture.

The maidens of the tribe were all anxious to marry a great warrior or an expert hunter, though I do not think it was essential for a man to have taken a head before gaining a wife.

The highest ambition amongst the youths and boys of the tribe seemed to be to distinguish themselves in tribal warfare, and they would practise for hours, merely aiming at a leaf placed fourteen or fifteen yards off, imagining it to be some enemy.

They never fired at long distances, and rarely fought fairly, except when surprised in the thick jungle by an unexpected encounter with some party belonging to another tribe. This *contretemps* had occurred just before I arrived, between the Ban-tau-lang and the Sibukun, with the result that the former tribe lost several of their warriors.

CHAPTER XIII

MY VISIT TO THE BAN-TAU-LANG TRIBE

THE Bangas were not at all favourable to my intended visit to the Ban-tau-langs. I smoothed the way, however, by a liberal promise of gifts to be received on my safe return to La-ku-li; and, after an interval of four or five days, we were ready to proceed.

Another day's delay occurred, caused by the arrival of a party of Tunas, who had their settlement half-way between the tribes of the Bangas and the Ban-tau-langs, and were eager therefore to make the acquaintance of the 'red-haired kinsman' who had come so far to visit them.

High festival was held to celebrate the auspicious occasion. The Bangas and Tunas had a great carouse, which lasted until ten at night.

The Tunas then took their departure—men, women, and children being equally intoxicated. Some were scarcely able to stand, and I dare not imagine the fate of one poor baby, who was slung behind its mother's back by a strap over her forehead. It had a perilous and unsteady home-going, I fear.

We marched at daybreak, for the purpose of passing their village before they could be expecting us.

As the Bangas still disliked our project, we slipped out of the sleeping village without anything to break our fast; Pu-li-sang leading the way, and assuring us that she would procure us a meal somewhere *en route*.

Our way was difficult and rugged; we passed over rocks and hills of bare slate. At one place we were forced

MY VISIT TO THE BAN-TAU-LANG TRIBE

to pull ourselves up the side of a precipice by the help of rattans, and here we found a quantity of blood, which had evidently been caused by one of the drunken Tunas falling down the night before.

Presently we came upon a river-bed about half a mile in breadth. Here Pu-li-sang enjoined silence until we had crept past the opening in the rocky banks, where lay the Tuna village; and beyond this point we were compelled to cross and recross the river breast deep.

We followed the course of the river until noon. Its banks, alternately formed by sandy beach and frowning, precipitous rocks, obliged us to cross about every ten minutes, a by no means simple feat when the stepping stones were about a foot below the roaring current.

When, at one point, we chanced to be upon *terra firma*, we scared a fish-hawk, which obligingly dropped a fine fish; this Pu-li-sang secured, observing that it would make us a nice meal, in conjunction with some sweet potatoes which she had scratched up in the vicinity of the Tuna village.

About two o'clock we reached a place which was supposed to mark the half of our journey. This spot was a natural stony-bedded amphitheatre, surrounded by high wooded mountains; and here three branches of the river joined, forming a small lake clear as crystal.

Here Pu-li-sang assured us we were quite safe. We therefore decided to rest, and enjoy our long-deferred breakfast.

Pu-li-sang made a fire of sticks, and cooked the sweet potatoes, whilst the two Chinamen and I climbed to the top of a rock which jutted out into the lake.

To our surprise we could distinctly see some large fish swimming about at the bottom, which appeared to be very near the surface, owing to the deceptive clearness of the water. The instinct of the sportsman awoke; I was impatient to try my hand at the fish.

Hoan-a, indeed, feeling sure that the water was not

very deep, dashed his spear in amongst them. The fish all made off scatheless, whilst, to our astonishment, we could see the spear standing upright at the bottom, held fast by its iron head, but still some distance from the surface.

We were in a quandary. We could not possibly go away without the spear; but the two Chinese dared make no effort to recover it.

Pu-li-sang left her cooking to climb up to help us, and she was preparing to dive in, when I, feeling somewhat ashamed, dashed in off the rock. The shock was more than I bargained for! The icy coldness was so intense that the water seemed actually scalding, and my sole energies were employed in getting out again as quickly as possible. I struck out for shore, my teeth chattering as though from an ague.

Pu-li-sang promptly dived in, and triumphantly fetched out the spear; and she and I made up for our wetting by laughing at the two Chinamen, who could not swim.

After doing hearty justice to our *al fresco* meal, we started again on our pilgrimage.

We crossed mountains and forded rivers until I began to believe that we must soon reach the beach of the east coast, when, a little before dusk, Pu-li-sang pointed out a spot which she delightedly declared was the village of her tribe.

This settlement of the Ban-tau-langs was perched upon a crag high above all the surrounding hills.

We toiled up the side of a jungle-covered hill, which at last brought us out upon a path which led to the village.

It was now quite dusk, and we were nearly dead with fatigue and hunger and the discomfort of our wet clothes.

We sat still whilst Pu-li-sang reconnoitred, as she assured us if there was a fast in progress we could not hope to enter the village.

I waited thus for some time, my enthusiasm ebbing

MY VISIT TO THE BAN-TAU-LANG TRIBE 157

away from exhaustion and fatigue; and Pu-li-sang made me still more dejected when she returned with the report that the tribe were holding a silent fast, and would not speak to any one. We were therefore doomed to lay outside for the night. We were famished, and a heavy dew was falling. The prospect was not cheering.

I determined that I would make an effort to bring things to a more favourable issue. Firing off a seven-shooter Spencer's rifle and a revolver, I awaited results.

Very soon we perceived some figures moving through the gloom towards us. As they approached us, I flung off my shirt, and so looked very white indeed. Two or three men then came up, and, striking their mouths with their hands, uttered a grunt of surprise.

I pursued this advantage by reloading and again discharging my rifle. This broke the spell; the savages began to jabber away, and seized hold of me to examine my wonderful white skin.

Pu-li-sang whispered to me that there was now a possibility of our being received in the village.

I therefore shrouded myself in my shirt, and, calling to my companions, made as though I would go back to whence I came.

The savages made eager signs to me to stop; I was inexorable. I assured Pu-li-sang that I would not remain to be treated so inhospitably.

The savages had a hasty argument between themselves; then, motioning to us to be seated, the party disappeared.

There ensued a period of suspense, during which I cannot own to being comfortable in either mind or body, though policy did not lie in flight, even if it had been possible in the dark.

At last they returned with torches, and conducted us up a rocky path which led to the entrance of the Ban-tau-lang village.

Here they put us in a small grass hut, similar to those

used by watchmen in Chinese gardens. I realised that, having aroused their curiosity, they would not willingly lose me. I had them in my hands if I managed diplomatically. I therefore protested loudly in Chinese to Pu-li-sang that without suitable food and entertainment I could not think of stopping.

This had no immediate result, but the savages again consulted together, and went off to ask their chief.

Ultimately we were taken into the village, to the house of the aged chief, who, like most of the heads of the Formosan tribes, was too old and decrepit to do more than give advice to his warriors.

Here a large fire was blazing upon the floor, which was a welcome sight to me, for I was chilled to the bone. I revelled in its warmth, whilst an old woman gave us a few baked potatoes to eat.

The people began to swarm in, evincing their surprise at the unusual appearance of their guests by striking their mouths with their hands, as they had done before.

They entreated me to again discard my shirt, which I philosophically consented to do, and I underwent an astonished examination from them all.

Pu-li-sang informed them that I could sing. They immediately begged to hear a specimen of my talents, but I excused myself on the score of fatigue and hunger, upon which they regaled me with some dried venison.

After a little hesitation they gave me permission to smoke, although, they said, they themselves were debarred from that luxury by their fast.

About ten o'clock, when the moon was high, a deputation requested our presence outside the hut, where in the open a large party of men and women had assembled to see me and to hear me sing.

It was a wild and romantic scene. The quaint savage settlement with its slate roofs, distinct in the moonlight; the rows of dark expectant faces pressing round for a sight of their strange white-skinned kinsman; the confused chatter and movement amongst them; and beyond, the great dark mountains, baring their rugged breasts to the solemn night sky, whilst the roar of the hill-side torrents formed an unceasing accompaniment to the scene. How far away England, and even Chinese civilisation, seemed!

I was over-tired, and I had that day sown the seeds of ague and fever in my system. For a moment I felt strange and weak, but the thought that I had at last seen the famous Ban-tau-langs, and the ambition to scale the top of distant Mount Morrison, re-nerved me.

I excused myself from singing at first, begging them to open the concert, but they declared that their fast tabooed them from doing so. I started a Banga tune, in which some of the men joined, the women took up the refrain, and we were friends at once.

I sang all the old favourite home songs, both Scotch and Irish, that I knew, whilst some bold sea-shanties with rollicking choruses immensely took their fancy, and they delightedly declared that we white kinsfolk were really men, singing in manlike style, not screeching like women as the Chinese did.

Every now and then some new arrival would beg for a sight of my white skin, until at length I had to plead 'hiang' (taboo), upon which they desisted.

Pu-li-sang's brother and his two sons were away, we found, but they were expected back on the following day.

We at length retired to dry our clothes in front of the old chief's fire, an occupation which took us nearly all the night.

The next morning Pu-li-sang, with Li-gai's daughter and another girl, took us for a tramp to look for cassia trees. I shouldered my rifle, as the Sibukuns occasionally had an unpleasing habit of lying in wait close to the village.

The scenery was very grand; there were many dark

rocky precipices, whitened here and there by spraying waterfalls, a wealth of cool green ferns of endless variety, tall trees with their graceful drooping parasites, and, above, a cloudless blue sky.

We appeared to be close to the summit of Mount Morrison, but the girls judged that it would be dangerous to venture so far, as the Sibukuns had so lately killed men of their tribe.

We wandered about until afternoon amongst this wealth of wild Nature's beauty, learning the names of strange plants and picking up the Ban-tau-lang dialect.

On making our way back to the village, we found that Li-gai had returned. He was a plain-featured man, but wonderfully strong and active for his age, which seemed o be about fifty. His two sons, aged respectively twenty and fifteen, were fine young savages who had shown their prowess already, but had not yet taken a head, that hall-mark of the savage warrior.

Li-gai gave me a very hearty welcome, and informed me that, in consequence of my unexpected visit, the tribe had hospitably determined to break up the fast, and that a hunting party would sally forth in the evening to procure game for us.

He arranged that in the morning we should go to meet them, and have a chance to use our guns. Wherefore, the next morning at daylight we set out, with Pu-li-sang, accompanied by some of the men and women; and after about three hours' quick walking over toilsome mountains, down steep precipices, and through the rapid streams and torrents, we at last reached the rendezvous.

Here we found Li-gai and about a dozen hunters. They had killed a bear, a wild boar, and some small deer; and they were busy smoking the flesh.

When we had rested awhile, we tramped on for some distance, hearing afar off the barking of dogs and the shouts of men. Our guides therefore hurried us on, until

MY VISIT TO THE BAN-TAU-LANG TRIBE

we came in sight of another party, who had seen a wild pig, and were then beating for it.

Li-gai's son was the head of this party, and I was stationed at a spot whence I hoped to have a chance of trying my skill. However, at the end of an hour or so, the animal still declined to come forth and be killed; and as the savages had already slain one boar, they came to the conclusion that sufficient meat had been procured. They therefore proposed returning.

The savages all gathered round me, and we spent some time in trying my rifle and revolver at a mark. They seemed thunderstruck at the great distance the rifle would carry, and at the rapidity with which I could load and discharge. They averred that with one white man and such weapons they would soon put the Sibukuns to rout, and make themselves lords of the surrounding country. They entreated me to dwell amongst them, and to procure ammunition and arms from the place that seemed to them the greatest in the world—Taiwanfoo!

They were all so eager to sample my gun that I had hard work to keep my ammunition from being entirely expended.

When we reached home the meat was cooked, and distributed in portions amongst the entire population, even the dogs receiving their share.

I found the native hospitality somewhat oppressive, as, directly I had been feasted at one house, I was dragged off to another. To refuse would have been ungracious; and, my Chinese companions thoroughly appreciating all the good cheer, I felt compelled to resign myself to politeness and inevitable dyspepsia.

The Ban-tau-langs still maintained their fast to the extent of abstaining from tobacco and spirits; there was therefore none of the disgusting intoxication which I have too frequently witnessed amongst other tribes.

Their etiquette of hospitality was decidedly curious. I

was made to sit down beside the lady, or daughter, of the house, who, with a large wooden spoon, fed me with beans, millet, or broth, after just tasting each spoonful herself. Then with her own fingers she picked out for me the choicest morsels of venison, pork, bear's fat, or sausage from the common dish.

Upon the conclusion of the meal, a long bamboo full of water was handed to me to drink from; but, being unaccustomed to this peculiar vessel, more water ran over me than I drank. These water buckets are about six feet long, and are formed of the largest kind of bamboo.

Two or three of these are slung in a frame, and are carried on the back by a strap slung over the forehead. It can, therefore, easily be imagined that it is no light task for the women to toil up the rugged mountain paths with these loads of water.

So far, the weather had been fine and bracing; but I began to feel the need of a blanket and a change of clothing, although the hope of ascending Mount Morrison, and the prospect of returning to La-ku-li within a day or two, had enabled me to be somewhat careless about the discomfort of damp clothes.

Unfortunately, during the fourth night of my sojourn the weather changed. Next day the wind was very boisterous, and it was also wet; they therefore all agreed that we could not think of going out until the weather cleared up; so I had perforce to content myself with observing the habits of my savage friends. The men, I found, spent their whole leisure time in eating and sleeping; the women had to cut wood, cook the food, and draw water.

The rain, sleet, and cold continued, which, with the discomforts of savage life and my continually damp wardrobe, made me very wretched, and brought on dysentery.

The savages warmed themselves by making a large fire on the ground, lying round it nearly naked. Our apologies

MY VISIT TO THE BAN-TAU-LANG TRIBE 163

for beds were arranged like berths in a ship, and I was forced to huddle up in a few skins.

I felt extremely ill, with no available medicine but chilli pepper and hot water, and I began to speculate whether I should ever get back to civilisation again. I therefore determined to make an effort to return whilst strength remained; and even their pressing invitation to wait until the rains were over, that we might visit Mount Morrison, had no effect upon me.

Keng-le and I arranged to start on the following morning, whether Pu-li-sang would conduct us or not.

When we announced our intended departure, it was strenuously opposed by all our savage friends, and Pu-li-sang emphatically declared that she dared not return.

However, Le and I would not be deterred, and in spite of a great deal of argument we prepared to start off. Hoan-a also wished to return with us, but his spear was not to be found; the savages had hidden it.

Pu-li-sang promised that if we would only wait a day or two she would recover the missing spear and accompany us, but I felt too ill to stay. I told her that Keng-le and I would start at once, and press on to La-ku-li for medicine, and that there I would make ready a stock of presents for her to bring back.

This diplomatic arrangement had a good effect upon the savages. They agreed that we should go; and I parted from them in a very cordial manner, receiving from them several presents of skins, venison, and native cloth.

Then we departed, feeling sure that we could find our way back to La-ku-li. We reached the Tuna village without any *contretemps*; but, just as we had got past the opening in the bank where the village is situated, we heard a shout, and, turning, saw a man of the Tuna tribe running after us.

His shouts had a contrary effect upon us, making

us hurry on; for a detention amongst the Tunas, especially without presents to propitiate them, would have been inconvenient, if not dangerous in my state of health.

We contrived to dodge the man, but in doing so we lost our way, and we were about an hour regaining our track.

At last we reached the Banga village, about four o'clock, where we found a party of Soa-mohais and Lanis, two tribes whose settlements lay to the south, opposite Takao. These visitors were gorgeous in all the splendour of savage finery, such as beads, shells, red cloth, boars' tusks, brass wire, flowers, and oranges.

I found that their language differed much from that of the Bangas, being more like the Tagala dialects of the South Cape.

As I have stated before, my opinion is that Formosa has been populated from several different countries, such as the Philippines, Japan, and perhaps Mexico.

The new-comers were delighted to see me, as they had never before seen a white man. I, of course, was made to pledge friendship in the orthodox savage fashion, by putting our arms round each other's necks, and mutually drinking, at the same moment, out of one basin.

These Soa-mohais and Lanis desired me to return with them to their village, but I was obliged to decline for the present.

I went off to Chau-po, who had always been my very good friend, and informed him of my state of health, begging him to convey me down to La-ku-li on the following morning.

This he promised to do; but to our astonishment Pu-li-sang and Hoan-a appeared upon the scene, just when we had arranged everything for our departure. It appeared that the old woman feared that, since we had left the

MY VISIT TO THE BAN-TAU-LANG TRIBE 165

Ban-tau-langs, we might forget our promised presents, or that the Bangas might possibly monopolise them.

The spear was therefore speedily forthcoming; and Pu-li-sang and Hoan-a hastened in our wake, to overtake us, and to accompany us to La-ku-li, that I might not be tempted to forget my promise.

The next morning I proceeded safely to La-ku-li, accompanied by an escort consisting of Chau-po and others of his tribe.

Here I made both the Bangas and the Ban-tau-langs happy with very inexpensive, but, in their eyes, very valuable, curiosities, and many common articles for daily use. I bade them farewell at length, feeling genuinely sorry to part with them, as they had all been exceedingly kind to me.

It chanced about three years later that some gentlemen from Takao visited La-ku-li, and there happed upon a party of Bangas who had come out to barter. Amongst these was Chau-po, who, upon discovering that these gentlemen were my friends, sent to me by them a beautiful long knife, with ornamental sheath and tassels of hair, and a handsome pair of deer's horns. These gifts, he intimated, were to remind me to ' tsap-tsap-lai ' (to make haste and come), and that I ought to ' k'o-lian ' (pity) my poor kinsmen, who longed to see me again.

Some twelve years after I had been settled in Singapore, a gentlemen one day called at my office, and informed me that he had been stationed at the South Cape, Formosa, to erect a lighthouse there.

During this residence he had made the acquaintance of the savages and the Chinese of that district. Upon hearing that he was returning to England, a deputation of more than a hundred of the inhabitants waited upon him, and entreated him to find out ' Pi-ki-ling,' and beg him to come back to Formosa and fulfil his promise of returning to visit them again.

Only a month ago I had the pleasure of hearing from the Rev. Mr. Campbell that, even in the most remote parts, my name is still kindly remembered by the natives.

This goes to prove that it does not require civilisation to give one a long memory for one's friends.

CHAPTER XIV

AN EXCEPTIONAL CHINESE MERCHANT. GENERAL
LE GENDRE TO THE RESCUE

THE firm with which I was now connected, Messrs. James & Neil McPhail, had their head-quarters at Takao; our Taiwanfoo branch being in the absolute control of our Chinese compradore, or 'shroff.' Branch books were indeed kept by me at the Taiwanfoo house, of out-going and in-coming goods, with cash account, etc.; all the rest, however, was unreservedly in the hands of the compradore, in whom the two brothers had the most unbounded confidence.

This compradore, as I have remarked elsewhere, was a Celestial *sans peur et sans reproche*. He was presumably of good family, with apparently a private personal income. He had crossed to Formosa from Amoy, bringing with him a small tribe of retainers, and his wife and family. His house was luxurious, his generosity and hospitality unbounded. In appearance he was refined and mild; his manners were courteous, and his business abilities undoubtedly great. He neither drank, gambled, nor smoked opium; his morals were unquestioned; and he spoke favourably of the European missionaries.

A pocket edition of all the virtues! So immaculate a man, in fact, that I, with the perversity of audacious youth, waited vaguely to find some flaw in this piece of perfection.

Meantime the brothers James and Neil admired and trusted him unboundedly. He was such a credit to our firm. He was a man of so much enterprise, of such resource. He had always some wondrous scheme on hand which was to raise the firm to dazzling heights of prosperity. I believe they would have listened to no word against him, had any unwise person had the temerity to suggest caution.

So time went on, until I returned from my adventures amongst the Ban-tau-langs, and the New Year of 1867 opened.

My habitation was fixed outside of the west gate of Taiwanfoo, the only European house of business, and it was my custom, after I had dined, in the evening to stroll down to the compradore's quarters to see how things were progressing ; for it is the general habit of the Chinese trader to sleep through the legitimate working hours of the day, and to arouse himself to transact his business and smoke opium in the evening, the night, and the early hours of the morning.

Thus the evening was the time when our worthy compradore was busiest, explaining to his wily countrymen, with a bland smile, and in his sonorous voice, the advantages of dealing with our firm ; and thus it was that, though my business was done, I derived amusement and information from the conversation of the Chinese traders.

I found that there was one man working there whose occupation seemed scarcely relevant to Messrs. McPhail's business. This man was an exceedingly clever woodcarver ; his work was an unfailing delight to me, it was so infinitely delicate and fine. Thus I frequently watched his carving ; and to my mystification I discovered that he was forming 'chops,' or stamps for seals—'chops' of exquisite workmanship. Moreover, I found on closer examination that these particular stamps were for receipts for the Likim, or government tax, which was levied upon all import goods after they had paid the usual Customs duties.

I found occasion to inquire of the compradore what we could possibly have to do with the Likim.

AN EXCEPTIONAL CHINESE MERCHANT 169

He beamed upon me; he interrupted my queries with a frank burst of confidence. I was to wait and see. We should shortly have *all* to do with the Likim. He had it all planned in his head. We should make an agreement with the Tao-tai, and we should 'farm' the Likim. Then our firm would become great indeed! But when that time came we should want 'chops' for the Likim receipts, to be pasted on the bales of opium, so he had engaged the engraver to prepare them.

This sounded very plausible, and I was glad to hear that we were going to gain such an advantageous position; but an incident a few weeks later aroused my vague mistrust again.

Our firm had daily couriers from Taiwanfoo to our head-quarters at Takao. The Tao-tai, being on most friendly terms with Messrs. McPhail, often availed himself of our messengers to convey his official despatches also.

Now a Chinese missive is not of inviolate security. The large official envelope is merely closed, and sealed down with rice, sago, or any glutinous matter that chances to be handy; then the part thus closed is stamped with the official seal, it is addressed, and sent on its travels.

I was in the compradore's office one day when such a despatch came from the Tao-tai to be forwarded to the consul at Takao by our courier.

'Good,' said the compradore, 'we will see what is in it.'

Whereupon this man of rectitude moistened the mucilage and opened the despatch.

I was horror-stricken. For such an act a Chinaman's throat was in peril.

'Why, compradore, you dare die?' I cried in the vernacular.

He shrugged his shoulders with an easy smile.

'This belong Chinaman fashion,' he replied carelessly.

That was possibly true, I thought; but a man who

could play so low as that—white man *or* yellow man would do or dare anything. I felt that at last I had reason for my distrust.

Moreover, as the months passed on, the smallest, vaguest rumours began to be stirred up, and hovered mysteriously around our immaculate compradore. There was just a breath of a whisper that he had been seen gambling with one or two merchants in some low den. That he was somewhat too extravagant for prudence; that his word was not quite above suspicion. How did I learn these things? Who first whispered them abroad? I could not tell. Suffice it that in my mingling with the people, speaking their talk, and always trying to get at the back of their affectation and guile, I somehow grew still more uneasy about the doings of our firm in Taiwanfoo; vague, intangible, but very real trouble seemed to loom ahead.

At last I mustered up courage to lay my suspicions before Neil McPhail. Alas! how little foundation of real proof my assertions seemed to have when I gave them voice. 'They say'—'I have heard'—'It is whispered.' My chief was indignant. He would, could, and should not believe anything against his friend the compradore. What right had I to suspect him? He would trust him as himself. He was devoted to the firm's prosperity.

I ventured to point out that, though we were presumably doing such great things, yet these large profits did not appear to pass through our books.

That was the compradore's affair entirely, he replied. The whole business was in the compradore's hands, and he had every confidence in its being so. Let him hear no more of it.

Well, I had done what I could, and had received the usual reward of the prophet who predicts evil things. I could but wait and watch.

So the days passed on until May, the time of the breaking up of the monsoon, and the vessels ceased to

AN EXCEPTIONAL CHINESE MERCHANT 171

come to Anping. James McPhail had come up from Takao. He was with me in the office at the close of the day, when the compradore came in to speak with him. The subtle change which had mysteriously taken place in his reputation seemed curiously reflected in the man's dress and manner. He seemed indefinably to have lost his old assertiveness, his former strong grip of things. His face had changed, his very clothes hung differently in their silken folds.

He had come, he said, to say that it would be well to send some store of treasure, opium, and piece goods down to Takao, and that he was going with them that night on board the small cutter, which we were in the habit of using as a lighter between the two ports.

I was surprised at this arrangement. It was somewhat *infra dig.* for our compradore to personally take down the treasure. It had usually fallen to my province to accompany the cutter upon these journeys.

However, it was arranged, and no more was said. The following morning I was aroused by my boy, who rushed into my room in great excitement, saying that there was a big row down below, that the compradore had 'tsau' (run away), and that the soldiers were outside our warehouses, sealing the 'hong' up. I hastily got into my clothes, and hurried down to the Chinese quarter of our house.

Sure enough, when I had made my way through the chattering, gesticulating idlers, I found a group of the Tao-tai's emissaries busily engaged in pasting huge proclamations and seals upon our big doors, and searching in the well, where they found false Likim brands used to mark opium.

No time was to be lost. They must be bluffed. Therefore I tore down the papers with great appearance of indignation, and fiercely demanded an explanation of their proceedings.

'Oh!' they replied, with unction, 'your great compradore! If we but had him here, his head would soon be under the sword of the executioner! What has he been doing these many months? Forging the Likim seal! and stamping the goods himself, thus cheating our Celestial emperor of his revenues! If we but had him here!'

Turning them into the street until they could produce an order from the British consul, I rushed within. The office was bare; all the compradore's men, his creatures from Amoy, had gone. Only two quaking Taiwanfoo clerks remained, stupid with mingled fright and guile. They knew nothing—nothing! Ai-yo! what should they know?

Then I spoke strong words to them, and would have proceeded to stronger action if fright had not loosened their tongues.

'Yes,' they said, 'it was true. The compradore had run away. He was not coming back. He was a great criminal. More they did not know.'

I rushed upstairs into the compradore's private establishment. Bare, dismantled—everything gone! Even the women's sacred suite of rooms was not respected by me in my excited progress. I tore the silken curtains aside. Deserted, emptied of all their grandeur! Evidently there had been a hurried flitting. Then it was all too true. I retraced my steps, and made my way to Mr. McPhail's apartment, to break the news to him.

He appeared dazed. He scarcely seemed to comprehend my hurried narrative. He could suggest no line of action. I got him up on to the roof of the house, where a kind of observatory had been formed under an awning, for peaceful evening smokes after the heat and burden of the day.

He sank into a cane lounge, and hiding his face in his hands would mutter nothing but 'Ruined! ruined!'

AN EXCEPTIONAL CHINESE MERCHANT 173

I was at my wits' end. I had already posted off a messenger to Neil McPhail at Takao, but, even if he started immediately on receipt of my news, he could not reach us until the following day. Meantime steps must be taken to protect our firm from the zeal of the Tao-tai and his emissaries. What was I to do?

Even as I asked myself this question, gazing despairingly over the sea, my answer appeared on the horizon. Just a little stream of smoke, which drew nearer and nearer, until the outline of a big man-of-war, flying the American flag and making for Anping Roads, was clearly visible across the blue waters. Nothing could have been more opportune. It was the 'Ashuelot,' bringing from Amoy General Le Gendre, who was American consul for that port and for Formosa. Never before had I been so gratified at the advent of Europeans.

Within an hour or two a party from the ship was below, knocking loudly at our closed doors for admittance. The General's lips formed a silent, long-drawn 'whew-w!' when he viewed the collapsed McPhail, and I told him of our plight.

'But there is still the opium in the warehouse below,' I concluded. 'We are not quite done for.'

'Let us go and see,' replied the General.

So we went down in a body to the warehouse where the opium chests stood, twenty-five or thirty of them, piled up, and all neatly sewn up in gunny bags as if they had never been opened since they left Calcutta.

'Let us open them,' suggested somebody.

And we did. Full chests indeed, but filled with bricks and rubbish. Of opium there was not left enough to send a cat to sleep.

Then followed a hurried consultation. General Le Gendre was a friend of the firm of an American merchant of Amoy, one of our chief creditors; therefore it was arranged that he should step in and take things over on their behalf, thus saving us from the tender mercies of the Tao-tai.

Next day poor Neil McPhail joined us from Takao. He was heart-broken, not only at the wreck of his business, but principally at the perfidy and treachery of the man in whom he had placed such absolute trust.

The compradore and the cutter seemed to have vanished from the Formosan seas : we could obtain no tidings of them. The probability was, however, that the compradore had crossed to the Pescadores, and was there in hiding, waiting for a favourable opportunity of slinking over to the mainland.

General Le Gendre, greatly to our benefit, had been a lawyer at some earlier date in his career, and his wise advice, and practical assistance with the Tao-tai, was invaluable.

He obtained from that dignitary an authority for me to search the Pescadores for the criminal, with a despatch to the chief mandarin of the islands to assist me by all the means that lay in his power, and a warrant empowering me to arrest the compradore when discovered.

Though I received information that the compradore had touched at one of the islands to burn incense, it was a vain quest ; either the people of the Pescadores really knew nothing of the culprit's whereabouts, or they had been heavily bribed to be ignorant. I stayed about a week at the mandarin's house, and then returned baffled to Formosa.

Events moved rapidly then. The peculations and entanglements of the dishonest 'shroff,' combined with some previous heavy losses consequent on the purchase of a tea cargo wrecked on the Pescadores, etc., were too much for the solvency of our firm.

Messrs. Elles & Co. took over what remained of the business, and for the first and last time in my life I played the part of auctioneer, selling off all remaining stock, with the compradore's goods and chattels, and obtaining good prices for them. After which I was placed in charge of the Taiwanfoo branch of Messrs. Elles & Co.'s business.

The two brothers, Messrs. James and Neil McPhail, quitted the island shortly afterwards : I believe both have now joined the great majority. Nothing could exceed their kind and considerate treatment of me whilst I was in their service; they were highly esteemed in Formosa, and it seemed a curiously bitter thing that these heavy misfortunes befell them through their single-hearted confidence and trust in an unworthy Chinaman.

CHAPTER XV

WRECKS AND WRECKERS

CRUEL were the tender mercies of the Chinese fisher-folk, even amongst the law-abiding population scattered along the sea-coast between Taiwanfoo and Takao. Further north, the wild and lawless settlers cultivated wrecking as a profession, and woeful indeed was the fate of any unfortunate vessel which chanced to be stranded upon the sand banks near their villages.

I have known the catamarans to put forth from Anping river in the morning, ten or twenty of them, bound for the fishing ground, when some sudden gale would cause them to return, and they would be capsized in the surf, on the treacherous bar.

These drowning wretches would be clinging desperately to spars and wreckage, drifting fast to death past the fishing villages where their friends and relations lived; whilst these fraternal folk would stand clustering upon the shore, or lie off inside the surf in their catamarans, by signs and shouts, above the roar of the waves, bargaining with them 'how much' for a rescue.

Sometimes the tables were turned, and one of these inhuman bargainers perchance coming to Anping to buy twine or nets, one of the rescued fisher-folk might hap upon him, and would give him rough greeting with a bamboo.

A short time before the Customs service was established at Takao, when the place and its inhabitants were more barbarous and wild than when I first settled there, a German vessel was blown by the violence of the typhoon upon the shore without the harbour below Ape's Hill.

Instantly the beach was alive with wreckers eager for the spoil. When the stout-hearted Teutonic captain dared to expostulate, they promptly settled *his* side of the question by killing him.

Nemesis followed in this instance. The Europeans of Messrs. Jardine & Dent's receiving ships, in their righteous wrath, took the law into their own hands, and, marshalling their crews of Malays and Manilamen, speedily burned the villages of the wreckers, as a gentle hint that European life must count, even to a Celestial.

Whilst I was first at Takao, living in the 'Ternate,' a fleet of big junks came to the harbour from the mainland, and were lying up for a long time taking in cargoes of sugar for the northern ports. They remained thus at anchor, waiting many weeks for the south-west monsoon.

The crews of these vessels were naturally much on shore during these weeks of enforced idleness, fraternising with their countrymen in Formosa. At last a morning dawned which seemed favourable for their departure. The sea lay calm in the sunlight, and no angry surf was to be seen. They hurried through their preparations, and bade their friends adieu. But, as the hours passed, the elements began to mock them. A cruel head wind beat upon their sails, wild clouds scudded across the stormy sky. A typhoon arose, which beat the junks, helpless as cockleshells, upon the rugged, deadly rocks of the Saracen's Head.

As the hours of darkness came on, bringing death each moment nearer, these unfortunate Chinamen cried in agony to their fellow-countrymen on shore to help them. But these were too busy on their own concerns, when the wild waves were washing in a rich harvest of wreckage to their feet.

All the good things from their former friends' junks were not to be wasted. They pushed, and fought, and scrambled, wading up to their necks in the white surf to secure some bit of spoil.

And if perchance some of the poor drowning wretches were dashed upon the shore, more dead than alive—well, a quiet blow from some handy piece of timber disposed of any inconvenient claim *they* might have made, at once.

Along this dangerous and treacherous west coast of the island the sea yearly claimed a heavy number of victims.

Each year, beating down the Formosan Channel against the full force of the south-west monsoon, would come unlucky vessels which were cast on the sand banks and shoals to the north of Taiwanfoo. In almost every case, directly the ship grounded, she was surrounded by hundreds of catamarans filled with jubilant wreckers, who swarmed over her as their lawful prey. The unfortunate crews were stripped naked, and sent on shore; whilst, in one or two instances, as the wedding rings of the German captains did not come off their fingers easily, the Chinese just cut off the fingers, as a direct method of saving themselves trouble.

One day, to our consternation, some twenty or thirty Europeans were brought to our house in Taiwanfoo, in a state of almost perfect nudity. It appeared that, having been stripped by the wreckers, they passed the night covered with sand to keep themselves warm, and they then had wandered disconsolately to a small town, where the magistrate, compassionating their shivering plight, gave them some food and a small sum of money, and supplied each with a new rice bag.

Cutting a hole in the bottom of these, they thrust their heads through, and were thus decently, if not artistically, clothed.

The humane mandarin also supplied the men with

a guide to conduct them to the European's house at Taiwanfoo.

Unfortunately, however, on their way thither, they were obliged to pass through a robber village on the coast, where the inhabitants decided that they could not permit such valuable property as new rice bags to pass unappropriated. They therefore stripped them of their single covering, and the men at last reached me in the primeval state I have described.

One day, early in 1867, two miserable Chinese soldiers were brought into the British consulate at Takao. They had a tragedy to relate. They stated that they were the cook and steward of an American barque, the 'Rover,' of which vessel they were the sole survivors.

It transpired that their ship had gone down off the South Cape, Formosa; and that the captain, with his wife, officers, and crew, had taken to their boats, landing upon the beach near the extreme south point of the island.

Here these unfortunates were set upon and murdered by a savage tribe called the Ko-a-luts. All had perished but these two men, who contrived to escape along the beach to a Chinese village.

H.M.S. 'Cormorant' was lying at Takao at the time this news arrived, and Captain Broad, accompanied by the British consul, proceeded at once to the South Cape to make an investigation.

They went on shore to hold communication with the savages, but were inhospitably greeted with a hot matchlock fire. Two of the boat's crew were wounded, and some of their oars were broken. They were forced to retreat on board the vessel, and returned to Takao, having accomplished nothing.

It was to avenge the massacre of the 'Rover's' crew that General Le Gendre, the U.S.A. consul general, had come over to the island in the warship 'Ashuelot.' He endeavoured to induce the Tao-tai to send Chinese troops on a punitive expedition to the savage Ko-a-luts. The governor, however, declined to interfere; arguing that Liong-kiao, the district in which the 'Rover' people were murdered, was outside Chinese jurisdiction, although it contained many Chinese settlers, both Hak-kas and Hok-los.

General Le Gendre therefore steamed away to lay the matter before the American minister and the Tsung-li-yamen at Pekin.

In the meantime the American frigate 'Hartford' and the corvette 'Wyoming,' under Admiral Bell, were sent from Japan to avenge the murders. Upon these vessels arriving off Takao, where at that moment I chanced to be, Commander Mackenzie, of the 'Hartford,' came on shore to invite me to accompany the expedition as interpreter. I was nothing loth to go and see some fighting, and the British consul asked to be allowed to accompany our party.

We started the same afternoon. Admiral Bell having asked my advice, I suggested that we should anchor for the night in Liong-kiao bay, on the west side of the South Cape. Here, I knew, was a Chinese village of Hak-kas, who supplied the savages with arms, and who had intermarried with them, thus acquiring a knowledge of their ways and haunts.

I suggested that by moral pressure of superior force, and by offering them monetary bribes, we might possibly induce the corruptible Chinese to provide us with guides, in order that half our party might attack the Ko-a-luts on land from their rear, whilst simultaneously the other half marched upon their village from the sea beach.

The admiral, however, doubted whether the Chinese might not be more likely to inform the savages of our intentions.

The following morning at daylight we reached the South Cape, and anchored off the scene of the massacre.

The admiral proceeded to land about one hundred and eighty blue-jackets and marines, under the leadership of Captain Belknap and Commander Mackenzie.

I was attached to Mackenzie's party, who went on ahead on skirmishing duty.

We could perceive no signs of any inhabitants, and progression was difficult; the country was covered with thick jungle, excepting a break here and there, where we came upon open spaces of grass and rocks.

We had not penetrated a mile from the beach when our unseen foes fired a volley upon us, but did no harm.

The sun grew very hot as the day advanced, and our track was uphill and very rugged.

The men grew exhausted; the lurking savages began to fire upon us from all quarters, both before and behind, whilst chasing them was difficult and futile. So far there had been no casualties, with the amusing exception that a marine shot away his major's epaulet or shoulder-strap.

The savages ceased firing for some time, and we could see no signs of any village or native track.

At last the captain halted the force under some rocks for a brief rest and refreshment, as the men were greatly distressed by the heat and the difficulties of our progress.

No sooner had we cast ourselves down in the shade, than another volley came from the bush close by, but it fortunately did no harm to our party.

Mackenzie then called for volunteers to drive the enemy from their haunts in the thick jungle. We rushed up the hill, firing wildly at the points whence the smoke had issued; but though we heard great howling, when we reached the spot, no bodies were to be found.

On coming to some high rocks, we few volunteers halted, to see if it were possible to obtain the solace of a pipe. I happened luckily to have a match or two upon me, and Mackenzie, with my companion, gathered closely round me to lose no flicker of the precious match for their waiting pipes.

At that instant our hopes of a soothing whiff were frustrated. There came another volley, right upon us.

Mackenzie, in deep exasperation, cried:

'Come on, my lads! Let us give a rally, and finish off these rascals!'

We all rushed ahead, cheering loudly. Our greeting was another volley through the green leaves. We were wild with excitement and wrath, pressing forward with all speed. I only had time to see Mackenzie turn; his hand sought his breast, and he just said in a queer, quiet voice, ' Somebody please go down and call the doctor.'

Then I was borne ahead by my excited companions, and we rushed on until we were suddenly arrested by the sound of the recall.

When we rejoined the main force, it was to find poor Mackenzie dead. He had been shot through the heart when he had asked for the doctor.

As there seemed to be no chance of our finding the Ko-a-lut village, Captain Belknap decided to return to the ships, whilst our party covered the retreat; whereupon the Ko-a-luts, emboldened by our retreat, followed us down to the beach, but their weapons did no harm.

The surf had grown very violent, and we had considerable difficulty in reaching the boats.

On arriving on board, and reporting matters to the admiral, he decided to return to Japan until the time of the north-east monsoon, the dry season, when the jungle would be burned.

He landed the consul and myself at Takao, and buried poor Mackenzie in the cemetery there. It was pitiful that, after passing unscathed through the whole of the war between the Confederates and Unionists, this gallant officer should be killed at last by the chance bullet of a wretched savage in Formosa.

WRECKS AND WRECKERS 183

A man-of-war came to Takao shortly afterwards, and conveyed his body to the States.

When I got back to Takao, I found awaiting me there a Mr. James Horn, who had come on behalf of the relations of the wife of the unfortunate captain of the ' Rover.' He desired to obtain her remains, for the purpose of conveying them to her friends in America.

He accordingly went down to Liong-kiao, but after spending time and money in a vain effort, he returned and requested me to help him in his melancholy task.

It being the time of the south-west monsoon, I had leisure to assist him. I therefore accompanied him on his return to Liong-kiao.

For an account of how we fared in our quest, and of the adventures which befell us at the South Cape, I cannot do better than quote some leaves from a journal kept by my friend Mr. Horn at the time, and published in the *China Mail* newspaper.

Extract from Mr. James Horn's Journal.

'On July 30 I returned to Takao from Sialiao, a village in Liong-kiao Bay, after a stay down at the South Cape of upwards of a month, endeavouring to obtain information regarding the "Rover." Not being satisfied with what information I obtained, nor with the interpreter, I called on Mr. W. Pickering of Taiwanfoo, a young gentleman who is reckoned one of the best authorities regarding the savages on the island, and a good linguist, and he kindly agreed to accompany me to the South Cape, and try to recover the remains, etc., for me.

'On August 3 we started for Sialiao, and on the 4th entered the little river there, and put up at the same house I had before.

'August 5.—We got here in time, as a typhoon came on, and two junks were wrecked off the cape and three drove out to sea from Liong-kiao. Mr. Pickering found a great deal of difficulty in obtaining information regarding the bodies, as the interpreter (Atowat) had tried to frighten the people by telling them that the Americans were coming to punish them for the murders. In the afternoon went to the Hak-ka village, Poliek; found that the remains and sundry articles were in the hands of a tribe of savages named Ling-nuan, living near the Ko-a-luts (the murderers of Captain Hunt and crew). Here we saw several savages who are kept as slaves to the neighbouring tribes; engaged a guide to take us to Toa-su-pong, a village in the bay, about two miles from where Captain Hunt landed.

'7th.—Started on our journey south. At 4 P.M. came in sight of a fresh-water lake, about two miles long by one broad, which the Chinese say abounds in fish, and in the winter is covered with wild-fowl; about 6 P.M. arrived at Sin-keng, a farm-house near the sea-shore, where we put up.

'8th.—Started, and arrived at Toa-su-pong about 6 P.M.

'9th.—Went to the house where Atowat had his information. Here we saw three of the Ling-nuan savages, who told us that the bones were still with them, but in a very bad state, as Atowat had only offered fifteen dollars for them, and told them that, if they would not give up everything belonging to the "Rover," in a few days a steamer would come and destroy their village, also the Chinese villages around; so, being frightened, they had thrown the bag containing the remains under a tree near the Ko-a-luts, and that since then the wild pigs had destroyed a portion of the bones. These savages speak Chinese. Mr. Pickering had a long talk with them. They told him that they were very much frightened when the steamers were there; also said they were honest men and never killed any person, and that had Captain Hunt come three hundred yards further to the westward to their village, they would have saved them all. They also said that every year they save some Chinese from the Ko-a-luts ; that about ten years ago they rescued three European sailors from the Ko-a-luts, who had just killed eighteen of them. The names of the sailors were Jim, Alex, and Bill ; they belonged to a vessel wrecked off the cape. The three sailors stayed with them and the Chinese for upwards of a year, and were taken off by a ship passing round to the eastward. The Chinese say that about a year afterwards Alex came back and gave them a present of two hundred dollars.

'In the afternoon we went to the Ling-nuan village, which is situated on the west side of the same hill that the Ko-a-luts inhabit. We only saw three savages there, the others had gone to the mountains. The savages showed us the place where the body was buried, under a tree near the beach, a little distance from the village nearer the Ko-a-luts ; the skull, breast bones, ribs, etc., were there, but the large bones of the legs and arms were gone. The savages had heard from Atowat that Mr. Hunt was a mandarin, so they demanded an enormous sum for the bones ; they also reasoned that she must have been some great lady or the men-of-war would never have come here. Mr. Pickering very patiently explained everything to them, also showed them how much it would be to their advantage to be friendly, and what benefits they would derive from trade with the white men, and that no harm would come to them from the arrival of vessels, and that they would be rewarded for any assistance they rendered to the American vessels in punishing the Ko-a-luts or in assisting shipwrecked seamen. They promised to do all in their power, and agreed to bring the remains of Mrs. Hunt to a hut near Toa-su-pong in the morning.

'August 10.—Heard that there was a Bashee islander in the village, who, with nine companions in a canoe, had been driven on the east side of the island. On nearing the land they had been fired on by the Bootan savages and one killed. They came further south and landed near the Tilasok village, where they met a deaf and dumb savage, who took them to his house. When there the rest of the tribe demanded their heads, but the deaf and dumb man placed himself in the doorway and defended them with a club, and showed the other savages that they must kill him before the islanders. This deaf and dumb man, being brother-in-law to the chief, was allowed to keep them, but afterwards the savages got one of the men out and took his head. We got this information from the Chinese, to whom one man had been sent to see if they could understand him and get a boat to take them back. The Chinese wanted us to see the man. Thinking we might be able to speak to him, we went to the house where he was, but of course could not understand him, and were going away when Mr. Pickering remembered that the Spanish traded with the Bashee Islands, and tried Spanish. To our surprise he answered, and informed us he was a Christian, repeating the Lord's Prayer, etc. He corroborated generally the Chinese account. Mr. Pickering promised to do all he could to get them liberated, and told the Chinese to send and request the savages to treat them well and they would be rewarded.

'From there we went to the place where the remains had been brought to. It was there ready for us. As we had no money to pay for it, Mr. Pickering had some difficulty in making arrangements; after some trouble, got one of the Chinese to be security to the Ling-nuans, and another to secure him; I, agreeing to stay at Liong-kiao until the money was paid, gave them the bargain money. We had to assure them that this was the last they would hear of the matter before they would give up the bones. We then got the bones put into a grass box with a lot of gilt paper to pay the spirit's way to heaven, as the Chinese said, and strapped on my back, as the Chinese would not touch it. We had to fire off all our arms towards the

Ko-a-luts to show our indignation against them. After we got them pleased, we started for Sialiao, and arrived there about 7 P.M. Both on the way south and back we were very well treated by the people. They are more than one-half savage, very little Chinese blood amongst them. Should shipwrecked mariners land to the westward of the Ko-a-lut Rock, they would be well received and kindly treated, but should they land to the eastward, they would be sure to fall into the hands of the savages.

'Just to the westward of the rock is a tribe of savages named Ling-nuans, who are comparatively civilised, but are not to be trusted too far, as they would not scruple to rob foreigners could they screen themselves.

'Mr. Pickering started for Takao, promising to send or come down soon.

'12th.—Went in company of a guide to a Pepo-hoan village on the banks of the lake in search of the trunk and sundries belonging to the "Rover"; got the trunk for five dollars. Made search after the chronometer and portrait that I had seen before; found that the savages wanted a large sum for them.

'17th.—Mr. Pickering returned from Takao, being commissioned by Mr. Carrol, the English consul, to obtain the release of the Bashee islanders.

'August 18.—Proceeded to Toa-su-pong, where the islander we had seen before was staying. Paid for the remains of Mrs. Hunt; called at the house where the islander was; found that the savages had sent another out. Mr. Pickering tried everywhere to get a guide to take us into the Tilasok village to see the chief concerning their release. We could not succeed in getting a guide, as we should have to pass through the Ko-a-luts (the tribe who murdered the crew of the "Rover"), and the Chinese would not go with us, as they said that if any harm came to us they would be held responsible for it. Mr. Pickering offered rewards to some of the Ko-a-lut women who came to

Toa-su-pong to show us the way, but they said that they dare not, as, since the steamer left, the savages' crops had been severely damaged by wild pigs, and one of their men had been bitten by a shark, also they had had a quarrel amongst themselves, in which two men were killed. The Ko-a-luts, after holding a religious ceremony to inquire into the reason of all these calamities, found that the Americans had left an evil spirit behind them to destroy the savages, so they had determined to be revenged on all white men. Finding it was in vain to think of going inside, we sent a savage woman to offer the chief of the Tilasok the sum of seven dollars each for the islanders. In two days she returned, saying that the chief wanted more, as the islanders had made signs to him that if he would send them back they would give him two rice measures full of dollars. Mr. Pickering then offered two hundred dollars, and said it was all we could give, and explained to the savage woman how foolish it was to expect people who had only a strip of cloth round their waists to have dollars. In two days the woman again returned and said that the chief demanded five hundred dollars for the men, and that there were four Chinese from Liong-kiao who had offered four hundred dollars, as they said that the foreigners would buy them from them, as they wanted to take them to Takao, to make opium of or sell them as slaves (the people there have some very strange notions about the Roman Catholic missionaries making opium of their converts). Mr. Pickering sent word to the chief that he had better sell the men to the Chinese, as we could not offer that sum, knowing that the Chinese had only offered four hundred dollars in the hopes of selling them to us for five hundred dollars. We then returned to Sialiao, and kept quiet for two days, giving out that we had returned to Takao in disgust, and gave a Chinese, who was married to a savage woman, two hundred dollars on security, telling him that if he could get the savage to give up the men the money was his. In the meantime, having an invitation from the Labosee tribe, about six miles off in the mountains, went in to see them. Were very well treated; had a grand feast, and on leaving the next day got a present of a bag of millet and some fowls; also about a dozen savages well armed accompanied us as an escort until we were clear of the mountains. On returning to Sialiao found that the chief had sent word that he would not take less, that he had just heard that the mandarins were coming down with 7,500 men to destroy the Ko-a-luts and other savages of whom he is the chief, some of the Hak-kas having gone in and showed him the proclamation and explained it to him, warning him to get ready.

'The savage woman said that the Bashee islanders were kept in strict confinement, and when she made signs to them that the chief would not let them go they cried much. Mr. Pickering was anxious to get back to Takao, and yet, not liking to go back without the men, agreed to pay the sum demanded. The woman took the money in on the 30th on good security.

'On the 31st seven men came out, accompanied by two old savage women and the wife of the deaf and dumb savage. They dilated very much on the goodness of their chief in letting the men go for that sum. These women promised to bring the remaining man from Toa-su-pong the next day, and pay all the expenses the Chinese might demand for keeping him so long. We waited two days for the arrival of the man, and the two women came back saying that the Chinese would not deliver him up. Next day we went down, well armed, and took the man away from the Chinese, telling them to settle with the chief. They at first made a great disturbance, but we explained everything to them and parted on very friendly terms.

'We then returned to Sialiao, and Mr. Pickering intended to start directly for Takao (I agreeing to stay as security for the money we had borrowed from a Hong).

He was going on board the boat about 11 P.M. on September 6, but, seeing the weather was very unsettled and the wind commencing to blow from the north-east, decided very fortunately to stay until morning, as the typhoon began directly afterwards and continued constant gales of wind and rain, no boats being able to go out.

'Sept. 8.—To-day the head of the Fokeen Chinese here came to Mr. Pickering and said that he had heard that the mandarins were coming down to Liong-kiao with 8,000 men to fight the Ko-a-luts and savages, and the Fokeen men were much afraid that the soldiers would cause a good deal of distress and do no good, as the savages all knew of their designs (the mandarins having foolishly circulated proclamations announcing their intentions), and had all joined together, eighteen tribes, under one leader named Tok-e-tok (the same man who had the Bashee islanders), and could muster eleven hundred men armed with guns, besides about fifteen hundred other savages called Amias, who are servants or slaves, with bows and spears. These tribes had determined to resist the mandarins, and if they found that they were too strong for them, they would go up north and wait until the mandarins went back.

'The Fokeen men said that the Hak-kas, who, as well as themselves, hold their land from different savage chiefs, had great influence with the different chiefs and thought they could influence Tok-e-tok to agree hereafter not to hurt any foreigners that were shipwrecked.

'The Hak-kas and Fokeen Chinese say that they are very comfortable as they are (they pay a certain sum of money every year to the different chiefs under whom they hold their land), but that if the mandarins came down the soldiers will do all the damages to them, their crops, etc., etc., and not be able to do anything to the savages; they also say that they do not want to fight against the mandarins, but if the latter do not destroy all the savages, when they return to Taiwan, the savages will come down and be continually at war with them for not helping them against the mandarins.

'The Fokeen people and Hak-kas were continually fighting amongst themselves, but the latter, living amongst the savages, are very friendly with them, and do all their trade for them.

'The two races of Chinese have agreed to make common cause now with regard to the Ko-a-lut business, and the head of the Hak-kas, Lin-a-kow, came to Mr. Pickering and said that he would call out the chief of the Tilasoks, Tok-e-tok, and get him to agree that after this the Ko-a-luts and all other tribes under his command should abstain from murdering any foreigners who might be cast or land on their shores, and assist them as far as lay in their power. Thinking that such an agreement would do no harm, but save a deal of expense and loss of life, Mr. Pickering agreed to see the chief, but told them that he could only report the matter to the proper authorities.

'The mandarins had sent to request the Hak-kas to assist them against the savages, but the Hak-kas said that, from what they heard of the mandarins in the north of Formosa and in the mainland, they treated friends and foes alike. Hitherto the Hak-kas and Fokeen men never agreed, but that they were all so much afraid of the damage that the presence of bodies of mandarin soldiers would cause in the country that they now agreed together to call the chief Tok-e-tok out, and make a treaty to help all foreigners who might fall into their hands. The Hak-kas and Fokeen men agree to be security for anything that Tok-e-tok agrees to, and should anything happen any government could easily find them.

'The Hak-kas have great power over the savages, as they can deprive them of ammunition, but they say they are unwilling to go to war with them, as they have always been at peace and hold their land from them.

'11th.—To-day we have had a meeting of all the heads of Hak-kas and Fokeen men at Poliek, and after a long discussion, in which the principal point was that the Hak-kas feared the foreigners would not agree to anything until some lives were lost in revenge for the murders of the "Rover" crew, Mr. Pickering told them it was out of his power to promise anything, but that from what he knew of foreigners' hearts he thought that if such an arrangement was not too late they would accept it, as slaughter was not an object with us.

'They begged us to send up as soon as possible to the proper authorities and try to get the soldiers delayed until some arrangements were made with the savages.

'12th.—Being tired of waiting for a chance to get up by boat, and no signs of the weather clearing up, we determined to start by land for Takao; the Chinese tried to dissuade us from it, as we had to pass through the savage territory; but we managed to get guides and started with the Bashee islanders; passed through the village of Cha-sia; found a petty mandarin had arrived—Mr. P. heard him telling the people to have nothing to do with us. He was astonished when Mr. P. went up to him and spoke in the mandarin dialect.

'Got to Hiong Kang about 6 P.M., after walking about fifteen miles over a hilly country, through the savage territory: raining the whole day. Started in the morning; came to a rapid river too deep to ford; had to return towards noon; got a boat on to Pangliao; arrived there about 5 P.M. Could not get further, as it was blowing fresh; found that the Chinese troops had arrived here, and that some foreigners were here. A Chinese conducted us to a house, where we met General Le Gendre and a French gentleman. General Le Gendre informed us that he was going down to Liong-kiao on account of the "Rover" business, and engaged Mr. Pickering to go with him as interpreter. Mr. P. gave him every information we had received, and proposed the treaty to him. There were between four hundred and five hundred soldiers here, but they could not get down for some time.

'Next day I proceeded to Takao by land, the Bashee islanders being forwarded by boat.

' 16th.—Arrived at Takao. The Bashee islanders were sent by Mr. Carrol, per the gunboat, home to the island.

' On the 26th I returned to Sialiao, and found General Le Gendre and the Chinese troops there, but nothing done yet, as the mandarins were putting every obstacle in the way. The whole of the business lay upon Mr. Pickering's shoulders. He was the first to go, in company of some Hak-kas, in to the Tilasoks, and had an interview with the chief, and since then has had several interviews with him. I do not think that anything could have been done by General Le Gendre towards making a peaceable arrangement with the savages without Mr. Pickering. I know I would never have got the remains of Mrs. Hunt without his assistance.

' Mr. Pickering is well liked by both Chinese and savages, and been more among the savages of north and south than any other man on the island.

'JAMES HORN.'

Mr. Horn was so attracted by what he saw of the Pepo-hoan character, during our dealings with them at this time, that he ultimately returned to Formosa, and settled with a German friend upon the north-eastern side of the island, where they formed a colony of these simple-hearted people, for the purpose of cutting down and disposing of timber.

All went prosperously, until Mr. Horn one day went round by sea to Tamsui, to engage the services of more Pepo-hoans. He was returning with about a hundred men in a large native boat, when a sudden typhoon arose, the vessel capsized, and every soul on board was drowned.

CHAPTER XVI

THE TRIUMPH OF DIPLOMACY

DURING the time that I spent down at the South Cape upon this melancholy mission, I embraced every opportunity of making friends with the tribes of Hak-kas and Hok-los who had settled in the savage territory of Liong-kiao. They were exceedingly hospitable, and inclined to fraternise with the red-haired barbarian within their gates.

I also was so fortunate as to rescue (on two occasions) some twenty or thirty shipwrecked Spanish sailors from the tender mercies of the savages on the east coast.

Just as I was about to return to Takao, there came a rumour throughout the country that the Chinese commander-in-chief and the American consul were coming down with a large army to punish the Ko-a-luts.

This prospect created great consternation amongst the Chinese settlers. They called me in, and entreated me to assist them. They argued: 'We have no desire to be under the yoke of the mandarins; whilst as to Chinese soldiers, you know what they are! They are worse than locusts. If we should be good to them, they will take all we have; while if we do not find them supplies, they will seize our women and kill us. They will never be able to stand out against the savages; they will be compelled to flee at last; then the savages will revenge themselves upon all of us who wear tails; they will stop our irrigation water, and our lives will not be safe by day nor night.'

THE TRIUMPH OF DIPLOMACY 195

The headmen assured me that both races of Chinese settlers had determined to abandon all their feuds, for the purpose of bringing united pressure to bear upon Tok-e-tok, the chief of eighteen savage tribes, to make it worth his while to spare all shipwrecked crews who chanced to come ashore on their coast, and to hand them over to the Chinese villagers, who would forward them to the consul at Takao.

They informed me that the savages were entirely dependent upon them for guns, ammunition, and salt. They therefore did not think that it would be very difficult to bring them to terms.

These same headmen besought me to go up to Tai-wanfoo, to lay their proposal before the consul and the commander-in-chief, General Lau, a gallant man and distinguished officer, who had been rewarded by the emperor with the honour of a yellow jacket for services under General Gordon.

I accordingly started off overland, and had the good fortune to meet the invading force half-way. It consisted of two hundred disciplined Hunan braves, armed with Enfield rifles, men who had fought under Gordon, and who were clansmen or fellow provincials of the commander-in-chief. These were accompanied by three or four hundred militia, armed with matchlocks, spears, etc.

The valiant commander-in-chief, and another general who had gained much credit in a rebellion some twenty years before, were in charge of the expedition; and General Le Gendre, with the sub-prefect,—the civil administrator and diplomatist of the island,—was also with them.

It transpired that General Le Gendre had been to Pekin, and had frightened the Chinese government into tardy action, by threatening that if the emperor did not exercise jurisdiction over Formosa, the English would take the island. He had called at Amoy, *en route* for Formosa, and had obtained the permission of the head of our firm for me to accompany the expedition. This gratified me exceedingly.

I ventured to lay the proposition of the Liong-kiao Chinese before General Le Gendre. He appreciated their motives, and affirmed that he should be only too glad if such an arrangement could be carried out. He proposed that I should accompany him to the Chinese generals, to consult with them.

These gentlemen, unfortunately, were not so pacific. They at once expressed great indignation. They said that 'they had received the emperor's commands to exterminate the barbarians, and they were going to do it.'

Possibly prudence came with reflection. Just after dark the commander-in-chief sent his secretary to request my attendance. I went over to his tent, and found the other general (who was an old acquaintance of mine) and the sub-prefect all in consultation.

They desired me to repeat the proposal that I had made to General Le Gendre. We had a long council, lasting through the night; and ultimately the commander-in-chief agreed that if I could fulfil that which I had promised on the Chinese settlers' behalf, he on his part would keep his men out of Liong-kiao, and would engage to help in every possible way.

'My braves,' he said, 'are all gathered from the north of China, and they cannot long endure this climate. They are already beginning to die of fever. I know too well that the local troops have no fight in them. Moreover, I do not desire to hurt the poor Chinese who are living in savage territory.'

The roundabout methods of Chinese diplomacy had, however, to be respected. The following morning we visited General Le Gendre in a body. I had, of course, informed him of all that had passed; and he again made proposals that they should accept my terms. This the mandarins opposed for some time, in order to 'save their

THE TRIUMPH OF DIPLOMACY 197

face,' but after a discreet resistance they ultimately allowed themselves to be convinced.

The army was accordingly marched down south, and encamped just without the borders of Liong-kiao. Inevitably the soldiers began to plunder the villages near, but the commander-in-chief promptly had two men arrested and led out for execution. General Le Gendre interceded on their behalf, and they were let off with one or two hundred blows with the bamboo.

Leaving the army thus bivouacked on the borders, the sub-prefect and I went down amongst the Liong-kiao people. We were introduced to their great chief, Tok-e-tok, to whom I was made a sworn brother in the usual mode, by mixing blood.

The result of our pacific diplomacy was that a treaty was negotiated which was satisfactory in character to all parties.

When all was in train for ratification, General Le Gendre joined the sub-prefect and myself, whereupon, accompanied by the Liong-kiao Chinese headmen, we all proceeded in state to Tok-e-tok's village, where the Chinese produced buffaloes and pigs to celebrate the occasion by a great feast.

The treaty was signed by the Chinese sub-prefect, the American consul, myself, and the Liong-kiao headmen, whilst the savage chief made a daub with his hand, as his mark.

I may here say that this treaty was faithfully respected during the three years in which I remained in Formosa. It saved the lives of many unfortunate shipwrecked crews, who were thenceforth spared and forwarded to Takao.

We had considerable difficulty to induce the savages to complete their share of the making of the treaty. The Chinese settlers, in their joy at thus escaping from the ravages of their own troops, had brought quantities of rice whisky, in which the savages indulged to their hearts' content.

The result was that we were compelled to wait a day or two before they were in a fit condition to comprehend the terms of the contract.

It was just before this critical period of our negotiations that an amusing incident occurred, which might, but for my prompt measures, have had a grave result, indeed which might have rendered all our efforts nul and void.

On arriving at Liong-kiao, we Europeans were quartered upon some very good friends of mine, three fine-looking young Chinamen, brothers, who had previously shown me the sincerest hospitality, and with whom I had become very intimate.

General Le Gendre had fixed his tent in the courtyard of their house at Sialiao, and his Chinese cook from Amoy had joined the settlers in their gossip round a big blazing wood fire, away at the further end of the yard. I had been absent, busy on many things; and upon my reappearance in the courtyard, my hosts, the young Hok-lo brothers, drew me aside, with gravely perturbed faces.

'Pi-ki-ling,' one said, 'we always thought you a great man amongst the barbarians; we understood that your words had weight and power. But that Chinaman over there, the great general's man, he says you are no account at all!'

'Yes, indeed,' broke in another, 'he says that over in Amoy, such as you barbarians are just kicked about the streets.'

'Now, Pi-ki-ling,' concluded the third brother, 'what are we to think? We have treated you well, not only because we liked you, but also because we thought you a great man, and one who spoke the truth. But how are we to know? This man says you are nothing at all. He bids us look at your clothes; he says such as you would be kicked at Amoy!'

THE TRIUMPH OF DIPLOMACY 199

Well, there was some excuse for these simple fellows to doubt. My attire could not be taken as a just criterion of my merit, I was aware. It was useful, but scarcely elegant! And they had only my word to go upon, whilst their countryman was very plausible.

Yet, if my reputation were taken from me, there was an end of all hope for our negotiations. It was the moment for prompt action.

'Come and see,' I said indignantly to the brothers.

Striding into the chattering circle round the fire, I fixed a wrathful eye upon the cook.

'Who says he wants to kick a red-haired barbarian about?' I inquired of him.

The coward shivered in his seat. He shrank back in terror.

'My no savee; I no hear any man talkee so fashion, master; my no talkee nothing. How can any man talkee allo same so fashion?'

'None of your pigeon English for me,' I roared. 'Speak your own language, that all these around may judge between us. Who says that the red-haired barbarians are of no account in China? Who says they are kicked about the streets?'

'Ah, not I, not I!' he whined terrified.

The bystanders all corroborated the brothers' story, so I waved my arms right and left.

'Make room,' I commanded. 'Come along, brothers, and see; I will show you how the red-haired barbarians are kicked in Amoy.'

Whereupon I took this craven cook by the pigtail, and kicked him energetically round the circle, and round again, giving him a little lesson to respect barbarians in future days.

Then when I had finished with him, I went off in a great state of heat to General Le Gendre, and told him the whole affair, and when we had laughed until we could laugh no more, I grew cool, and felt much better for this salutary exercise.

But this slight *contretemps* increased our desire to bring the affair of the treaty to a speedy conclusion.

As I have previously mentioned, the difficulty lay with the savages, who, though ostensibly with us for the purpose of ratifying the treaty, had drunk 'not wisely but too well' of their hosts' potent rice whisky, and were therefore not in a fit condition to negotiate.

I at last hit upon a plan—not, I believe, wholly original on my part—by which we could perhaps arouse them to intelligence through their fears.

General Le Gendre had fought all through the American war, and was covered with honourable wounds; above all, he wore a glass eye. I held a secret consultation with him, and we arranged a little plot.

Then, seizing my opportunity, when the savages were recovering from a debauch, I summoned all parties before the general, who assumed an expression of fierce impatience.

I then proceeded, through the medium of a Liong-kiao Chinese interpreter, to harangue the savages.

'Come, my brothers,' I said impressively, 'we must trifle no longer. This great man grows angry. We must get to work. Beware of his displeasure : he is no common man ; he can do things you have never seen done before ! '

I looked intelligently at General Le Gendre, whereupon he spoke American phrases in a mighty voice, stamped his foot, and, taking out his eye, he cast it on the table before them.

The savages were absolutely dumbfoundered. They gave us very little more trouble, and the treaty was signed forthwith.

The Chinese generals were overjoyed, and thanked me enthusiastically. They bestowed a new name upon me, to be inscribed upon my visiting cards ! Hitherto I had spelt my name phonetically, with three Chinese characters, Pi-ko-lien, which had no special significance. The great yellow jacket now, however, decreed that in future my appellation must be the character of the *ki-lin*, or unicorn, that sacred, mysterious beast which only appeared at the birth of some great sage. In the Hok-lo dialect I was to be 'Pit-ki-lien,' in Pekinese 'Pi-chi-lien'; for surely, they said flatteringly, 'you must be indeed a *ki-lin*, to have been able to bring us such good luck!'

They also reported my deeds to Pekin as 'worthy of being written in letters of gold, and carved upon stone.'

The army returned to Taiwanfoo, and there I received the thanks of the American, the Spanish, and my own government.

It may be imagined how elated I was with my success. None needed to begrudge me one morsel of my satisfaction; for this was the last occasion upon which I was ever praised and had my doings appreciated by a mandarin, or, indeed, had any peace or comfort in Formosa.

I indirectly reaped some benefit, in the troublous times which now awaited me, from the fact that I numbered the commander of troops and the sub-prefect as my friends, which gave me several chances of escape during the perils that were before me.

CHAPTER XVII

THE BEGINNING OF THE CAMPHOR WAR

UPON my return to Takao, after the adventures at South Cape recorded in my last chapter, I found that orders had come from our firm in Amoy, instructing us to engage in the camphor trade.

There had gradually arisen a great demand for this article in America, and prices had gone up to a great height in consequence.

Hitherto there had been but little demand for camphor; in Formosa the Tao-tai's monopoly had therefore not been interfered with, and that dignitary had made great profits from farming the camphor sales out to wealthy natives.

In former years a good deal of the drug was clandestinely produced and smuggled across to the mainland, where it was bought up by European speculators and transmitted to Calcutta, where the Hindustani made considerable use of it.

The gigantic laurel (*Laurus camphora*) which yields the camphor is to be found covering the whole line of high mountains extending north and south through the heart of Formosa.

The method of obtaining the drug was primitive in the extreme.

The trees, as they were required, were selected for the abundance of their sap, for many were too dry to repay the labour of the undertaking. The best part of the felled tree was secured for timber, and the refuse was cut up into

BEGINNING OF THE CAMPHOR WAR

chips. These chips were boiled in iron pots, one inverted on another, and the sublimated vapour was the desired result.

The camphor was then stowed in large vats, with escape holes in the bottom, through which an oil slowly exuded, known as camphor oil, which was a much-valued remedy amongst Chinese doctors for rheumatic diseases.

From the vats the camphor was placed in bags containing about a pecul each, or in large tubs holding three peculs (400 lbs.) each, and it was then ready for shipment to Taiwanfoo, where we packed it in air-tight cases for exportation.

When our firm decided to take up the camphor trade, we had offers from a wealthy landowner, the head of an important clan (Ch'oa), to supply us with any quantity of the drug. We accordingly contracted with him to do so, and our agreement was officially endorsed by the consul.

We also made large advances in cash, and established warehouses and Chinese agents at Go-ch'e, a small port lying about sixty miles north of Taiwanfoo. Thus an extensive fresh field for British enterprise seemed opening in the south.

We reckoned, however, without the cupidity of the Tao-tai, who would not let his valuable monopoly go so easily. That worthy, with the other officials, quickly took alarm. They tried clandestine opposition, and at first contented themselves with inciting another powerful clan to attack the clan of our agent. In the course of this feud our camphor that was ready for shipment was plundered to the value of 6,000 dollars.

This could not be endured passively, and I was proceeding to Go-ch'e to investigate the matter, but the wily Tao-tai refused to sign my passport, though he was bound by treaty to do so at the consul's request. The consul, in spite of this opposition, gave me his permission to proceed to Go-ch'e, and informed me that he would send over to Amoy for a gunboat, to bring the mandarins to reason.

The Tao-tai's next move was to cause researches to be made in the musty official records, in order to find ground for some trumped-up case against our Go-ch'e agent.

This was speedily accomplished. It was found that Ch'oa's late father, when but a youth, had been concerned in some forgotten rebellion of long ago.

However mythical this might be, it gave the necessary power to the Tao-tai to harass our agent. That amiable official forthwith ordered two hundred soldiers to march to Go-ch'e, to arrest Ch'oa, on the plea of his father's complicity in the ancient rebellion.

I contrived to reach the place in a few hours, going round by way of the sea, in a large European-built boat, rigged with Chinese sails; whilst it took the troops some days to march overland.

I had a Malay employé of the firm with me, named Assai, who was worth many a Chinaman in a fight, as we had soon occasion to prove.

On arriving at Go-ch'e, we found our warehouse besieged by the clan Tan; but, with the help of our seven-shooter rifle and two boat guns, we and our agents, Clan Ch'oa, succeeded in routing the enemy for the moment.

Go-ch'e was practically populated by these two clans, Tan and Ch'oa, each of which, according to North Formosan fashion, possessed a strong loopholed mud tower, into which the warriors could retreat during a clan fight.

Things quieted down for a few days, but, when I had been up there about a week, the Tao-tai's troops, composed of militia under the district magistrate of Lok-kang, came in sight.

The Clan Tan's evaporating courage returned to them, whilst our clan, on the contrary, promptly removed their

CAMPHOR DEPÔT GO CH'E
From a Drawing by the Author

BEGINNING OF THE CAMPHOR WAR 205

women and children and furniture in carts, and ran away, leaving me, with our old agent, the Malay, my servant, and a leper, to defend the fort.

We thereupon proceeded to load the boat guns with chain, nails, and shot, and, the tower being situated in an open plain extending for three miles in the direction the troops were coming from, we were able with these and our rifles, to make a great deal of noise, without doing any material harm. We, however, thoroughly and completely cowed the approaching troops by the fierce 'whiz' of the chain, and the 'ping' of the rifles at a range incomprehensible to the Chinese mind.

The terrified chair-bearers dropped the mandarins and took to their heels, whilst the troops wavered in their march, and their commander sent messengers to propose a parley, the result of which was that he engaged to do us no harm, if we on our part would let him alone. He then valiantly turned his attention to wrecking all the Clan Ch'oa's deserted property.

As the soldiers marched into the village, we completed our preparations for a defence of our fortress.

We barricaded the principal entrance with the large tubs of camphor, whilst behind a small side door we placed one of our boat guns, loaded to the muzzle with nails and small bits of chain and iron, and we lighted joss-sticks ready to fire it in the event of the enemy trying to get in.

Very soon a crowd of the rabble militia collected round our enclosure. They began testing the doors, shouting and demanding to see the 'barbarians.'

I harangued them reasonably from above. I told them that if they pushed the door down they would inevitably be blown to pieces, and I advised them to go to their official, who had taken up his residence in a large house in the debatable ground between the Tan and Ch'oa quarters of the town.

Whilst I was thus engaged, an inferior official appeared upon the scene, bearing the mandarin's card, inviting me to visit him, to talk matters over. Our agent and my Malay entreated me in terror not to leave the fort, as they were convinced that I should be captured, and that so they would all be ruined.

I thereupon scribbled off a reply in Pekinese colloquial, to the effect that I dare not quit my present place of security whilst he was so powerful in troops and in the assistance of the Clan Tan fighting men. I reminded him that I was but acting in accordance with the treaty; that the Tao-tai was illegally oppressing Europeans and breaking the treaty, wherefor he would certainly suffer in the end.

After a short interval the messenger returned with a letter, guaranteeing my safety if I would call upon his honour.

As the mandarin was the lawful authority, and therefore possessed the right to summon me to explain matters, I determined to accept his assurance, in all good faith.

Leaving my Chinese servant in charge of the gun, I took as my attendants the Malay and the leper. I was armed with my revolver and a seven-shooter Spencer rifle, whilst the Malay had a rifle and revolver, and the leper carried a spare double-barrelled fowling piece. As a pacific weapon, I took with me a copy of the Tien-tsin Treaty in Chinese, to back up my arguments.

Directly we were without, the door was barred behind us. The streets were crowded with an excited throng of the Clan Ch'oa people and the militia.

The Ch'oas upon seeing us waxed triumphant, cheering us and abusing the soldiers, shouting, 'Look out now! Pi-ki-ling is here! You will see how he will wipe out your "braves" and the Tans.'

I was fearfully embarrassed by this. The least *contretemps* just then would probably do for us, or cause a fierce

BEGINNING OF THE CAMPHOR WAR

fight. I therefore appeared indignant, and, smacking some of the loudest shouters on the face, I called out:

'You braves need not waste your feelings! You are good soldiers. I have no quarrel with you. Take no notice of these beasts of the Clan Ch'oa. They dare not fight themselves, and they want to make us fight.'

We made our way into the main street, still followed by a hooting, chattering crowd, until we reached the mandarin's house.

Here we found a guard of some twenty men, armed with spears fifteen feet long, with banners attached, whilst behind them was gathered the whole of the Clan Tan.

Then some of the Ch'oas shouted:

'Hut, Pi-ki-ling! Hut!' (Attack, Pi-ki-ling! Attack!)

The spearmen immediately charged wildly. A matchlock went off from the Tan side, whilst our leper fired his gun, but no one was hurt.

At this critical moment the mandarin himself rushed out, in full uniform, long boots, peacock feather, and other official paraphernalia, whilst he grasped a horsewhip in his hand.

He hurriedly dragged me into the house, the Malay and the leper bringing up the rear.

I pulled out my revolver, and with the treaty fast in my other hand, I followed the mandarin upstairs, where we sat down upon a bed to begin our diplomatic interview.

I informed him that I should hold him responsible for our lives, and that if any treachery was attempted I assured him that his life would be the first to go.

Having thus put matters on a comfortable and straightforward basis, we proceeded to enjoy our pipes and tea together; after which we had a long argument, in which I proved that I was supported on all points by the Chinese text of the treaty, signed by the Emperor of China.

The mandarin, whilst owning all this to be so, said that

he had but to obey the Tao-tai's commands. He entreated me to leave the place, and return to Taiwanfoo.

This I absolutely refused to do. I assured him that I was prepared to resist all attacks, but I agreed to compromise the matter, by promising to buy or ship no camphor until I had communicated with the consul; meantime I advised him to write to the Tao-tai putting all the circumstances frankly before him.

The official was very cordial throughout the interview. He was an old acquaintance; I had visited him at Lok-kang on my first arrival, and had shown him my passport. During the whole of our conversation there was a great hubbub and shouting in the street outside.

After gaining his promise to write to the Tao-tai, and to take his soldiers away next day, on condition that I would cease buying camphor, I brought our interview to a close, and rose to return. I took the precaution to pull the mandarin with me to the door, and made him clear a passage for us.

We had not proceeded far from the house, however, when the soldiers and Tan men gave a mighty howl, and went for us, whereupon our patience gave out. We faced round, and firing down the street, at first above the level of their heads, we made a dash at them, which sent them flying hither and thither for shelter from the terrific barbarians. We drove them all into the houses, whilst some of the soldiers actually held children up before them, using them as shields, behind which they fired after us; but fortunately they were too terrified to aim correctly.

We cleared the whole of the Tan quarter, and returned to our tower by a new and devious way.

The following morning the wives of some of our wounded adversaries came to us, and had the impudence to ask us to give them some medicine to cure the slight wounds their husbands had received in the *mêlée*.

I supplied them with some pills, assuring them that

they were very lucky to have any husbands left alive at all.

We kept guard all that night until the next day, when the mandarin and his troops left the town with a great noise of tom-toms and waving of banners.

I then drew up a report of the whole affair, which I sent to my employers and to the consul, and waited for further instructions.

Meantime, the retirement of the Lok-kang mandarin impressed the Clan Tan with some slight respect for my power. They ceased open hostilities, contenting themselves with pot-shots from the roofs of their houses when we chanced to exhibit our heads above the parapet of our tower, and by annoying our leper whenever he visited the market to buy provisions. This leper, by the way, was the man who once cut off his own tail to save his life.

They, however, gradually wearied of this one-sided enmity, until at last we ceased hostilities to the extent of joining in a model yacht or junk race upon a big pond outside our fort—competitors on both sides being armed in case of misunderstandings arising.

Thus the days passed, while I waited for instructions until I was quite down-hearted. We were living on a diet of rice and water, with roasted peas for coffee. I could not return to Taiwanfoo, as at sea the weather was fearful, whilst I dared not attempt the journey by land on account of the risk of falling into the hands of the troops.

At length, after I had been in Go-ch'e a week or two, a courier secretly conveyed to me a letter from the consul, begging me to escape any way I could, as, he wrote, the weather prevented any communication with the mainland of China, and he had received secret information, on good authority, that the Tao-tai had determined either to have me poisoned, or to accuse me of murder; in which case, after securing me by treachery, he would feign to send me down, according to treaty, to the consul, for investigation, a prisoner in a sedan chair. He would then, probably, order the chair-bearers to stumble, and thus to let the chair fall into one of the rivers, swollen by the late rains. Thus, of course, by a most regrettable accident, I should be got rid of without further trouble or inquiry. General Burgevine, the reader may remember, had been quietly disposed of in this manner two years previously.

I communicated all this information to my trusty Malay, Assai, who had so bravely supported me through all my troubles in Go-ch'e.

His cheery countenance fell as my narrative proceeded; he seemed to become a changed man.

Going in silence to his box, he produced a kind of amulet which he ceremoniously strapped round his arm.

'Master,' he then said, 'it is of no use doing any more. Let us "amok," and kill as many of the Chinese beasts as possible before we die.'

I had read of 'amok,' but I was not at all inclined to finish my career in that manner. I therefore made answer.

'Assai, I don't believe in "amoking." I just want to get back to Taiwanfoo, and not to kill any Chinamen, nor to be killed, if we can help it. Cheer up! You believe in Allah; so do I. You believe in Ibrahim, Isaac, and Yakub; so do I. What's the use of caring about those Chinese? Let us get on board the boat, and trust to Allah to take us somewhere. There is no good in dying before we are obliged.'

I communicated the news I had received to our agent. He was by no means loth to get rid of us, as he said that he and his clan would then contrive to make peace with the mandarins.

I forthwith sent a man to order our boatmen to prepare to receive us on board, as the weather was somewhat improving. To our dismay, the messenger returned with the news that the boat had been taken out of harbour

BEGINNING OF THE CAMPHOR WAR

that afternoon, a man having given the crew orders, as from myself, to convey her up a small creek for the purpose of loading camphor.

I felt desperate at this news, for I could trust none of the Chinese about me, since there were evidently such traitors around.

Our agent continued to urge me to depart, proposing that he should take charge of all our store of opium, and render an account for it when affairs were settled. I could not agree to this, but I smoothed matters over by arranging that he should retain half, whilst he should put the remainder in baskets, and obtain coolies to take it and our traps to the boat immediately.

The Malay somewhat sulkily acquiesced in my plan, and we at once set off in the dark, arriving about midnight at our boat, which we found high and dry in a narrow creek.

I railed at the boatmen, but I found that they had merely obeyed what they believed to be my orders, but which really was a ruse of the officials to prevent our escape.

We waited impatiently for the tide to rise, but at high water we found that she was still aground. By the promise of a ball of opium, I bribed the fishermen of the place to try to get her off. We took every bit of ballast out of her, and at length managed to get her afloat. When we desired to replace the ballast, however, the rascals refused to allow us to do so; and they also appropriated the remainder of the opium.

The tide was ebbing, there was no time to fight nor to argue. We poled down the creek into the harbour, where we speedily discovered that the boat could not stand up at all against the strong breeze which was blowing, and which was increasing every minute, with squalls and rain.

Assai worked like a man, and between us we contrived to get a heavy caboose, or cooking-place, down into the

P 2

hold, which steadied the boat somewhat. We then put her before the wind, and scudded swiftly to the northward under bare poles, before the gale and the heavy sea.

We could not distinguish the land for the enshrouding mist; and we could only steer, with three men at the tiller, guided by the sound of the surf.

Assai despairingly decided that fate was against us, and went below to await the final catastrophe in sleep. The Chinese crew were all good sailors, with no opium smokers amongst them; but our case seemed hopeless, as unless the land showed out we must scud past the island. The heavy seas followed us, each moment threatening to swamp us.

I knew the men and their families personally, and I endeavoured to keep their hearts up as much as possible by supplying them with pipes, filling and lighting them for them whilst they wrestled with the tiller.

We scudded wildly along through the seething water like some possessed thing—the steersmen praying and crying, working for their lives—until the afternoon, when the peaks of the highest mountain ranges began to peer through the mist, giving us some idea of our position.

About five o'clock the wind fell, and the sea abated; the sky cleared, and to my joy we saw two high hills, which my boatmen told me formed the entrance to the port of Tamsui.

The Malay recovered his spirits as soon as the weather cleared. He reappeared on deck, and seemed to take a renewed interest in life, whilst I took care not to offend him by any untoward remarks regarding 'fate' or such things, for he certainly had behaved splendidly until he had good reason to believe that there could be no further hope for us.

As for the Chinese crew, they had surprised and delighted me with their skill, their endurance and patience. The Chinaman is an unfathomable creature!

BEGINNING OF THE CAMPHOR WAR 213

a mixture of every best and every worst quality in human nature.

Our little craft sailed calmly into harbour before sundown ; and in Tamsui port I received a hearty welcome from Mr. John Dodd and his partners, Messrs. Crawford Kerr, and Bird.

We learnt that the British consul had sent down a gunboat to Go-ch'e to inquire after us, but owing to stress of weather she had been unable to communicate with the shore.

I stayed with Messrs. John Dodd & Co. until a favourable opportunity occurred of crossing to Amoy.

Upon my arrival on the mainland, I found that a new consul had been appointed, who with Lord Charles Scott in H.M.S. 'Icarus' was just about to cross to Formosa to endeavour to bring the authorities to terms. I therefore returned to Takao in our schooner, the 'Eliza Mary.'

Lord Charles Scott, the consul Gibson, and an escort marched into the city of Taiwanfoo for the purpose of interviewing the Tao-tai.

I was included in the party, and I remember an amusing incident which occurred on that occasion.

Lord Charles Scott's escort consisted of some twenty blue-jackets and marines, under the command of the boatswain or gunner.

When we had passed through the big city gate, and we were threading our way through the narrow, slippery streets, it occurred to me that it would be dangerously easy for the mandarins, if they so chose, to cut off the whole party.

Upon arrival at the yamen, we marched into the courtyard, and, after being made to wait sufficiently long to prove that the Tao-tai was not at all disposed to be respectful, our party was at length admitted into his excellency's audience hall.

Here again we endured an ominous delay. At last

a body of Cantonese guards appeared, armed with wonderful mediæval halberds, tridents, and spears, and clad in gaudy uniform. These silently entered, and formed two sides of a square around us, the other sides being the great gates and the Tao-tai's judgment seat. The great doors slammed to with an ominous 'clang,' and we were shut in.

Our trusty boatswain started forward, with his hand on his cutlass, exclaiming:

'Get ready, my lads! There's bloody treachery here, my lord!'

We could not refrain from smiling, although the situation certainly did appear critical.

Just then, however, there was no time for thought. The great man entered with his retinue, and took his seat most majestically.

The consul argued our case with him. It was of no avail, however. The Tao-tai insulted the consul and naval officer in every way possible. He refused to listen to reason, evinced an utter contempt for any treaty, and insisted that no European should buy camphor except through him and upon his terms. I think the warrant officer and escort were disappointed that affairs passed off so tamely.

As the weather would not permit the 'Icarus' to remain lying off the coast, and as she was too large to get into Takao, nothing further could be done until the north-east monsoon. Lord Charles Scott therefore returned to China for further instructions, after handing the Tao-tai a protest and ultimatum.

This temporary evacuation of the position was regarded by the mandarins as a great victory, of which they took every advantage, seeming to lose their senses. They incited the people all over the island to rise against the foreigners. The mission houses, both Roman Catholic and Protestant, were plundered and burned, and converts were persecuted and murdered. European firms in Takao and

BEGINNING OF THE CAMPHOR WAR 215

Tamsui were wrecked by the irresponsible mob. One European merchant was stabbed, and an ambush was set to waylay and kill the consul himself. Messrs. Elles & Co.'s worthy compradore at Taiwanfoo was arrested. His beautiful house was plundered; the women's sacred apartments were sacked, and costly furs, silken robes, and jewellery were ruthlessly appropriated by the Tao-tai's soldiery.

Our compradore was a man of good family and of official rank. His arrest was on the customary frivolous plea of some political offence, and upon an accusation brought by his uncle, concerning some law-suit regarding the division of the family estate.

This uncle was a notorious character, who had himself been concerned in a rebellion some years previously, upon which occasion he had only escaped decapitation by feigning death. It was rumoured that some wise Chinese doctor had administered to him some strange potent drug which caused all the appearance of death; and so he was carried out in his coffin for burial, lying quietly in his tomb until the rebellion was suppressed. This was done in the usual way, by buying over the leaders, and punishing the unfortunate followers. When this was accomplished, the man was resuscitated, and lived to practise more mischief.

He had now discovered reasons for accusing his nephew, in order to gain favour with the Tao-tai, and in the hope of sharing in our unfortunate compradore's confiscated property.

When, however, the cases of merchant and missionary outrage were tried before the Chinese commissioners and the new Tao-tai, our compradore was completely vindicated, and his accuser received two hundred strokes with the big bamboo.

But I am anticipating: the end of the troubles was not yet. In fact, a reign of terror and disorder existed in the island until the end of December, when news arrived that in consequence of the grave reports made by Lord Charles Scott of the condition of affairs on the island, the China fleet under Admiral Keppel had been ordered to proceed to Formosa from the Yangtse, where it had been engaged in quelling outrages. The Pekin government was evidently roused to action by this order, as two Wei-yuans, or high commissioners, promptly came over from Foochow, armed with full authority to inquire into all complaints, and, if necessary, to remove the Tao-tai.

Then a little stern justice ensued. After several sittings the commissioners promised full compensation for all outrages and damage caused by the Tao-tai or the people; that all offenders should be brought to judgment; that Messrs. Elles & Co.'s compradore should have a fair trial, and also that proclamations should be circulated, containing a full apology for the Tao-tai's past conduct, notifying the legality of the camphor trade, and assuring freedom and protection to the missionaries for preaching Christianity. Subsequently, after due inquiry, it was decided that the Tao-tai should be removed, and an official more amenable to reason was appointed in his stead.

The old Tao-tai, however, seemed unaffected by these drastic measures; he ignored the commission and waited, trusting to his influence at Pekin.

Even whilst the commissioners were arriving at these decisions at Takao, and whilst I was attending in court with the other Europeans, the news was brought that the Anping forts were manned by the Tao-tai's soldiers, and that the garrison had fired upon the boats of H.M.S. 'Algerine.'

Her commander, Lieutenant Gurdon, forced to action by this daring insult, landed with a few blue-jackets in the night and attacked the fort, which speedily surrendered, the Chinese commander, or Hiap-tai, evading his share of the consequences by committing suicide.

BEGINNING OF THE CAMPHOR WAR 217

Then did Lieutenant Gurdon and Consul Gibson proceed to demand righteous damages, and an indemnity, which was forthwith paid, with a heightened respect for the barbarians who would brook insult no longer.

When the fleet arrived, Admiral Keppel found that events had marched so rapidly that, beyond the moral effect of the presence of a few vessels in Formosan waters, there was but little remaining to be done; so leaving the 'Rinaldo,' 'Pearl,' and a gunboat, the admiral took the rest to Hong Kong, his flagship not appearing in Formosa.

Unfortunately about this time a change of government took place in England, and what was then called the 'free breakfast-table' ministry came into power.

Orders were sent to our minister at Pekin that in future all grievances were to be redressed by diplomacy, and that our vessels of war were no longer to be used as persuasive methods. Consul Gibson, who a few years previously had been decorated by the Emperor of China with the famous yellow jacket for his bravery in action against the rebels in Manchuria, was removed, Lieutenant Gurdon quitted the navy, and the indemnity was returned to the Chinese officials. Indeed it appeared at that time that the home government was determined to have no trouble with China, however British subjects might suffer loss.

The American minister, Mr. Burlingham, had undertaken a mission to Europe to show that China was anxious 'to enter the comity of nations,' and 'to plant the shining cross on every hill!'

The British Government accepted this vapouring: they professed implicit belief in the Pekin Government, and would believe no ill of things Celestial.

As a proof of this, I may mention one anomaly. The governor-general of Fuh-kien and the Tao-tai petitioned the emperor against me, for the many outrages I had committed during the camphor troubles; more especially for resisting the armed force sent against me at Go-ch'e.

According to them, I had a dangerous influence over the people, through my knowledge of their language and customs. I aroused them to revolt and rebellion against the mandarins. I was now no longer likened to the classic and mystical unicorn; I was degraded from my high estate, being now said to resemble a restless and interfering little mongrel Manchurian terrier. The favour of the great is but fleeting!

Our minister at Pekin thereupon sent two commissioners, Messrs. Adkins and Swinhoe, to the island, for the purpose of investigating the affair.

The result was that I was cleared from every charge, and that all the trouble was proven to be the inevitable result of the Tao-tai's unscrupulous and illegal action against British interests and British subjects who were carrying on their business according to the Treaty of Tien-tsin, and with the knowledge and sanction of their consul.

Notwithstanding this, before returning to Pekin, the two commissioners summoned together the European residents, merchants, and missionaries of Taiwanfoo and Takao, and regretfully impressed upon us that, although we had been acting legally and as good subjects, yet— there must be no trouble! If disputes arose, even in defence of our just rights, the person who caused the trouble would be deported from the island!

In the face of such a policy as this, can there be any wonder that the Chinese have been emboldened to disregard the rights of British merchants and missionaries in the Celestial Empire?

We gradually resumed our dealings in camphor, but we removed our agencies to a place called T'ai-kah, and ultimately to Aulang, some fifteen miles to the north of that port, in the Tamsui district.

Fortunately camphor represented but one small portion of our business, for the old Tao-tai, who had never left the

BEGINNING OF THE CAMPHOR WAR 219

island, was reinstated, since the moral persuasion of our fleet was withdrawn. He immediately renewed his persecutions, and I had to undergo a new course of troubles.

The Tao-tai this time confined his anger to the camphor trade. Our warehouses and boats were repeatedly plundered, the Chinese agents were arrested and imprisoned, whilst all the redress we could obtain from our consul was that he would refer the matter to the minister at Pekin.

Now, it is curious and instructive to notice that while the Tao-tai was in possession of the decision of our government even before our consul got his mails, yet it took six months for the Chinese Government at Pekin to receive news from the Tao-tai with which to reply to the questions of the British minister!

The true inwardness of this was that the Tao-tai exerted his privilege of communicating directly with the emperor, ignoring the viceroy at Foochow; and thus the Chinese foreign office excused their delays by stating that the governor of Formosa was subordinate to the viceroy, and that they had received no despatches from Foochow. Wherefrom it was apparent that they possessed a flourishing branch of the circumlocution office in the Far East.

CHAPTER XVIII

FURTHER CAMPHOR TROUBLES. A REAL GHOST STORY. THE ULTIMATE TRIUMPH OF THE TAO-TAI

As I have mentioned, after being driven out of Go-ch'e, we had established our fresh branch of the camphor business at T'ai-kah, and things progressed fairly smoothly until the south-west monsoon ensured an immunity from the presence of the British gunboat, when our old enemy renewed his attempts to destroy our intercourse with the camphor districts.

The T'ing, or magistrate, of the sub-district of Lok-kang, who was an old acquaintance of mine in the time of the troubles at Go-ch'e, was despatched to T'ai-kah, under the pretence of examining into the validity of our contracts with our agents and also to inspect my passport.

The mandarin arrived in pomp, accompanied by the usual official retinue, and an escort of some fifty 'braves,' or local militia, fiercely armed with rusty knives, spears, and matchlocks.

After taking up his residence in the small 'yamen' of the place, his honour sent me a card, courteously inviting me to pay him a visit for the sake of our old acquaintance-ship at Go-ch'e.

I accordingly visited him, accompanied by my trusty Malay, Assai, taking the precaution that we should each be fully armed, not only with our usual weapons, but also with our passports. I also bore with me my *vade mecum*, an official copy of the Tien-tsin Treaty in Chinese.

I was most honourably received. The mandarin and I

had a very pleasant conversation on indifferent topics; but no allusion was made to the real motive of our meeting, the camphor business, excepting that the magistrate assured me that he would be happy to assist me, as he was bound to do by the terms of the passport, and we parted very good friends.

Some days after this interview, one of my people brought me a placard, bearing the seal of the district magistrate of Chiang-hoa, which had been posted all over the country, accusing me of many breaches of the treaty, and offering a reward of five hundred taels (160*l*.) for my arrest, in order that I might be handed over to the British consul for punishment.

This district magistrate had been formerly sub-prefect at Taiwanfoo, but when the Tao-tai was removed he also had been degraded, and appointed to the inferior post at Chiang-hoa.

I had known him very well in the old days, and he and I had worked most cordially together during General Le Gendre's expedition to the South Cape, where, it will be remembered, he accompanied us.

I was therefore not a little shocked to find that he could issue such a proclamation, and I determined to proceed at once with the notice to our consul at Takao.

Whilst making my arrangements for leaving T'ai-kah, the Lok-kang mandarin's secretary waited upon me, and begged me to go to the 'yamen' at once, as his master urgently desired to speak to me. He added that I need not trouble to wait to dress, as his master was in so great a hurry. I foolishly hurried off with the messenger, omitting, in my haste, to take any weapons but a knife, which was hidden in my stocking.

The magistrate received me most pleasantly. He said that he merely wished to see my passport again. I had left it behind, and offered to go back for it, but he smiled and said, 'Oh, never mind, never mind, *we can do without it!*' He then began to discourse upon the camphor trade. He entreated me, as a friend, to quit the business, as it would only cause me much trouble, the Tao-tai being, he assured me, determined to retain the monopoly in his own hands.

In reply, I quoted the treaty, and said that I was but a servant, and must do my duty. I also brought the placard to his notice, but he asserted that he had nothing to do with that; the Chiang-hoa magistrate was alone responsible. He continued his argument by saying that the treaty was very good for China, but that Formosa was different. It was a peculiar place; the people were wild and turbulent, and that if I obstinately persisted in my course I might lose my life. Whereupon I represented to him that if I were killed it would but make it unpleasant for the authorities, as the gunboats would come, they would be punished, and ten better Englishmen would proceed to take my place.

The mandarin called for tea and pipes, but even with the aid of their soothing influence we could arrive at no satisfactory conclusion.

I therefore asked permission to take my leave of his honour, as I desired to proceed to Takao, to consult with my consul.

The mandarin, however, paid no heed, but continued talking, until I assured him that I must really return home. Upon my rising with this intention, he began talking very loudly, and pushed me back into my seat. At the same instant I observed a number of 'braves' entering the 'yamen' enclosure.

My suspicions were aroused. I administered a push to the mandarin, which knocked him backward, and with my knife unsheathed in my left hand, and my right hand in my bosom as though grasping a revolver, I dashed out amongst the braves, shouting, 'Look out! Pi-ki-lien is coming! If any of you come near me,

I'll kill you with my seven-mouthed pistol! Pi-ki-lien's coming!'

The cowards scattered right and left, and I managed to get safely back to our warehouse.

After this warning I would linger no longer. I immediately started off on foot for Takao, with my Malay and a coolie guide.

We arrived about dark at the walled town of Chianghoa, where we put up for the night at a coolie's lodging-house in the suburbs. Here, as we had been advised to do by our Chinese agents in T'ai-kah, we ate our rice and fish out of the same bowl as the coolies, for fear of poison.

I engaged sedan chairs for the Malay and myself, and we drew down the blinds to screen us from the public gaze.

We started at daybreak, taking a circuitous route outside the walls.

We had not proceeded far, however, when, as fate would have it, we heard the sound of a gong, and our chair coolies shouted, 'Lo-tia-lai!' ('His honour is coming!'), and, sure enough, we saw approaching us on the narrow path the district magistrate in his official chair, followed by a small retinue.

There was nothing for it but to put a bold face upon the matter. The path was so narrow that our chairs had to be put down in the fields at the side to permit the official to pass. I knew my coolies would court discovery by saying that they had barbarians within. I therefore sprang out of my chair, and, assuming as unconcerned an air as possible, I said, 'You are very early this morning; good morning, your honour. You see, I have come to give you a chance to take me.'

The mandarin looked extremely surprised, but he quickly regained his composure, and replied smilingly, 'Pi-chi-lien! I am glad to meet you again. Where are you going?'

I replied that I was on my way to the consul, regarding the proclamation which he himself had issued. I upbraided him, saying :

'How could your honour offer a reward for the capture of the man who was your great friend when you were in trouble, and the man who saved you from disgrace in Liong-kiao ?'

'I only obey my orders,' he replied. 'I don't want to hurt you, Pi-chi-lien, but you must take care of yourself. The Tao-tai will certainly punish you, treaty or no treaty. Taiwan is not China, you know.'

I assured him I should continue to do my duty, and to obey the orders given me by my superiors. I also bantered him discreetly, proposing that, as he had six or seven soldiers with him, he should effect the capture of the Malay and myself, and thus personally secure the reward he had offered.

The old gentleman laughed good-humouredly, and proposed, in his turn, that we should each pursue our journey ; so, shaking our own hands to each other, in the approved Chinese fashion, we parted amicably.

I was not, however, disposed to trust too much to official friendliness. I thus considered it best to push forward boldly on foot before emissaries could be despatched to Taiwanfoo.

I accordingly dismissed the sedan chairs, and by walking hard all day, at dusk the next day we reached Hm-kang-boe, a village some ten or fifteen miles from Taiwanfoo, having given a wide berth to all the towns and large villages on our route.

I decided to leave Assai behind me there, to follow the next morning to Taiwanfoo, where his wife lived, whilst I would push on in order to pass the capital under cover of the night, and so make my way to Anping, whence I could take boat to Takao.

I started alone directly the moon rose. The road was a familiar one to me. Shortly after leaving Hm-kang-boe,

UNIV. OF
CALIFORNIA

THE SCENE OF THE GHOST
From a Drawing by the Author

for several miles of the journey, my way was along the top of a high dyke, the path broken by sluice-gates and hummocks which had formerly been rocks or small islets of the sea, but which, the sea having receded, the Chinese were draining and reclaiming for cultivation. For the whole length of the dyke there were no houses, whilst the hummocks had been utilised by the Chinese as graveyards.

The night was most beautiful ; the brilliant moonlight made every object appear almost as distinct as by day. It was very still too, and, but for the hoarse croaking of innumerable frogs in the surrounding marshes, it seemed as though I had the world to myself.

I walked briskly along for some time, keeping up my spirits by whistling, and marching quick-steps to the tunes.

At length I felt that I had earned a rest and a smoke. I thereupon squatted down on my hams, Chinese fashion, beside one of the tombs, and searched in my badger-skin sporran or purse for my iron pipe.

This I proceeded to fill with cut cavendish from a compartment of the sporran. I lit my pipe with my flint and steel, and began to smoke contentedly whilst I reviewed my position.

My prospect of getting past Taiwanfoo city undiscovered and in safety was somewhat hazardous. I was overwrought by the strain and excitement of the day. Trouble lay behind me, and vexation and danger lay ahead. How far I had wandered from Old England, from home and security! I looked around me, with a half smile, at the old Chinese burying-ground, the tombs showing white and distinct in the glorious moonlight. Ah, what a change danger and adventure had worked in me! In those long-ago days of my boyhood no possible bribe would have served to induce me to sit in our village churchyard at midnight, that ' witching hour '

> ' When churchyards yawn
> And graves give up their dead.'

I should have dreaded the sight of some ill-resting 'boggart,' and the less I saw the more I should have feared.

Then my mind wandered to all the stories I had ever heard of ghostly visitants, of sights and sounds that made men's blood run cold. Could such things indeed be? I, in all my wild life, had never had any experience of the supernatural, but I had heard strange tales of ghostly appearances from people who, I had every reason to believe, were serious and truthful.

I, however, came to the philosophical conclusion that if the ghosts of the Chinese were no more courageous and dangerous than their living descendants, I had not much to fear, even should the whole company around me appear upon the scene.

One should beware how one speaks disrespectfully of ghosts, even in self-communion. I had but just arrived at this valiant decision regarding them, when a sudden wild flame burst before me; I saw stars innumerable; my pipe was whirled from my mouth; and I fell sprawling on my back, utterly helpless from fear, my limbs trembling and my heart beating violently. When at length I regained my scattered wits I exclaimed inwardly:

'If I can but get out of this, never, never again will I speak slightingly of ghosts!'

I was powerless to stand up, so scared was I; so, sitting on a grave, I waited until I grew calmer, when my reason reasserted itself, and I, base sceptic, began to doubt whether any ghost had been concerned in the matter.

Nature lay so still and calm around me; no being was in sight, either human or supernatural.

Suddenly a thought struck me; I grasped my sporran, and examined it carefully.

It contained several divisions or pockets. In the lower one was loose tobacco, with my flint and steel, and in one of the upper divisions was a quantity of small metallic

A REAL GHOST STORY

cartridges for use in my Smith & Wesson's revolver. I eagerly searched amongst my tobacco, and to my relief I found amongst it one or two of the tiny cartridges which had fallen through an unwary hole in the upper pocket.

The whole affair was thus made clear. I had unwittingly stuffed, with the tobacco, a cartridge into my pipe, and, having smoked on until it became red-hot, it had exploded, producing the mysterious shock which had given me such a severe fright.

I searched around in vain for my pipe, and proceeded on my journey at last with very weak knees; in fact, I did not completely recover from my shock until I reached Anping, and was able to lie down in the boat, which the next day landed me safely at Takao.

Before removing our camphor business from T'ai-kah to Aulang, one of the partners of Elles & Co., Mr. Randall Pye, determined to visit the camphor districts. Accompanied by myself, he left Takao in our large boat, with a quantity of treasure for the purchase of camphor. We also enlisted the services of two Manilamen as guards, in case we might chance to encounter any of the coast pirates.

Soon after passing to the north of Taiwanfoo our progress was arrested by a head wind, which forced us uncomfortably near the sand banks, whilst, to add to our discomfort and danger, heavy showers of rain obscured the coast.

We were tossed about helplessly through the whole of one long night, and before daybreak we were beginning to feel very apprehensive as to our position.

Providentially we had a skilful Tai-kong, or steersman, who was acquainted with all the intricacies of the dangerous shoals.

After dodging about until the dawn, he ran us in-shore at high water, and brought us up in a kind of lagoon formed by the sand banks, where we were able to lie in safety.

In spite of this relief from the dangers of the sea, we were in an awkward predicament, for our quiet haven was close to the notorious Po-te-ts'ui, and, as the day advanced and our presence became known, we were surrounded by hundreds of the merciless Chinese wreckers, who, when the receding tide left us high and dry, came alongside our vessel.

They observed that we were well armed; they therefore contented themselves with asking our Chinese crew who we were, and what cargo we had on board.

'We know nothing,' our men discreetly replied. 'We are only "hands and feet"; ask our "heads," the red-haired barbarians. We merely eat their rice.'

We meanwhile held a consultation as to the wisest mode of procedure. Wind and weather rendered it impossible to continue our voyage north to Aulang, yet we were reluctant to return baffled to Takao. At the same time we were convinced that the wreckers would plunder us if they dared.

Eventually we determined to put to the test the Chinese traditionary sense of reason and righteousness.

Personally, I maintain that no people in the world understand these two principles so thoroughly as the Chinese of all classes, from the lowest coolie to the highest mandarin; that is, that the fundamental principles of reason and justice are due to themselves, and to their neighbour, when he has power to enforce their practice.

Heaven, reason, righteousness, and mutual sincerity are continually on the lips of a Celestial, especially when he is about to act contrary to these principles; but he will submit to the strictest rule of government, and will endure any punishment whatsoever if it only be enforced in pursuance of reason and justice.

As the men crowded round, every moment increasing in numbers, I stepped forward to address them in accordance with our policy.

'Well, brothers,' I began, 'what business have you here?'

'Oh, nothing,' they replied. 'What business have *you* here in our place? What are you come for?'

'For a sail. To amuse ourselves.'

'This is a queer place to amuse yourselves,' they laughed. 'There is nothing but salt water and sand here! You barbarians are queer people in amusing yourselves.'

'Well! you can all go away,' I responded. 'There is no need for you all to stay here. Go home to your wives and children. It is cold here. We have no wish to trouble you. We need nothing from you.'

'No, no, we shan't go away,' they said knowingly. 'Oh, is it you, Pi-ki-ling? What have you got on board?'

'Why do you ask? Are you come to plunder?'

'Plunder!' they virtuously replied. 'No! how dare we do such a thing! You know we never plunder, do we?' There was a general laugh. 'We are all most respectable people here!'

'Well, of course I know that,' I responded unconvinced; 'but I tell you, you won't get any plunder here. We are not wrecked. We shall go away next tide.'

'No, you won't! The weather is coming on bad. You won't get away,' they cheerfully assured me.

'Now listen, brothers,' I said. 'I will tell you all about us, and we will talk reason.'

'Yes, yes,' they cried, 'let us talk "cheng-li" (correct principles of right). It is worthy of us that we should talk reason.'

'True, it is. Now if you have come to plunder, we have plenty of dollars on board, which we are taking to Aulang to buy camphor,' I said; 'so there is plenty of plunder. But then there are two red-haired men and two black-faced Manilamen. We have thirty or forty barrels of guns between us, six and seven shooters. We shall not let you plunder us before many tens of you are killed. That would be a great trouble and waste of life for you, whilst at home your wives and your children would grieve not to see their men again. Shall we talk reason, now, and save all this?'

They hastily consulted together, and then they said, 'Let us hear what you have to say; we will be reasonable.'

'Well now,' I continued, 'supposing all you brethren will carry the treasure to the nearest village where we can hire sedan chairs and coolies, we will go overland, as it would be a waste of time to turn back to Takao. We will pay you what is proper, and give you drink money besides.'

'How much will you give?' they inquired.

'Here is our compradore, who knows the proper charges,' I said; 'he shall settle, and whatever he fixes we will make it double.'

'No, no, you fix the amount yourself,' they cried. 'We Chinese folk are clever at "eating men" (imposing upon each other). You barbarians are straightforward; one sentence is one sentence with you!'

'Oh, no,' I protested, 'we are foolish, and not up to you "men." We must not go on foolish principles, but upon Chinese rules of justice.'

Ultimately it was agreed that our compradore should fix the price, and that we should give a good amount of earnest money.

The chiefs of these ruffians soon brought themselves prominently to notice by taking charge of the negotiations and receiving the advances.

The dollars were forthwith apportioned into burdens, and slung upon the men's shoulders.

When this was done I said to the headman, 'Now we are trusting you. Heaven is above and sees us all.'

'Yes, oh, yes,' all cried. 'Heaven is above our head; we dare not deceive you; trust us!'

'We trust you,' I replied; 'but the Manilamen have

UNIV. OF
CALIFORNIA

TAMSUI (TREATY PORT, NORTH FORMOSA)—BRITISH CONSULATE

ULTIMATE TRIUMPH OF THE TAO-TAI 231

orders to shoot the first man who leaves the line of carriers.'

These preliminaries arranged, we all got on shore with our baggage and servants, and trudged along in line through the heavy sand for some miles, until we reached the large market town of Pak-kang, where we put up at the house of a Chinese merchant, a friend of our compradore.

The wreckers were well paid for their novel experience of honest labour; they were made happy by an extra bonus, and went home well satisfied. Meantime our boatman had availed himself of their absence to get the boat away to sea, and had returned to Takao.

Two days later we arrived at Aulang, having travelled chiefly through the night, to avoid the intrusive and curious villagers *en route*.

After completing the necessary business in connection with the future transaction of our camphor trade at Aulang, Mr. Pye determined that, as we were now so conveniently near the port of Tamsui, we should proceed thither to visit our good friends, Messrs. Dodd & Co.

In two days we reached Bang-kah, the chief inland town in the north of the island, at the head of the Tamsui River.

The inhabitants of this town were extremely anti-foreign in their sentiments; we were therefore relieved to arrive there in the early hours of the morning, when the town was wrapped in slumber.

Here we left our chairs and coolies, and took boat to Tamsui, which place we reached at daylight, much to the surprise of our friends. Having spent a very pleasant day at Tamsui, we started to return at sunset, Mr. Dodd accompanying us as far as Bang-kah, and his partner returning with us to Takao.

I had with me my Highland military pipes, and I well remember that we amused ourselves, whilst passing up the river, by serenading a gentleman who was suspected of Nationalist (or, as they were then termed, 'Fenian') sympathies, with the tune of 'Boyne Water.'

I had some time previously adopted a kilt as the best costume for my continual excursions into the mountains, and for wading through rivers, etc., whilst others of our party had followed my example, having improvised these garments at Tamsui.

One of us bore a claymore which had seen service in 'the Forty-five,' and with this formidable weapon, our kilts, and the bagpipes, we flattered ourselves that we had a truly Highland appearance.

We reached Bang-kah about midnight, hoping to get to our sedan chairs as unobserved as we had come; but to our disgust we found that it was the night of some special feast, and that the whole population was abroad in the streets.

Our landing was the signal for a rush by the shouting mob, who cried, 'The barbarians are coming!' We started our attendant coolies off to wait for us with the sedan chairs outside the town at the further end, for we dared not render ourselves helpless by taking our seats in them.

Retaining one of the bearers as a guide, we endeavoured to push our way through the howling, excited crowd. When we reached the market-place we came upon a grand theatrical stage, lighted brilliantly by flaring lamps, where one of the interminable native plays was in progress. The actors were, however, at that moment enjoying a brief rest, for their audience had rushed off upon the fresh excitement of our arrival.

A happy inspiration struck us—to turn the tide of hostility into more congenial sentiments.

We jumped boldly on the stage. I struck up a rollicking Strathspey, and my three companions danced heartily to its measure, the claymore and the kilts having a fine effect in the lamplight.

W. A. P., 1869

ULTIMATE TRIUMPH OF THE TAO-TAI 233

At the unaccustomed sound of the skirl of the pipes the actors fled, but the music and the dancing brought down the house, which was now crowded indeed.

The mob was delighted, and encored us enthusiastically in Chinese, until we grew weary, and began to fear that they appreciated us too well.

We at last seized our opportunity, and, jumping down in the midst of them, we hastened out of the town before they had recovered from their surprise.

Mr. Dodd bade us farewell, and started to return to Tamsui. He had no apprehension, being well known all over the Tamsui district, and being liked, respected, and feared both by the Chinese and the aborigines.

We all arrived safely at Takao, having had a most pleasant journey through nearly the whole length of the island.

In spite of the proclamation which had been issued by the authority of the viceroy of Fuh-kien, to the effect that the camphor trade was open to all Europeans complying with the consular regulations and paying the tariff duties, the Tao-tai renewed his persecutions.

Our firm, in partnership with Messrs. Tait & Co., had, upon the settlement of the troubles, advanced large sums of money for the purchase of camphor; and early in the year 1869 six small junks, containing 500 piculs [1] of the drug, left the port of Aulang for Taiwanfoo.

One evening shortly afterwards, the captains and crews of these junks appeared before me, camphorless, and full of trouble.

Their story went that, soon after leaving Aulang, they had been compelled by stress of weather to put into Po-te-ts'ui, that noted haunt of pirates and wreckers.

Whilst our boats were lying here for shelter from the fury of the storm outside, the Po-te-ts'ui men swam off during the night and cut their cables.

[1] A picul = $133\frac{1}{3}$ lbs.

Thereupon the boats drifted with the tide on to the shore, where the crews were stripped of their clothing, and the camphor was plundered to the value of nine thousand dollars, the pirates asserting that they were merely obeying the orders of the Tao-tai.

I had some knowledge of Po-te-ts'ui, having visited the village years before to recover goods plundered from a wrecked Dutch vessel by the inhabitants. The heads of Messrs. Elles and Tait having obtained the permission of the consul to visit Po-te-ts'ui for the purpose of investigating the matter, we organised an expedition consisting of four Europeans, Messrs. Pye, Masson, Taylor, and myself, accompanied by three Malays or Manilamen carrying guns and a plentiful stock of ammunition; for, to venture with any degree of safety into such a district, it was essential to be well armed.

We arrived at Po-te-ts'ui just before daylight, completely taking the ruffians by surprise.

They had hitherto been accustomed to view Europeans as their helpless victims, shipwrecked and at their mercy : our appearance therefore, belligerent, fully armed, determined if possible to regain our property, completely cowed them.

After some searching amongst nets, sails, and foreshore rubbish, we discovered the greater portion of our camphor; whilst, with a little gentle persuasion, we induced the headman to give us receipts for the whole amount, and a written promise to deliver it all in our boats at Taiwanfoo.

To ensure the due fulfilment of these contracts, we took three or four of the chief men back with us to Taiwanfoo, the result being that we received the greater part of the stolen camphor within forty-eight hours of our leaving the village.

We returned in triumph to the consul, reporting all

ULTIMATE TRIUMPH OF THE TAO-TAI 235

things to him, expecting his congratulations upon our successful raid.

To our astonishment and chagrin we were informed that we had been guilty of a great crime, and that the Tao-tai had sent in a complaint against us, accusing us of a cruel attack upon the port of Po-te-ts'ui, and of forcibly abducting peaceable subjects from their homes.

I immediately hastened to our house, where the 'abducted' chiefs were detained.

I spoke good words to them. In my kindly consideration I feared that they might find the hours long, I therefore gave them a few dollars each, and granted them my permission to go forth to see the sights of Taiwanfoo, the capital, and to enjoy themselves. Of course, I suggested I should hope to see them again in the evening.

They were delighted, thanking me for my kindness, and assuring me that the evening should see them again on my doorstep. I departed, rightly convinced that they would not return to perplex me.

The Tao-tai having formally presented his official complaint of our conduct, our consul took up the matter seriously, and established a court, in which we were all respectively tried, judged, and fined various sums each, from 2,000 dollars for the Europeans to 100 dollars for the Malays.

This was my first visit to a European court of justice of any kind, and the whole scene seemed very imposing to my unaccustomed eyes.

The consul occupied a bench covered with black cloth : there was a specially constructed witness-box, with a dock in which all the prisoners were placed.

Since those days a long experience of our legal procedure compels me to say that this trial was carried out in a peculiar manner.

There was no prosecutor, except that the Tao-tai had sent in his written accusation, with as many Chinese witnesses as he had been able to collect under fear of his dire displeasure.

The consul was to all intents and purposes the real prosecutor as well as judge.

I was the only defendant who understood Chinese, and was thus competent to explain what took place between ourselves and the Chinese Po-te-ts'ui; Messrs. Pye and Masson therefore requested that I, as a subordinate acting under orders, might be released and allowed to give evidence for the defence.

My release was permitted, but the consul immediately announced that he should use me as evidence for the prosecution.

The pirate headmen themselves, though brought forward as witnesses by the Tao-tai, acted very honourably, refusing to give evidence as to having been ill-treated in any way; but the fact of our having been able to bring such well-known pirates down to Taiwanfoo was pressed hard against us.

I gave my statement of the whole affair, and I was severely cross-examined to prove that force and intimidation had been used to bring the Chinese down to Taiwanfoo.

I was able with a clear conscience to exonerate all the rest of our party from the charge, and to take all the blame on my own shoulders, I being the only member who could communicate with the robbers. This did not, however, avail to prevent wholesale conviction of all but the forced 'Queen's evidence.'

We proceeded to appeal to the supreme court at Shanghai, where we gained our case against the consul, whose judgment was reversed.

We had also fortunately recovered our camphor; but the fact of four European gentlemen, who lived on terms of daily intimacy with the consul, having been marched through the public streets of Taiwanfoo by the consulate

BRITISH CONSULATE, TAIWANFOO

ULTIMATE TRIUMPH OF THE TAO-TAI 237

constable, and afterwards tried as criminals for merely recovering their own property from the clutch of pirates and wreckers, made the Chinese wonder with awe at the great power now exercised by their Tao-tai. Moreover that wily official was emboldened by his success to harass us still further.

Shortly after this I returned to Aulang to develop the business there. We purchased a great quantity of camphor, and contracted for large amounts; but the Tao-tai's exactions became more vindictive and arbitrary, until the people dared not fulfil their contracts, and our agents were persecuted until life was not worth living.

At length the situation became so impossible that I was obliged to go down to Takao to consult with the firm as to the advisability of relinquishing our camphor business.

I started off one morning overland, leaving our depot in charge of a valiant Chinaman, who, according to his own estimate of himself, was a very fine soldier.

This man possessed discharges and favourable notices as a sergeant in the U.S. army. He had been kidnapped in a New York drinking saloon, and had been sent into the army, serving there throughout the war. He had risen by merit to the rank of a non-commissioned officer, so he apparently had some reason for his belief in himself. Be that as it may, a few days after I had reached Takao he, with the rest of our staff appeared, with a sorry tale to tell.

It transpired that, a few hours after I had quitted the depot, the local mandarin and a few soldiers appeared at the gate. My valiant sergeant meekly admitted them, after which the official drove him out, with the rest of our men, just as they were, and proceeded to plunder the depot and to burn my clothes and books.

A somewhat amusing incident occurred at this time. An American merchant from Tamsui was visiting Aulang upon camphor business, and he had the curiosity to stroll round to look at the wreck of our house.

The mandarin's soldiers discovered him there. Before he could draw his revolver, they threw him down, secured him, and dragged him before their superior officer.

As the American could not speak Chinese, and had no interpreter, the mandarin actually sent for a Pepo-hoan to translate ; he in his ignorance of foreigners believing that one barbarian language was as good as another !

When it was found, however, that the gentleman had no connection with Elles & Co., he was permitted to go about his business.

This last outrage finished our connection with the camphor business. We were obliged to content ourselves with making our claims for due compensation to the consul, who forwarded them to Pekin.

It was not, however, until the year 1876 that our firm received the money granted by the Tsung-li-yamen as compensation for the losses we had sustained.

CHAPTER XIX

MY FAREWELL TO FORMOSA

I NOW resided at Taiwanfoo, in charge of the general business there, but my health was completely broken up by fever and dysentery; in fact, a chronic form of the latter terrible complaint was rapidly killing me. Providentially my good friend Patrick Manson had a year or two before settled in Formosa, and by his skill and kind care he not only saved my life, but practically cured me.

Since those days I have been in every circumstance calculated to produce a renewal of this fell disease; but, although I shall never recover completely from its effects, I have not had a recurrence of the attack. I rejoice to know that the medical career begun in far Formosa has, through indefatigable study and experimental research, prospered so greatly that to-day Dr. Patrick Manson, LL.D., is at the head of his profession as an authority upon tropical diseases.

By a most curious coincidence, whilst I was so unwell in August 1870, an old friend of mine, Captain Farrow, came into Takao, commanding the Chinese Customs steamer. This gentleman when a boy, in 1859, had been wrecked in the ship 'Chieftain' of Jersey on the Pratas shoals, and he was sent home as a passenger in the 'Lady Macdonald,' on board which vessel I was an apprentice.

I was desirous of visiting our firm at their headquarters, and Captain Farrow kindly invited me to share his cabin to Amoy, an offer of which I gladly availed myself.

On the passage thither we called in for a day or two at Foochow, where I received a most cordial welcome from those of my old messmates who still remained on board the Customs hulk 'Spartan' at Pagoda Anchorage.

When Messrs. Elles & Co. at Amoy saw my state of health, they most liberally gave me a free passage home, with twelve months' leave of absence. The Franco-German war had just broken out, and I determined to return home by one of the Messageries Impériales boats, in order that I might have an opportunity of seeing something of the state of things in France.

I accordingly left Amoy in the steamer 'Yesso,' commanded by that genial old China coaster, Captain Ashton. We reached Hong Kong in the morning of the day upon which the M.I. mail steamer 'La Guienne' was due to sail at noon.

I was in the very highest spirits, which was natural, with plenty of money and the prospect of a whole year at home with my friends, for whom I had brought large packing-cases filled with curios.

I proceeded to the Messageries' office, where I was informed that I must procure a passport from the French consul, as it was war-time. I spent so long at the consulate that when I returned to the office with the necessary credentials, I was informed that the accounts were closed, and that I must procure my ticket on board.

Accordingly I boarded the steamer with a small cargo of luggage, and was handed over to the commissaire, who escorted me below to choose my berth, there being ample choice, as there was but one first-class passenger. After my free, rough and tumble life in Formosa, the gorgeousness of the saloon appeared oppressive: I therefore requested the commissaire to show me the second-class. Here I did not find very much difference, so I roused the man's impertinence by demanding to be shown

MY FAREWELL TO FORMOSA

the third-class quarters. 'Oh, very good!' he said, 'but it is full of Spanish non-commissioned officers, and a sick Englishman being sent home by his consul from Japan.' It was quite a pleasure to me to contemplate spending some time amongst the Spaniards, and having the opportunity to rub up my knowledge of their language; so, upon finding that the third-class saloon was better than any cabin I had been used to in my old sailor days, I ordered my traps to be put there, and took up my quarters.

I had no reason to regret my decision. I saved half my passage money, and found the Spanish officers a very jolly set of fellows; whilst I was able to be of assistance to my sick countryman, and contrived to enlist the *maître d'hôtel's* services on his behalf.

Thus the days flew by until on a Saturday night we reached Saigon, where the pilot came on board. Then ensued a great chattering, with much excited comment. He brought a small bundle in his hand; the Messageries Impériales flag, 'M.I.,' was hauled down, and his bundle was hoisted to the mast-head in its stead. As it gradually unfolded itself to the breeze, we discerned the characters 'M.M.' (Messageries Maritimes). After this significant change was effected all hands united in singing the 'Marseillaise.'

Upon the vessel arriving at Saigon, tables were set all over the deck, officers and men embraced and kissed each other; the whole night was spent in conviviality, and the quiet hours were made hideous by the continual roaring of the 'Marseillaise' in every note of discord.

The following day was spent on shore, where the whole town seemed to have gone mad. All traces of imperial government were torn down and exchanged for republican emblems.

At Saigon we embarked a company of marine ar-

R

tillery, all Bretons, fine tall men, on their way to increase the garrison of Paris.

We had a very pleasant passage as far as Aden. I pleased the Bretons with my bagpipes; but, to their disgust and mine, the Provençals and the Corsican crew invariably insisted on the 'Marseillaise.'

As soon as we dropped anchor at Aden, news of the Metz disaster was brought on board.

At first none would believe it to be possible. 'It is English news,' they cried. 'Perfidious Albion desires it!' When it was confirmed beyond possibility for doubt, there was a terrible scene.

The southerners vowed that it was the work of the priests and 'Madame La Cæsare,' who had betrayed France.

The Bretons retorted that God was but punishing France for her atheism. Whereupon they came to blows, and the officers had some trouble in separating the two enraged parties.

At Aden we took on board a crowd of the most disreputable people I have ever seen.

They were described to me by one of the officers as the scum of Mauritius and Bourbon: card-sharpers, touts, billiard-markers, who were bound for France to fight as *franc-tireurs*, and the Messageries Company was giving them free passage and food.

Henceforward we had but little peace on board.

Every one seemed wild with excitement; wine was apparently served out *ad libitum* to these volunteers, who gambled, fenced, and quarrelled throughout the passage.

The Suez Canal had just been opened. I went on shore at Ismailia for an hour or two during the night we stayed there. The place appeared to be a rendezvous for all the bad characters of the Levant and the Danube States.

MY FAREWELL TO FORMOSA 243

We found on arrival at Marseilles that the railway communication with Paris was cut. I therefore had to wait for an opportunity to go round by Gibraltar.

Upon presenting myself at the *douane* with my luggage, I had an amusing adventure.

All my boxes and cases were placed for inspection, and the first one to be opened was my cabin trunk, wherein, on the top, reposed my beloved bagpipes in a disjointed condition.

The *douaniers* gazed at the curious instrument as though it were a species of infernal machine; but they would not touch it, fearing consequences. 'Mais qu'est-ce que c'est cela, monsieur?'

'C'est une cornemuse, messieurs,' I responded.

'Cornemuse! Cornemuse!' they repeated puzzled.

'Oui, messieurs, une cornemuse. Les Bretons l'appellent un binion.'

They either could not or would not understand; so growing impatient I put the instrument together, inflated the bag, and striding about amongst them I struck up the 'Marseillaise,' an air which the pipe gamut can compass, with the exception of the highest note.

The effect was electrical. Enthusiasm rose to a high pitch. 'Bravo! Bravo!' shouted the small crowd which had collected. 'Encore! Encore! Monsieur, que vous êtes un brave garçon!'

I was made to blow until I was wearied out, and my mind reverted to the scene on the theatre at Bang-kah.

At last I was obliged to desist, and the bag groaned out its collapse.

'Embrassons! Embrassons, monsieur!' I was forced to undergo a lot of oppressive affection. Some wiseacre informed the crowd that the 'cornemuse' was a Scottish instrument; they therefore saluted me as 'un brave Ecossais!' Although I knew what an honour I was declining, truth compelled me to confess that I was but a poor Southron—'un Anglais'—which lowered me somewhat in the general estimation.

I overheard one or two say, 'You know, the Scotch are friends of France. Have you not read?'

I almost began to regret my candour; but I was comforted subsequently when I heard a Frenchman describing the Scotch to his friends as 'montagnards; une espèce de sauvages' who wore no 'pantalons'!

After the fraternal embraces were over, the chief *douanier* cried out, 'Laissez passer monsieur et son bagage'; so my pipes served my purpose well.

Some of my fellow-passengers, Italian silk-worm dealers returning from Japan, advised me to accompany them to a cheap and comfortable inn, the Hôtel de Danube. I had not been installed there long, before the *propriétaire* waited upon me to say that the people had collected outside, and that they prayed that I would step without on to the balcony and play them a tune upon my wonderful instrument.

I thought it prudent to acquiesce. I found, however, that there was but one tune which would satisfy their patriotic enthusiasm, and during my stay in Marseilles I was continually liable to this friendly tyranny.

I remained two weeks in Marseilles, unable to get a passage to England. I spent this time in seeing as much as could be seen of the French character and habits at this crisis in the national history.

The people apparently had completely lost their heads.

It was dangerous work at times to visit the cafés: my fair skin and light hair rendered me liable at any moment to be pounced upon as 'un Allemand,' but I always managed to convince them of my nationality.

The *maire* was summoned by the restless people almost

MY FAREWELL TO FORMOSA 245

daily to address them, and to give them news of some victory.

The papers announced daily French successes, and no idea of defeat seemed to have place in the national mind.

I at length decided to proceed to Bordeaux, as the sick Englishman had already made his way there, and wrote assuring me that we could get home by that route.

I started one night at ten o'clock, and did not reach Bordeaux until twenty-six hours later. We were continually detained at the stations by trains arriving with wounded soldiers, but no hint was given that French affairs were not prospering.

We found the Bordeaux people excitedly preparing to receive the Chamber of Representatives from Versailles.

We remained a week in this port, and then left for London in a steamer trading in arms.

I arrived in London on December 6, 1870, and to my surprise, upon opening the *Times*, I received the first ntimation that France was at the feet of the German conqueror.

When I had been at home for some nine months, I received an offer from Sir Harry Ord, governor of the Straits Settlements, inviting me to join the civil service of that colony ; and through the kindness of Messrs. Elles & Co. I was enabled to accept that offer.

After sixteen years' service in the Straits, as Chinese interpreter and Protector of Chinese, I retired on pension in 1890.

If my readers have had the patience to follow me through the adventures recorded in the foregoing pages they will, I am sure, agree with me that I have great reason to be thankful to God for all the preservation and prosperity that He has vouchsafed to me.

My memory recalls with gratitude the innumerable acts of kindness from my own countrymen and the genuine hospitality I received, not only from the aborigines, but also from the Chinese of all classes in Formosa. These pleasant memories, and my appreciation of the scenery and the climate, in the north-east monsoon, often fill me with a keen desire to revisit the island. This is now, however, out of my power, and I must perforce conclude my account of old times with the sincere expression :

> 'Absence makes the heart grow fonder;
> Isle of Beauty, fare thee well!'

APPENDIX

WARNINGS AND PROPHECIES WITH REGARD TO BRITISH INTERESTS IN THE FAR EAST

EXTRACTS FROM JOURNALS AND MAGAZINES, 1883-4

THE FRANCO-CHINESE WAR

To the Editor of THE TIMES

SIR,—Would you kindly grant space in *The Times* for some remarks on the Tonquin question by one who, in consequence of a residence of more than twenty years in China and the East, passed in intimate communication with the Chinese of all classes, has gained a fair knowledge of their ideas and language, and who has also in the course of duty during the last two years been brought into contact with Annamese officials now opposed to the French in Indo-China?

The unanimous tone of the British press at this moment seems to be one of sympathy with China, combined with an unaccountable solicitude for France, and a fear lest she should ruin her already declining fortunes by a conflict with the increasing power and resources of the government of the Celestial Empire.

As far as we are concerned, the French occupation of Cochin China has been beneficial to our trade and colonies, and any extension of their power must augment the commercial importance of Hong Kong and the Straits Settlements. French rule means security for life and property, which cannot be ensured by China or any other Asiatic government; and, notwithstanding the protectionist views expressed by individuals, the mass of intelligent Frenchmen must be aware that it would be impossible to develop the wealth of Indo-China and the trade of the Red River except by giving every reasonable privilege to the merchants and shipping of America, Germany, and Great Britain.[1]

[1] These opinions have not been justified by subsequent facts. The French have endeavoured to strangle our trade with their Colonies in the Far East by enforcing a protectionist policy.—W. A. P., 1898.

Having endeavoured to show what, in my opinion, are a few of the just claims of France to our sympathies as the representative of progress and civilisation, I will, with your permission, in a future letter examine the case of China, and hope to be able to prove that the imperial government at Pekin, by interfering with France in Tonquin, is actuated merely by the fear of European influence, and represents a retrograde policy, opposed not only to European commerce, but also to the best interests of the millions of industrious and oppressed natives of the Celestial Empire.

Yours,
W. A. PICKERING, Protector of Chinese,
Straits Settlements.

41 Cavendish Place, Eastbourne, Nov. 23, 1883.

To the Editor of THE TIMES

Sir,—Being encouraged by your kindness in inserting my letter of the 23rd inst., I will now try to prove the correctness of some of the statements contained therein. In doing so I must confess that the wind has been considerably taken out of my sails by the able telegram from your Paris correspondent published in your issue of the 24th. He at any rate seems to have discovered that the war in Tonquin is being waged by the French 'against a band resisting at random,' and that China is 'as puerile in military as in diplomatic matters.' I trust that his suggestions as to England insisting on the trade of the Red River being kept open to all the world will have their due effect, and that the French in carrying out their laudable mission of restoring order to Tonquin will, by keeping a mental equilibrium, avoid making enemies of the only people in the world who are inclined to wish them well.

Before proceeding, I would explain that when using the words 'France' and 'China' in the following remarks, by France I of course imply the French people as represented by a ministry and parliament, virtually elected by popular vote. In speaking of China, on the other hand, I do not include the people of China, or the numbers of talented foreigners now in Chinese government employ ; I mean an oligarchy of Tartars and Chinese, including a few able and patriotic ministers, but containing a majority of conceited, ignorant, and prejudiced old men and women, who from Pekin try to rule the Celestial Empire in the name of Kuang-Sü, the young Emperor of the present Manchu dynasty Ta-Ts'ing.

In considering the probability of a rupture between China and France this, in my opinion, is the proper view of the question. The French cannot, after having declared war, be expected to tamely submit to their movements being checkmated through assistance rendered to China by European mind and matter. I submit, too, that it would not only be unjust but also impolitic were

APPENDIX 249

the Western Powers to extend any protection to their subjects who for mere pecuniary considerations might choose to remain in the service of an Asiatic government; and especially so as that government has always opposed European influence and the improvements of civilisation, excepting just as far as these seemed to offer China an ultimate prospect of ridding herself of the foreigner, and of returning to her former state of isolation.

France cannot be accused of undue haste in her dealings with Tonquin and Annam, as the present operations originated in a treaty signed, I believe, in 1874, when China could, if she wished, have entered a protest against the transaction. There is no doubt that, had the French been wise and known their own minds, a well-conducted expedition of 15,000 men despatched to Tonquin in 1874 would have enabled them to annex the whole country up to the frontier of China, and we should have heard very little of the claim of suzerainty.

Since then, however, China has had the benefit for some years of instruction in western political science, and has also acquired some superficial knowledge of modern military tactics and discipline; she has also carried out a successful campaign against rebels in Kansuh, and disputes with Russia and Japan, which she, no doubt, considers victories. Besides having purchased the newest style of vessels and guns from Europe, China has also arsenals and dockyards of her own, and troops disciplined after the European manner. To the short-sighted ideas of the Pekin oligarchy, all these acquisitions are rendering China more capable of resisting European nations; the insane policy of France at home and abroad having isolated her from the sympathy of most nations of Europe, the Pekin government, no doubt, has some idea of trying conclusions with her on this favourable opportunity of the suzerainty question.

The presence of her ambassadors at the European courts has also, no doubt, given China much encouragement; but it is a question whether this has not injured the real interests of the Pekin government. There is no doubt that the high tone taken by the Marquis Tseng, and his statements as reported in the daily papers, have placed his superiors in a position from which (unless they receive the help of some great European Power) they can only extricate themselves by either appearing ridiculous before the world, or by entering into a conflict which will waste the already impoverished revenues of the empire, injure European trade, perhaps cause a rebellion in China, and certainly end in a defeat for themselves. Besides this, China now appears as sponsor for the Black Flags (really rebels against her authority): the French will soon drive them out of Tonquin, and then they will appear in China, where the Pekin government must waste more money in their purchase or extermination. As long as the French keep to their programme in Tonquin and do not enter China, they when at Marseilles are almost as near the seat of war as are the Chinese in Canton (of course I mean as far as the facilities for transport, etc., are concerned). We hear much about the legions of troops which China could bring to bear on France in Tonquin. I do not know where the Chinese military depôts for war material, stores, etc., are supposed to be placed, or what number of disciplined troops they are prepared to bring into action. As far as raw material goes, in spite of opium, I suspect China can show as fair a proportion of well-built men as most countries in the world. It may, however, be taken for granted that, if the military depôts are superintended, the artillery handled, and the troops drilled and led by Europeans, then the Chinese army will give some trouble to the French; if, on the contrary, affairs are entrusted to native officials, then the stores will be embezzled, the arms ruined, and the troops, however well disciplined before, will, by the time they reach Tonquin, be only dangerous to their Chinese officers and countrymen, and they certainly will be inferior to the Black Flags in fighting power.

Tso-Tsung-Tang, no doubt, is a most talented man for a Chinese, and with unlimited funds, no scruples or law to fetter him, he has been and would be a formidable man against Chinese rebels badly armed, without resources, and, above all, fighting against the law. When, with these advantages, he gives himself two or three years to perform his task, he has every chance in his favour; but supposing these rebels to have on their side a European like Colonel Gordon, I am of opinion that General Tso would not reappear before his imperial master at Pekin.

What can Tso-Tsung-Tang expect to do against France, when the latter Power (content merely to hold its own in Tonquin) can in a very short time attack the coast of China with an overwhelming fleet, and, with a *minimum* of damage to European commerce, cut off one of the chief items of the imperial revenue, take the Chinese arsenals and their new gunboats, torpedoes, etc., and, while Tso-Tsung-Tang is blundering through the mountains towards Tonquin, force the Pekin government to come to terms?

My sympathy is altogether with the people of China, and I feel that it would be a real calamity were the present dynasty to be overturned by a rebellion. The rulers now at Pekin have the machinery for carrying on the government of the empire, such as it is. Were a revolution to take place, it could only be accomplished after temporary anarchy and damage to the country. After all, too, there would be no improvement in the general state of affairs, as the fault does not lie so much in any one set of officials as in the low state of the people from whom they spring. My sympathy with France only goes as far as the operations demanded by her position in Cochin China; but I feel deeply that any

APPENDIX 251

person who would encourage China to risk war for the sake of a punctilio is an enemy to the welfare of the Celestial Empire.

Within the Chinese Empire, as far, at least, as the three southern provinces, Kwang-tung, Kwang-si, and Fuh-kien, are concerned, there is no doubt that the local officials are powerless to keep order or to protect their people from lawless oppression. I do not, of course, mean to say that in a comparatively civilised nation like that of the Chinese there are not some really conscientious and able officials; but I think it will be acknowledged that in the provinces I have named the majority of mandarins are either weak and corrupt or cruel and oppressive. In the rivers piracy and dacoity almost universally prevail; brigandage and clan fights defy the law; torture is used by the mandarins, not only to extort evidence, but to procure squeezes of money; the local authorities are almost always found powerless to protect European missionaries, even if they do not often themselves excite the feelings of the populace against the strangers.

Under these circumstances China now appeals to European sympathy on the ground that France is attacking her honour by extending influence in Annam, and she is ready, for a question of suzerainty over an outlying State over which she cannot exercise any beneficial influence, to rush into a war which will not only end in her own defeat, but will also injure European commerce and other western interests.

I cannot think how China can expect any assistance from Europe in this matter. Western interests on the coast of China are identical, and any reverse suffered by the French would only increase the arrogance and opposition of the Pekin government towards all foreigners.

The old *régime* of ignorant bliss and conceit received its first real blow when we came into collision with the empire some forty years ago; since then China has been thoroughly humiliated by foreigners twice or three times, and the present dynasty has really been kept in its place, and the empire kept together for the last twenty years, solely by European influence—chiefly by the power of Great Britain. To England the Pekin government owes the inestimable services of Colonel Gordon and our fleet, which crushed a rebellion that otherwise would have utterly ruined the empire. At the present day everything that is worthy of being called good government is performed by Europeans, and Western Powers have a perfect right now to dictate to China as to the course she should pursue in a matter concerning their interests.

It has been advanced by some writers that China cannot run the risk of losing prestige and humiliating herself in the eyes of the people by withdrawing from the position she has now taken up. As I intend, if the patience of yourself and your readers has not been already exhausted by the prolixity of my present letter, to make some remarks as to the interest the Chinese people can have in the dealings of Pekin with Europe and America, I will merely say that, supposing my statements in the preceding paragraph to be approximately correct, then China's prestige is *nil*, and she has been already sufficiently humiliated in the eyes of her people without recklessly seeking further disgrace.

France, on the other hand, in spite of her faults and misfortunes, has a prestige to maintain which is of importance to herself and the world, both in Europe and Asia. In Europe the effacement of France would certainly have a disturbing effect on the balance of power; in Asia, if France were to succumb to China, she would endanger the interests of all Western subjects in the East, and entail on Great Britain or some other Power the burden and expense of repressing the increased arrogance and assumption of the Pekin government.

With regard to the present state of China, I am not afraid to maintain that, bereft of foreign advice and assistance, she is less capable of either keeping good order in her own dominions or resisting invasion than she was fifty years ago.

Were the European and American governments to decide to withdraw from the Celestial empire their fleets, ministers, and consuls, China would not only be unable to oppose even a second-rate European Power, but would be vulnerable at a hundred points to the attack of a strong filibustering party, if led by men such as the late General Ward, who are to be found in numbers in the cities of Europe and the United States.

Within two years of the departure of the European fleets, etc., the Chinese Empire would be in a state of anarchy, torn by rival factions, each anxious to destroy, but unable to reconstruct on any firm moral basis. The leaders of each faction would bid high for the services of European or American military adventurers; no doubt a splendid trade in munitions of war would spring up, but China would be ruined. Although such a catastrophe cannot be expected from a war with France, yet there is reason to fear that, besides the inevitable defeat, some parts of the empire would break out into petty rebellion, the suppression of which would entail loss of life and ruin of thousands of the poor Chinese; and in my opinion the best advice a friend of China can give to the Pekin government is that it should cease to cherish any hopeless schemes of opposing French progress in Annam by romantic antiquated claims of suzerainty over outlying countries, but should by a scrupulous fulfilment of treaty obligations enlist the assistance of Western Powers while paying its whole attention towards the consolidation, good government, and moral elevation of its people dwelling in the eighteen provinces. That such advice would be followed I can scarcely hope, as, however talented and far-seeing may be some Chinese officials, civil and military, there is no doubt that the Pekin majority only appreciates Western science, political, military, or engineering, just as far as the adoption of it will, at some future and not far distant time, enable the present dynasty to expel the hateful foreigners with their missionaries and traders, and allow it to fleece three hundred millions of people under the pretence of 'following the maxims of the ancient kings.'

The venerable officials who rule from Pekin see plainly that the nations of Christendom, however intellectually inferior they may be, certainly enjoy an immense physical superiority to China and the rest of the world; they in their ignorance attribute all this to the fact that we possess splendid steam vessels, enormous guns, and scientific appliances for war, manufactures, and commerce; they also vainly hope that in a few years (already possessing a superiority in intellect) by a smattering of scientific knowledge, military discipline, and engineering skill, they will be able to more than equal us in material strength.

The Chinese government, like other nations, and individuals too, is apt to mistake effect for cause, and cannot be expected to know (what some of us are trying to forget) that the source of any superiority we may possess over the rest of the world is to be traced chiefly to the advent of the Divine Man whose birth we are now commemorating this Christmas-tide.

Could China know this she would leave off her abortive attempts to exclude Western ideas and men, and cease from a wasteful expenditure of money on arsenals, forts, vessels of war, etc., and would instead devote her attention towards a course of progress which alone can enable the Middle Kingdom gradually to take a position among the nations commensurate with its geographical extent and the undoubtedly sterling qualities possessed by its enormous population.

Your obedient servant,
W. A. PICKERING.

41 Cavendish Place, Eastbourne, Dec. 30.

THE WAR BETWEEN CHINA AND JAPAN, 1895

PALL MALL GAZETTE, *February* 25, 1895

MR. W. A. PICKERING ON CHINESE AFFAIRS

Some months ago Lieutenant-General Sir Andrew Clarke informed me, writes our representative, that no European knew more about the Chinese than Mr. W. A. Pickering. I approached that gentleman, therefore, recently on the subject of the present Oriental embroglio.

'You know a good deal about China, Mr. Pickering?' said I.—
'I have had,' he returned, 'an experience of about thirty years

among the Chinese, in China, Formosa, and the Straits Settlements. I speak tolerably well four dialects as well as the mandarin, and have a fair knowledge of the written character. My experience of the Chinese ranges from the highest officials to pirates and rebels.'

'And you agree generally with the views recently expressed by Professor Kennaway Douglas in the columns of the *Pall Mall Gazette*?'—'Yes,' replied Mr. Pickering, 'my opinions entirely coincide with those of Professor Douglas, and I think that the Japanese are the benefactors of the world, though, in their turn, they will have to give way to Russia.'

'And what of Russia?'—'*Well, it is no way in the interest of Russia* that there should be a *strong government at Pekin ;* neither is it in the interest of the civilised world nor of Christianity.'

'And why not, please?'—'A strong government at Pekin,' observed Mr. Pickering, 'means non-fulfilment of treaty obligations, and the continuance of the policy of shutting up the Celestial Empire to trade and commerce.'

'But might not a crash at Pekin produce grave disorders and danger for European residents?'—'Whatever danger,' resumed Mr. Pickering, 'to the lives of Europeans may result from the downfall of the present dynasty would be more than compensated by the nuts which the Japanese would, if finally victorious, get out of the fire for all nations. If, as I have reason to believe, General Le Gendre is advising the Japanese from the United States, I feel sure that this is the end he will pursue.'

European Mouth-pieces

'You are acquainted with him?'—'Yes, I was with him in Formosa. Now, ever since—in the sixties—Burlingham brought forward China to enter the comity of nations, and in the name of the mandarins talked bunkum about erecting the shining cross on every hill and in every valley, the Chinese have used Europeans to talk our language, and to utter the sentiments of Christianity and civilisation.'

'In order to deceive us poor Westerns?'—'Yes, quite recently I imagine Lord Rosebery to have been taken in by listening to European mouth-pieces, while the Chinese official is really thinking in Chinese, and has pagan and semi-civilised sentiments in his heart.'

'And how does that work out?'—'Well, if you come to reflect, you must be aware that the Chinese now frighten us—by Chinese, I mean the literary class, who, by so-called competitive examinations, rule the masses or unlearned—by saying : "If the government should be overthrown, we cannot secure the safety of your missionaries and traders."'

'And that is humbug?'—'Yes, they never have done this ;

but the literary class has always egged on the mob, in the hope that by continued acts of violence they may frighten Europeans from the interior. You will have noticed that before the Chinese had got chastised by the Japanese, their soldiers began to murder European missionaries. Now, since they have found out how utterly helpless they are, the officials take every possible step to protect the lives of Europeans ; and though, a few years ago, the Pekin government professed their utter inability to protect foreigners from the savage hate of the ignorant common people, now they protest that the government are quite able to protect our missionaries in the interior, that is, for a consideration that the Japanese do not take Pekin and upset the government. The fact is, the Chinese government are helpless—and have always been helpless—to protect us from the people, if the people hate us ; but the people have never hated us very much more than ignorant people in most countries hate strangers.'

'Then the literati are at the bottom of the whole mischief?'— 'Yes,' went on Mr. Pickering, 'from the beginning of our intercourse with the Chinese government it has been the official class, the literati, who have set the people against the foreigners ; and I feel sure that our people are quite as likely to live safely in China, when the mandarins and the expectant officials are so frightened for their own lives that they have no time or spirit to incite the common people against quiet, law-abiding missionaries and merchants. As I believe that the Russians, French, and Americans know this, I do not wonder that they refuse to interfere, and I only wish our government would withdraw all our people employed by the Chinese, and keep them in our service. They would honour our service, and would deserve the highest rewards ; now they must either serve two masters or not serve us.'

'And what further points would you make, Mr. Pickering?'— 'Well,' he replied after a few moments' pause, ' I think I have said perhaps more than enough already ; but my great wish is that our government may not, through any misplaced sympathy with the Chinese, neglect the interests of our own countrymen. *Every year the power is inevitably getting more and more into the hands of the working classes, and every day the working classes are becoming more and more dependent on the enlarged scope of our foreign markets for the disposal of the manufactures which they sell, in order to procure the necessaries of life, and not only for this, but for the supply of the food they eat. These markets can only be secured by the increase of our influence in such countries as China.'*

Chinese Military and Civic Virtue.

'And what do you think of the Chinese as soldiers and civil servants?'

'Well, though I say this in opposition to most people, I hold that the Chinese are eminently pugnacious, at any rate in the way of clan fights and provincial jealousies; yet I believe that the influence of Confucius and of other ancient sages has kept them from being sufficiently warlike to be dangerous to any robust race which has got past the educational system of Confucius and Mencius.

'Yes, the latter touched on military matters. He describes the classical mode of warfare as follows : "The two armies approach each other at the sound of the drums ; they meet, and after the weapons cross one side throw away their coats of mail, trail their arms, and run away." Excepting when they have been cooped up in the island at Wei-hai-wei, the Chinese throughout the present war appear to have followed faithfully the maxims of the ancient sage.'

'Their officers seem to be no good?'—'They are honeycombed with vice,' returned Mr. Pickering, 'and generally venal and unpatriotic. Though the Chinese fought well under Gordon, it must be remembered that they were fighting in the cause of the Son of Heaven, the cause of law and order, under the command of English gentlemen against rebels forsaken of heaven and forsaken of Confucius. The rebels, too, were led by ignorant, dissipated, and unscrupulous runaways from the merchant ships at Shanghai, or—in many cases—deserters from the ranks of European and American armies and navies.'

'What as to the civil service, Mr. Pickering?'—'No doubt there are good officials, loyal and faithful, just and benevolent, in the Chinese civil service ; but the majority are corrupt, rapacious, and cruel, who only fill office with a view to enriching and repaying themselves and their relations for the capital spent in gaining office and promotion, although these are supposed to be gained by competitive examination and merit. In fact, competitive examination holds the heterogeneous population of China together—that is, the desire to keep intact the sheep to be fleeced by the officials and the class from which the officials spring.'

'Then China generally is in a bad way?'—'For all that I have said I believe that were China Christian, and granted a set of officials like we possess in our Indian civil service, then the Celestial Empire, ruled by Chinese law, would be the happiest in the world. I have spent most of my life among the Chinese : I like them very much, and feel that they are the best specimens of the human race under the conditions set forth in the first chapter of St. Paul's epistle to the Romans, and I don't believe that any other nation left in the same condition for, say, five thousand years would have remained a nation so strong and so good as the Chinese are to-day. This, however, is not much to say for human nature.'

APPENDIX

[April 27, 1895]

ENGLAND AND THE TREATY OF SHIMONOSEKI
An Interview with Mr. W. A. Pickering, C.M.G.

There are not many men, we imagine, who have had better opportunities of forming a sound judgment on the present situation in the Far East than Mr. Pickering. In 1878 Sir Robert Hart said that no single European had ever possessed such opportunities of learning the Chinese character in all its phases; and though we dare say that some of Mr. Pickering's present opinions would make Sir Robert doubt his capability of learning wisdom by experience, yet the experience remains a fact. From 1877 to 1888 Mr. Pickering was virtually the ruler of some hundreds of thousands of Chinese in the Straits Settlements and in the native States. In 1883 he was asked by the Intelligence Department of the War Office to write a paper on the state of the Chinese army, and again requested to make suggestions as to the best mode of attacking China in case of war. For this paper he received the thanks of Lord Wolseley and of the commander-in-chief, and certainly all his statements and opinions have been more than confirmed in the course of the present war. 'My whole life,' says Mr. Pickering, 'since I was eighteen years of age, has been spent with the Chinese or in studying Chinese affairs, while at the same time I have kept up my interest in European affairs, and have always remembered first of all that I was an Englishman.' From this record it will be evident that Mr. Pickering's views on any matter affecting China are not without value and authority; and a representative of *The Westminster Gazette* waited upon him accordingly to learn what he thought of the Treaty of Shimonoseki and of England's attitude thereto :—

China a Sponge and a Cancer

'There seems to be a conspiracy of lying spirits abroad,' said Mr. Pickering, 'regarding the terms of the peace between China and Japan.'

'Do you mean the story of the offensive and defensive alliance?'

'I am quite sure,' replied Mr. Pickering, 'that the Japanese will never enter into an offensive and defensive alliance with China. They know that to her allies China would only prove a sponge to suck up their resources, or a cancer to corrupt their bodies and eat out their vitals. I don't think China has stability enough to carry out the terms of any treaty.'

'Then what is the end to be, in your view?'

'The end,' returned Mr. Pickering, '*must be that she is divided between Russia, England, and France.* What have we, however, to fear from any favourable terms Japan may make? Surely we can't go to war because of trade rivalry!'

S

'And Formosa?'
'Well, we have had lots of chances to take Formosa. Certainly we can't allow Russia or France to take it, and it could not be in better hands than those of Japan, or in worse than those of China.'

Japhet and Shem

'And *Russia*, Mr. Pickering?'
'*Russia will stir up the water till she gets a port in the Pacific open all the year round, and some portion of Manchuria.*'
'And France—and Germany?'
'France will coquet with Russia to spite us, and Germany can do nothing but act as a cuckoo, and place her young ones in the nests of the other Powers, so that they may make money out of our markets and undersell us.'
'And as to our native land, Mr. Pickering?'
'If England be wise,' he replied, '*she will make ready to get her share in the coming inevitable scramble in China.* In the meantime our interest lies with Japan's successes. *Sic vos non vobis mellificatis apes.*'
'But what about an invasion by yellow men, and jaundice at a premium?'
'There is no fear,' returned Mr. Pickering, with a comfortable smile of assurance, 'of any Mongolian invasion of Europe by Chinese and Japanese, except in the way of cheap labour and commercial rivalry. Shem will never dwell in the tents of Japhet. The contrary must be the result of all this upsetting of the present state of things.'

THE OUTRAGES ON MISSIONARIES AT FOOCHOW, 1895.

THE MISSIONARY QUESTION IN CHINA.

To the Editor of THE TIMES.

Sir,—In addition to other excuses and pleas, the Pekin government will always take advantage of that complicated subject, the missionary question, and use it as a most powerful lever with which to force European Powers to recede from their treaty rights as to residence in the interior provinces of the Celestial empire.

This access to the interior by missionaries and traders must be ruinous to the tyrannical and corrupt official system by which China is closed to civilisation and progress, and its people ground down for the benefit of the literati and mandarins. The missionaries introduce ideas which, if accepted by the common people, must render them more accustomed to liberty of spirit, and make them dissatisfied with the present state of things political. Merchants and traders visiting the interior under treaty rights must also interfere with the squeezes and illegitimate taxes by which the officials exist and grow rich.

There is no doubt that the Chinese government, weak as it is, can and will keep order amongst its people towards foreigners, if it only be forced to do so by motives of fear or advantage to be gained. Both these motives have been removed by the interference by Russia and of France with Japan, and now the officials have resumed their old game of forcing the hands of foreigners to quit the country because residence will never be safe. The farce of a central government is held out to Europe, while really there is no central government, and the European advocates (as mentioned in a letter from Hankow in your Monday's issue) are fascinating Englishmen by benevolent platitudes unknown and unintelligible to their Chinese employers. The only way to keep China quiet and enforce the fulfilment of treaties until the inevitable partition of the empire arrives is to revert to the old gunboat system, and to make the viceroys, tao-tais, and prefects responsible for the peace and good order of their respective provinces, etc., and in case of riots to enforce good order and redress without reference to Pekin. This may be considered retrograde policy, but it is quite advanced enough for the present condition of the Chinese government, which has only improved since 1860 in the knowledge of fooling the European.

I regret that my opinions on religious subjects will cause hurt and offence to many old friends ; but, as I base my opinions on the only safe guide (the words of our Lord and His apostles), I am quite ready to stand *contra mundum*, if that *mundus* even be the whole religious world.

Yours faithfully,
W. A. PICKERING.

August.

To the Editor of THE TIMES.

Sir,—I have lived nearly forty years with the Chinese of all classes, from the highest mandarin to the lowest coolie, and have read most of the works written on China during that period. I have, however, never seen any description of the Chinese character equal to that given in your Article No. 2, on the state of 'China after the War.'

There is no doubt that, as far as our position in the East, England is in a very serious dilemma.

There are two important ingredients for a remedy for the present state of affairs :

First—A man like Sir Robert Hart as our British minister at Pekin.

Second—*A complete understanding with Russia as to what she demands, and what we can afford to give her in the Far East.*

I am, Sir, your obedient servant,

W. A. PICKERING.

September, 1895.

THE MEKONG TREATY.

ASIATIC QUARTERLY REVIEW, *April*, 1896.

Since writing my article in the last issue of this Review on the 'Straits Settlements,' Great Britain has signed a treaty with France regarding the affairs of Siam.

Under these circumstances I will venture to express my opinion as to our prospects in the Far East, as affected by the recent treaty.

There never could be a more unjust libel or a more undeserved compliment (according to individual opinion) than that contained in the accusation made by Continental nations, that Great Britain and her statesmen have persistently followed a Machiavellian policy to extend our rule over the face of the globe. There certainly have been, and we must hope that there always will be, administrators of provinces and governors of colonies whose knowledge and patriotic foresight have determined what ought to be our policy for the good of our race and for the benefit of the people over whom Providence has ordained that we should rule; but certainly it cannot be said that for many years any statesmen in charge of our Foreign and Colonial Offices have been aggressive or have been actuated by any other desire than to keep things quiet and to diminish the responsibilities of Great Britain as much as possible. Indeed, it has been diffidence, susceptibility to the criticism of the opposition, and a fear to offend foreign Powers that have caused trouble and expense during the past thirty or forty years—all of which might have been avoided by a bold and straightforward policy.

Fifty years ago we could afford to dally with the questions of extending our influence in Africa and the Far East; but the exhibition of 1851 and the German victories of 1866 and 1871 have changed all this.

Continental nations have not only learned from us and become able to compete with us successfully in manufactures and trade, but Germany, Russia, and especially France, have entered upon a career of colonial enterprise, and are now prepared to dispute with England for every square mile of unoccupied territory. We must be prepared to take what falls in our way or to allow other nations to appropriate it; but the difference is that, while we colonise not only for our own advantage but also for the benefit of every other nation, every colony established by France, Germany, or Russia, though primarily intended for the aggrandisement of each respective nation, is really used as a weapon against the prosperity of British trade—that is, the existence of the inhabitants of these isles. At the present time we cannot persist in our old policy without serious danger of involving this country with one or other of the Great Powers.

We must always bear in mind that if Germany, in spite of its many disintegrating elements, such as socialism, religious differences, capricious autocracy, etc., should continue to be a united empire, it will, on the first opportunity, absorb Holland, and with that country her colonies in the Eastern Archipelago.

Great Britain will then, in the East and Far East, be closely hemmed in—by Russia on the north and west, by France on the east, and by Germany on the south, east, and south-west.

The immense empire of China, too, is a 'sick man' awaiting partition. One of our statesmen has said that in the Far East there is enough for all the Western Powers; but only the Powers who boldly take will be allowed to possess; and it is a certain fact that while every extension of our empire means food and clothing for the working men of the British Isles, every appropriation of territory by any other nation means the shutting out of our manufactures from that market. If France and Germany were to lose their colonies, it would be rather advantageous than otherwise to the mother countries; but for Great Britain a loss of colonial trade or a restriction of her markets implies danger to her very means of existence.

This needs to be most urgently impressed on our working classes; for at a time when we have nearly attained to that *panacea*, universal suffrage, we can scarcely blame ministers of state if they hesitate to disregard or go beyond the mandate of their creators. In the republics of ancient Greece and Rome *demos* and *plebs* could indulge in politics, and enjoy their *panem et circenses* at the expense of the labouring hordes of helots or gangs of slaves; but their modern representatives, in our own country at any rate, must either work hard and steadily or starve, unless they choose the expedient of plundering the goods of the classes which supply them with capital, work, and wages: this last method would speedily reduce us all to an equality of poverty and barbarism.

Any class which is not intelligent enough to understand that under God, not only the prosperity but the very existence of our teeming population depends on the maintenance of an overwhelming command of the sea and the extension of markets in proportion to the increase of that population, is not worthy to exercise the franchise, and should be kept in tutelage until it can comprehend that the revision of the register, local veto, disestablishment, the higher education, etc., are luxuries, not necessaries of life.

Though the new treaty as to Siam seems to have effected one good result, the abolition of that greatest and most objectionable of all diplomatic shams, a 'buffer State,' yet it is to be feared that we have only got rid of a smaller evil for the probability of a greater.

The kingdom of Siam can never stand long by itself, as the government is hopelessly corrupt and effete; therefore the administration of the country must, at no distant period, be undertaken by France or England, and until this event occurs Bangkok will be the scene of intrigue and a continual cause of soreness between the two European governments. Indeed there can be no permanent and cordial agreement between Russia, France, and Great Britain in Asia until our sentry-boxes on the various frontiers stand back to back, and our officers and men fraternise in their messes and canteens, while our ministers at home negotiate face to face without the intervention of semi-barbarous Mohammedan or Buddhist kinglets.

If such an arrangement could be arrived at, there is a grand future for the hitherto down-trodden Asiatic races, and also great benefits in store for their European protectors. But England, above all, must take the initiative, by putting aside her fears, boldly declaring her policy, and abandoning the 'buffer State' idea, which so often has set up 'Monroe doctrines,' impossible and inadvisable to insist upon when the time came to enforce them.

With the present abnormally strong government, there ought to be every hope for the future; but nowadays, when the minds of the people move as it were by railway and telegraph, it will never do for statesmen to persist altogether in the old dallying style of diplomacy, although we have to be thankful that their minds are not quite so easily determined as they are pressed to be by would-be Little England advisers.

If our Foreign Office be inspired by the spirit of the illustrious Burleigh, and the Colonial Office by that of the patriotic and undaunted Cromwell, while the nation at large acknowledge God and His righteousness, we need not fear that England will be allowed to lose or diminish her proud position as pioneer of liberty and promoter of prosperity for the whole world.

And supposing the other Great Powers, through an unreasoning jealousy, should not choose to allow us to go on our way in peace, then—

> 'Come the *three* corners of the world in arms,
> And we shall shock them.'

APPENDIX 263

THE REVISION OF THE TARIFF IN CHINA, 1896-97

BRITISH INTERESTS IN CHINA

To the Editor of the LONDON AND CHINA TELEGRAPH

Sir,—I see in your last issue that there is a practical unanimity amongst British commercial bodies as to agreeing to the increase of customs duties in China, on the understanding that this increase shall be the sole charge levied, and cover *lekin*, transit, or any other duty or impost whatever. This unanimity of opinion shows clearly that we British must have forgotten everything and learned nothing during the past forty years' experience of China and its government. It will be the easiest thing possible to increase the customs duties, but no power in this world will ever be able to compel or induce the Chinese government to fulfil its part of the bargain. The only good result from the change will be that a state of things will be arrived at which will force on a war, and bring about the destruction of the imperial government. Whether Great Britain, France, or Russia acccomplish this end, there can be no doubt that the Chinese people will greatly benefit from such a catastrophe to their corrupt and utterly incorrigible oppressors. Yours faithfully,

LAU TAI-WAN.

64 Warwick Gardens, W., November 24.

Sir,—Referring to my letter of November 24, and to your appreciatory strictures thereon, I would call your attention to the most valuable series of articles now appearing in the *Times* on the subject of our commercial relations with China. I contend that, in spite of his agreement with you as to the comparative success of new regulations concerning such a special and decreasingly important article of trade as opium, Mr. Chirol says plainly that the Chinese are both unable and unwilling to give due compensation for the permission to increase the tariff duties on imports.

The special correspondent of the *Times* bases all the advantages to be hoped for by allowing the Pekin government to impose increased duties on foreign trade on such conditions as the following :—

1. That sufficient security be furnished by the Chinese for the effectual fulfilment of obligations which it undertakes to perform, *and which in the past have been a mere dead letter.*
2. The value of all provisions must necessarily depend upon the *good faith* of the Chinese in *carrying them out,* and on the ability of foreign governments to enforce their strict observance.
3. The transference of the *lekin* collection to the control and supervision of the Imperial Maritime Customs ; in fact, to

amalgamate the native Customs at the non-treaty ports and on native-borne trade with the Imperial Maritime Customs, *and entrust the latter with the collection of the whole revenue derived from trade.*

Now these conditions imply a radical and total change of the nature of the Chinese and their government, and a perfect European concert with regard to the Celestial Empire. I affirm confidently that such ideas are Utopian in the extreme. If it were possible for the central government to entertain such an idea as to allow the empire, as far as trade revenue is concerned, to be handed over to the administration of foreigners, that government has not the power to overcome the immense opposition of the provincial officials.

As to any European concert, it has been proved clearly in the case of Turkey that mutual jealousies prevent any united action, and that no member of the so-called concert dare take up his instrument and begin to play for fear that, while his eyes were fixed on the music, the other members of the orchestra would knock him down or rend each other. In the Far East, where the interests of Great Britain are far greater than in Turkey, and where, until within the last few years, we had gained, at our own great expense, almost a monopoly of influence, whatever England will propose is certain to be opposed openly by Russia and France, and, in an underhand manner, by Germany.

China is well aware of this, and will always take advantage of this state of things : she has no desire for anything but money to keep her going, and would willingly eject all barbarians (merchants and missionaries) from the sacred pale' of the Middle Kingdom, so that her officials may stew in the juice of the ' ancient sages.'

The fact is this, Mr. Editor, and you with your long experience know it : the only difference between China one thousand years ago and the present day is—then she was a powerful and comparatively civilised empire, surrounded by inferior races and shut out from the rest of the world ; now she is utterly helpless, bankrupt in patriotism, power, and available resources. All the king's horses and all the king's men cannot set China up again ; she must, like Turkey, fall from worse to worse, until she is partitioned by Western nations, and, if our people and statesmen will keep their heads, we deserve to get the British lion's share.

Even such a talented and far-seeing man as Mr. V. Chirol can only suggest, as the surest guarantee for the fulfilment of the conditions on which increased duties are to be granted, that in case of China's breach of faith we must return to the *status quo.*

Would it not be far better for British merchants to prepare for the inevitable crisis, and to endure the ills we know, than to hastily fly to those we know not of, but of which there is almost a certainty that they will be greater than those existing at present ? I am, etc.

LAU TAI-WAN.

64 Warwick Gardens, W.

Sir,—It is an encouraging sign during this critical condition of our most vital interests in the Far East that the affairs of China, with regard to Western nations, are being brought prominently before the public by most able writers in our magazines, reviews, and journals. During the present month the *Contemporary* contains an admirable article by Mr. Henry Norman, ' Down the Long Avenue,' and another on ' The Russo-Chinese Treaty,' by an anonymous writer. To *Blackwood* Mr. Michie has contributed 'The Chinese Oyster,' and the *Times'* special correspondent in the Far East continues his articles in the form of an excellent critique on ' The Mission of Li Hung-chang and its Sequel.'

Let us hope that all these timely warnings and sound advice so patriotically given may have the same good effect in arousing Englishmen to a due sense of their responsibilities and interests in the Chinese Empire, as the writings of talented pamphleteers and journalists have accomplished with regard to the question of strengthening our navy.

Mr. Norman, although—as he avows himself to be—pessimistic, seems to have most thoroughly grasped the whole subject. If the experience gained by him during his tour in the Far East three or four years ago, and given to the public in his book, had been availed of by our statesmen, there can be little doubt that Great Britain would still be the predominating power in China.

Mr. Michie states, with truth, that hitherto our 'solid interests in China ' have been but imperfectly recognised by the general public : he might have added that they have been scarcely realised at all by our statesmen of either party. Certainly with our Foreign Office, our ministers at Pekin, consuls in China, as well as by the people at home, attention has been too much turned 'to quaintness of custom or costume, to superstitions, cruelties, corruption, and things useful to put a spice into newspaper paragraphs, while the real, live China has been ignored.'

To the British official mind in the Far East, China has been chiefly interesting as a field of study in which to gain a literary distinction by learned works on the language or philosophies of the ' black-haired ' race.

But, as Mr. Michie observes, ' the China ' on which the feeding and clothing of our working classes must increasingly depend is 'the peaceable, law-abiding, *clothes-wearing*, industrious, frugal millions, whose willing muscles are a mine of wealth to themselves *and indirectly to us.*' 'A tithe of the energy spent by us on exploration amongst savages would have brought China near to our hearths and homes; a percentage of the good seed scattered in the howling wilderness would, if sown in the arable land' (until four or five years ago virtually in our own hands), 'have yielded rich harvests to *our workers.*'

This is a simple fact; and yet, while we are preparing to go to any expense, and to brave France and Russia for the subjugation of the Soudan (in the interests of a country which we are pledged ultimately to give up), we view with apathy these two Powers gradually depriving us of our political and commercial influence over more than three hundred millions of Chinese—those millions who, under our influence, might be rendered invaluable as contributors to the existence and prosperity of our working classes, who now hold the government of this empire in their hands.

Mr. Michie scarcely seems to realise our present position when he deprecates the importance of England being able and desirous to take her share in the partition of the Celestial Empire, which partition, he admits, has already begun; he rather recommends our ensuring a preponderance of the trade to be developed in China by railways and other improvements. I submit that to expect to retain a commercial superiority, if we neglect to take our share in the territorial partition, is unreasonable. Experience teaches us that the advance of France and Russia will be chiefly utilised for the detriment of British commerce. The writer on 'The Russo-Chinese Treaty' gives most interesting information as to the diplomacy which patriotic Russians have successfully carried out for the benefit of *their countrymen.* The treaty, however, is now a fact, with all its possible and probable injury to our interests and prestige, and has doubtless practically existed since we first heard of it twelve months ago. We of all people should have been prepared to meet this danger, as we have had enough experience that, when a fairly authenticated rumour of Russia's diplomatic encroachments has been followed by an official *démenti,* the rumour has always proved to contain a fact.

Mr. Chirol dwells chiefly on the corruption of Chinese officialdom, which, however interesting to those who do not know Chinese affairs, can have little bearing on the position of Great Britain in the Far East. Mr. Norman hits the nail on the head when he points out our fatal mistake in not coming to an understanding with Russia, when we occupied a favourable position, while we have supinely allowed the Tsar to become not merely the protector but the real ruler of China.

APPENDIX 267

Whether China be progressive or retrogressive, her officials pure or corrupt, her intercourse with Western Powers is *now* entirely in the hands and under the control of Russia, backed up by France, and foolishly encouraged by Germany through insane jealousy of England.

Whether we seek to share in the partition of the empire or demand a share of its commerce proportionate to our rights and absolute needs, we can only obtain our desires by showing the Pekin government that we have naval and military strength sufficient to enforce our just demands, and that we are more to be dreaded than France and Russia combined.

Even when our prestige was at its highest, our diplomatists have seldom been anything but children in the hands of those feeble but wily old men of the Tsung-li-yamen, and have never maintained any right or secured any privilege or advantage except when the Pekin authorities have come to the conclusion that an admiral was behind the British minister, waiting and anxious to enforce his demands. What can we hope from mere diplomacy at a time when the Chinese ambassador-elect, Lo Fêng-loh, is reported to have expressed his opinion that Great Britain is played out, and that Russia and China can conquer the world?[1] It is very certain that we have no chance of getting either territory or facilities of trade in China unless our government, forced by the people of Great Britain, shall take the necessary steps to prove that this is the fallacious opinion of a young man utterly ignorant of the world and spoilt by a thin veneer of Western civilisation.

Whatever we may demand will be resisted by the ruling powers of China, France, and Russia, who are now checkmating us in every part of the world, from Abyssinia to Washington, from Bangkok to Herat. It is more than possible that were we to attempt to enforce any demands on the court of Pekin, we should be confronted by the military and naval forces of these two nations, posing as guardians of the 'Son of Heaven.'

The coalition of these two Great Powers will not only shut us out from the trade of Manchuria, north, and south-west China, but they will also, by their supreme influence at Pekin, endanger our possessions in the Straits, the Malay States, and Hong Kong. The backbone of all these possessions is the large Chinese population, on whose industry and enterprise their wealth and prosperity chiefly depend. Now the great majority of these Chinese have left their parents, wives, and families behind in China; and I maintain that with Russia and France virtually ruling at Pekin, in case of a war between Great Britain and those Powers, the Chinese officials could bring such pressure to bear on our Chinese colonists, through their families at home,

---

[1] 'Russo-Chinese Treaty,' *Contemporary* Magazine, February.

that we should be most seriously hampered in the defence of our most valuable dependencies from Hong Kong to Rangoon.

Our chief general, some years ago, seemed to labour under an unreasonable fear lest the Chinese Empire should become a danger to Europe, and that the times of Tamerlane or Genghis Khan might be renewed. Left to herself China is contemptible, but the millions of robust Chinese, disciplined and led by France or Russia, would certainly prove a most serious danger to our empire in India.

There can be no doubt that we have lost, and more than lost, many advantages we gained in 1860 : we have thrown away our splendid opportunities with a light heart. When Sir Robert Hart shall, on account of age, be obliged to vacate his post, we shall be in a worse position still; while that gentleman has most loyally served his employers, and has for many years practically upheld the Chinese government at Pekin, he has at the same time been the embodiment of British prestige, more so than most of the ministers we have possessed. When the war between China and Japan broke out it was certainly not our duty or interest to interfere in order to preserve the Chinese government from the consequences of its own conceit and wrong-headedness, so long as the other European Powers preserved their neutrality. But, on the other hand, directly Russia and France showed their hands—two nations whose immediate interests in China were small and sentimental compared with our own—why did not the guardians of our people, the statesmen of Great Britain, at once seize the opportunity and make themselves heard, and felt if necessary? Why was not our minister at Pekin immediately ordered to declare that England was perfectly willing to act in concert with Russia and France for the common cause of civilisation and progress ; moreover, that we were ready to acquiesce in Russia's reasonable desire for an ice-free port, but that as the commercial interests on which the life and prosperity of Englishmen depend were paramount in China, so therefore the British government must have, and was ready if necessary to fight for, a paramount influence in all arrangements consequent on the success of Japan ? But what did we do? Lacking a mandate from an enlightened democracy, our government simply did nothing. While Russia—a country chiefly interested in China as far as the future is concerned—and the French—who are greatly actuated by love of harassing us—had grasped the situation, and taken the Chinese government out of our hands under their protection and guidance, we English, who have 70 per cent.[1] of the foreign commerce of China, who have a population of thirty millions almost entirely dependent on the extension

[1] According to Mr. Norman £32,000,000 = 3½ times trade of Continent, Russia, and United States combined.

APPENDIX 269

of foreign markets for their very means of subsistence, looked on the whole affair from a dilettante point of view !

It appears astounding that such an apathy can exist at a time when the condition and prosperity of our country are perhaps more critical than at any period of our history. At the beginning of this century, with a small population independent of foreign countries for food and for the raw material which, manufactured, enabled us to carry on a lucrative trade all over the world, we were able, with comparative impunity, to carry on wars with the nations of the Continent. These nations, too, were not serious competitors with us in our foreign commerce, yet our statesmen were most vigilant in securing every possible outlet in distant lands for the enterprise of Englishmen.

At the present time our agricultural population is disappearing : we do not grow enough corn for three months' home consumption, and, with the exception of coal and some iron, we are almost entirely dependent on foreign countries for all the raw materials which supply the means by which the majority of our population must gain the necessary wages in order to clothe and feed themselves and families. The truth is that both money and food are dependent on countries outside the United Kingdom. Any shrinkage of markets and trade areas implies increase of poverty to our working classes ; and a loss of command of the seas would result in speedy starvation and misery only comparable to the accounts we read of the siege of Jerusalem. We have freely given to the whole world every commercial advantage we possess in the mother country, and in our enormous possessions and colonies ; and, while Continental nations are successfully competing with us in all these markets, they studiously prevent us from enjoying any reciprocal benefits in their own states or in any new territories they may gain and colonise. Three-quarters of a century ago the government of the empire was held by an oligarchy composed of men possessing ample means from landed property or accumulated in trade ; but, at the same time, they were educated and able to take broad views of foreign policy. To-day power is in the hands of a democracy whose very subsistence depends on extension of markets for the works of their hands, and on the opening out of new fields for commerce ; these can only be acquired and secured by a continuous and spirited foreign policy supported by an overwhelming navy.

It is to be feared, however, that these most vital questions are those on which our working classes are most ignorant, and therefore in which they take the least interest. They require to be taught that prudent and just extension of empire and of imperial influence is not 'Jingoism,' but chiefly for their own benefit ; and that an insufficient or incompetent navy means their utter ruin. It ought to be made clear to them that any government, Whig or Tory, which fails in performing its duties in these matters should be considered as the enemy of the working classes. Ministers of any political party are always tempted to divert the attention of the people, and catch their votes by such questions as Extension of the Franchise, Education, Women's Suffrage, etc., all of which objects, though good, perhaps, in their place, can only be possible on the condition that the country continues to prosper materially, so that the voters may be able to live.

On questions which involve great responsibility and the danger of international complications, or the assertion of our rights by force of arms, statesmen will rarely move any farther than they are pushed by an enthusiastic popular voice. Now, if ever, it is absolutely necessary for the people to force our government to protect their important interests in the Far East.

Could our democracy only realise the potential advantages to be obtained from the development of British influence in China, our ministers would be obliged to make up their minds as to what are our just rights and imperious necessities in the Far East, and to determine that, whatever France and Russia may choose to do, Great Britain will never give up her share in any partition of territory, or participation in the benefits which may accrue from the opening up to foreign trade of the immense resources of the eighteen provinces and the outlying dependencies of the Celestial Empire. We shall then have no more British ministers at Pekin who will dare to say that they will never allow the interests of twenty-nine millions to over-ride those of three hundred millions;[1] or officials at our Foreign Office so ignorant of their duties as to object to the idea of our occupying the Pescadores because these islands belong to Spain.[2]

We must not content ourselves with monopolising the carrying trade of the world, or congratulate ourselves (as some would teach us) because we can build vessels and sell them to foreigners who are trying to cut us out of this monopoly. A very small portion of our people can be benefited by the fact that British vessels, manned largely by Scandinavians, Germans, and Lascars, are carrying raw materials and manufactured articles to and from the Continent and the United States. What we absolutely require for our existence as a nation is a steady expansion of our foreign trade which will keep in remunerative employment the whole of our mining and manufacturing population. If the greatest happiness of the greatest number be the true object of government, then British statesmen are bound to use all their power to secure the possession of the best and largest fields which will provide unlimited scope for the industry of our toiling millions. At the present time, China presents that field, ready for the harvest; but only on

[1] 'Cycle of Cathay,' Dr. Martin.   [2] Fact.

the condition that we all realise the necessity of seizing the opportunity before it passes irrevocably away.

I am, etc.

LAU TAI-WAN.

64 Warwick Gardens, W., February 6.

THE GERMAN SEIZURE OF KIAO-CHAU AND THE PROPOSED LOAN TO CHINA, DEC. 1897, JAN. AND FEB. 1898.

DAILY NEWS, *December* 30.

INTERVIEW WITH MR. PICKERING. 'WHY PLAY THE DOG IN THE MANGER?'

As the Far Eastern diary continues it does not lose its characteristics as a colossal Chinese puzzle, 'What Russia means, what Germany has done, what England may be expected to do ; what line of conduct may be looked for from Japan, what indefinite thing the United States will prefer, and the measures which will finally commend themselves to France '—these constitute the confused Briton's daily fare. There is a multitude of prophets, but few seers ; and it was in the hope of finding a counsellor (writes a correspondent) that I conferred with Mr. W. A. Pickering, C.M.G., yesterday. In 1888 Mr. Pickering, as Protector of the Chinese Straits Settlements, was virtually the ruler of some hundreds of thousands of Chinese. I have some recollection that in 1878 Sir Robert Hart declared that no single European had ever possessed such opportunities as Mr. Pickering of learning the Chinese character in all its phases, and certain it is that in 1883 the late Protector was requested by the Intelligence Department of the War Office to prepare a paper on the state of the Chinese army, embodying suggestions as to the best method of attacking China in the event of war. This he did, receiving in return the thanks of the commander-in-chief and of Lord Wolseley. But this is not all. Mr. Pickering has spent a lifetime in China since the age of eighteen. Here, then, was surely a wise man of the East to lighten the darkness.

'You ask me,' said Mr. Pickering, in reply to my initial question, 'what is the value of Japan in the present development of affairs in the East? Well, Japan is an Asiatic nation, in spite of her modern civilisation and her Western ideas. Against any European Power Japan can do absolutely nothing ; in fact, there is no European nation that has any reason to fear anything from any Asiatic race, however civilised. Japan, however, would be splendid as an ally; and, *per contra*, she would be just as dangerous in alliance with any other European Power. That she would be a splendid ally to us I have not the least doubt.'

'That being so, how do you expect present events to unravel themselves?'

'As to that point, why should we pursue a dog-in-the-manger policy? If we were prepared to bite it would be another matter. But if we growl without biting—if we protest against any other party trying to get a share while we ourselves do nothing—where is the use of it?'

'Then you think Russia must get her portion?'

'Certainly; why not? She must have a port free from ice, and what is more—she will have it. So what is the use of our protesting, with the certainty of having to give in at last? The only result of such a course of action must be to make us appear foolish in the end. France, again, has her interests in Tonquin; but why should we make a pother concerning any action she may take if we do not mean to act?'

'Then what do you suggest as the best course of action?'

'Simply this. We had better agree with Russia and France—for France must have her share—as to the sphere of which each shall take control.'

'Then you think that the partition of China is inevitable?'

'Undoubtedly; and, that being so, it should never be forgotten that our own interest in China is greater than that of all the other Powers who will be engaged in the scramble. There are thirty millions in this country who require to be fed. China is a market that enables them to earn food-purchasing wages. Have South Africa and other places the same marketable capacity as China's four hundred millions? No. Bear in mind there is no Jingoism in this; it is merely a matter of national necessity. Our working men have votes, but unfortunately they do not know how to use them in these matters of foreign policy. Why, a foreign policy is a necessity of our existence; but it is always lost sight of in our tremendous concern for Local Veto or Women's suffrage, or something of that kind. They are all good in their place, but they are possible only on the condition that the country continues to prosper materially, so that the voters may be able to live.'

'That being granted, what section of China do you suggest the government should indicate to the Powers as constituting the British claim?'

'Why, all that section of the country lying between the Canton River in the south and the southern portion of the province of Shantung in the north. That, let me tell you, is the very best portion of China. There our interests lie, and there dwell the Chinese population who give us our trade. Having done that, we should say to France and Russia, "Take your share with welcome."'

'And Germany?'

'Oh, she is there to give us a prick, and Russia and France

are helping her. Germany does not need to open fresh places in the same way as we are bound to open them ourselves.'

'Not open fresh places ! What do you mean by that ?'

'Simply this, that whenever we open a new place we make it free to the whole world. Germany comes along and benefits there almost as much as we do ourselves. My dear sir, perhaps you do not know that British-born Chinese prefer to charter German or foreign vessels. Why? Because foreign vessels are not hampered with restrictions and regulations as our own ships are in our own ports. The Germans know that well enough. So do the French. We open new country, and both of them are better off than they are at home. When they open a place they impose heavy protective duties, but the thing does not pay. Look at France and her enormous colonies ; she never gets a cent out of them. Yet a Frenchman sinks everything, even religion and party differences, immediately he hears the name of France mentioned. And that should be our kind of patriotism. Anyway you can believe me that Germany has no need of colonisation in the same sense as we have need of it.'

'From what you say, then, I presume your opinion to be that in the partition of China there will be no need for fighting?'

'None whatever. There is no reason to fear any serious result from the action of Russia at Port Arthur, or from that of Germany at Kiao-chau. If the foreign minister and the people know what they want, and if the country is intelligently informed by the press, there will be nothing to fear. Supposing Germany had the whole of her fleet in Chinese waters—what then ? Her fleet could never get back to Germany again. The only thing left for her to contemplate in that case would be an invasion of England, and she would never go to that length for the sake of securing a portion of China.'

'But what about our waning influence in the Chinese Empire ?'

'That is a serious fact that must undoubtedly be admitted. From 1856 to 1865 we could do anything we pleased in China, and the Chinese regarded it as right, for we were the only people who had expended blood and money in the country. In those days Pekin had little to do with matters, the provincial governments being dealt with direct. The result was that whenever murder or disturbance occurred it was only necessary to send a gunboat or a force to the spot to have things rectified at once, the viceroy of the province concerned being the chief authority. Since that time our influence has gradually waned. The ambassadors of Russia, Germany, and France have used their influence simply in the interest of their respective countries, while our own efforts have been almost solely directed towards the protection of the government at Pekin. The course we should follow now is

T

that which I have suggested : we should claim as our sphere the whole of the area which includes the province of Kiang-su in the north, and the province of Kwang-tung in the south. That would give us Shanghai : it would not interfere with the French sphere to the south of us, and it would not affect the occupation by Germany of Kiao-chau north of us under the Shantung promontory, or the occupation by Russia of Port Arthur still further north of us. If that were done, our sphere in China, you will observe, would extend right across the country to the Burmese frontier.'

'What about Yunnan ; would that come within our sphere ?'

'Yes, but I will not say anything about that. For the rest, let Russia and France fight it out between them. So far as the area I have mentioned is concerned, we should reserve our rights, and we should be prepared to back them up. China must break to pieces, and what we have to do is to accept the inevitable. We must have markets, and we should take the best we can while we still have time. Even Russia does not want all the land, and France has to pay dearly for everything she gets. The great difficulty is that the Powers cannot trust us. How can they, when they cannot tell whether Great Britain's policy will be backed up by the next government to come into power or not ? And how can they trust us, again, when we declare that we shall bite, yet when the time comes we do nothing of the kind ?' Foreign statesmen have no such conditions as those which obtain here to contend against, and they can therefore act as they think they will. What we should remember is that we have only six weeks' bread in the whole of the kingdom ; and, remembering that, we should support our statesmen when they reveal boldness and wisdom. And what I have said of China applies with equal force to Afghanistan. Like China it must go to pieces. It would be better to have Russia touching our boundaries at all points, for then both of us would exactly know each other's position.'

'Then I take it that you are no admirer of the principle of maintaining buffer States ?'

'Most decidedly I am not. Buffer States are of not the slightest real use. In a buffer State what do you have ? Why, simply a lot of barbarians who steal your women, raid your cattle, and give both of you no end of trouble and expense. A buffer State simply means that you are usually subsidising a tribe of blackguards, who play the very mischief over the borders on each side of them. No, let us understand each other ; let us come close together, and let us make the best terms with each other that we can. When the terms of peace were being arranged between China and Japan I said the end must be that China would ultimately be divided between Russia, Great Britain, and

France; and that partition must come. The present is the time to recognise that fact, and we should begin to act without delay.'

THE PROPOSED LOAN TO CHINA.

MORNING POST, *January* 12.

WRITTEN BY W. A. PICKERING, C.M.G.

For expressing to a special correspondent, who sought me out, my opinion that it is the duty and policy of the British government and people to amend their ways and to be prepared to uphold and develop British interests in the Far East by force if necessary, I have been stigmatised as a Jingo; and in one journal it has been declared that 'it is not the fault of the Pickerings of this world that the Armageddon referred to so apprehensively in the ministerial speeches of the last two years is not already in full blast.' I cannot believe that any amount of hostile criticism should prevent Englishmen who possess any special knowledge of China and the Chinese from pressing this knowledge on their fellow-countrymen at such an important crisis as the present. I am encouraged, too, by the opinions of Mr. Colquhoun, as given in the *Morning Post*, since that gentleman certainly accords a general support to my views. The very people who object to what they are pleased to sneer at as 'Jingoism' seem quite willing that the British people should with a light heart advance £16,000,000, a payment which would wellnigh certainly hasten the 'partition' of China, a necessary 'grab' of territory on our part, and an inevitable battle sooner or later between the European Powers interested in the Far East. Of course, if we clearly understand our position, if we have counted the cost, and if the whole nation is prepared to accept the risks, £16,000,000 will be a moderate sum to pay for the advancement of our immense interests in the Chinese Empire. But on what security is it proposed that we should lend this large sum of money? The only reliable asset of the Pekinese government, the Imperial Maritime Customs Revenue, is to a large extent already hypothecated, and even that security is chiefly dependent on the personality of Sir Robert Hart.

Supposing that the Chinese should promise the land revenue of the empire as a security for the proposed loan. To make this pledge of any real value would necessitate the presence of a British official, with a staff of clerks and interpreters, and a military force at each of the principal yamens of the eighteen provinces. Without this support our officials would be useless; for they would at every step be thwarted and opposed by the venal and semi-independent provincial mandarins. These with their underlings would oppress and squeeze the common people, in the name of the 'barbarians,' to such an extent that in a few years a general massacre of our officials would probably take place.

This would entail either our retirement from the country with loss of money and of prestige, or would oblige us to invade the empire in order to retrieve our position. What would Russia, France, and Germany say to this? If as security for the loan we demand railway, mining, or territorial concessions, these must be confined to the middle provinces. The Pekin government may promise, but dare not give us and protect us in concessions in the north or south-west of the empire. The partition of China has already virtually begun in these portions of the empire. We can hope for nothing there unless we are prepared to fight Russia, France, and Germany. In reply to our demands for fulfilment of engagements the Tsung-li-yamen officials would be perfectly justified in pleading *non possumus*.

We have since 1860 had a treaty with China which ought to satisfy our present needs. But this treaty, owing to the utter supineness of successive British governments, has never been carried out. We have never been able to induce the Chinese government to fulfil its stipulations as to residence in the interior, exemption of our trade from illegal and ruinous imposts, or indeed in any other particular obnoxious to Pekin, except by the use of force; no, not even when Great Britain was the paramount influence in the Far East. It is now stated that our government has decided on the policy of insisting on the strict fulfilment of the treaty of Tientsin with regard to every right and privilege of British subjects in China. What can the British people wish for more than this? Yet we must bear in mind that if we mean to carry out this strong policy we must be prepared to use force against China or to allow all our diplomacy to be neutralised by the intrigues of European powers in the Tsung-li-yamen at Pekin. If we decide to use force we must be ready for the eventuality of facing China, *plus* Russia, France, and Germany. Supposing that British interests are to be maintained as provided for by treaty, or to be developed in ratio with those of other European nations, we must count the cost of a decided policy with the risk of a great war—call it by whatever name we like.

To speak of British policy in China being merely 'pacific and commercial' is simply absurd. No European individual or community can exist in the Celestial Empire on such terms. We must be prepared to be treated as inferior beings, with whom no faith need be kept, to be driven out of the country, or to prove that we can more than hold our own by physical force if necessary. We must remember that all foreigners in Chinese estimation belong to races who, however powerful and wealthy they may be, not having received the teaching of the sages, are akin to the 'birds and beasts.' Finally, if we British are ready to hand over £16,000,000 to the Chinese under the impression that Pekin can give us any security for which we shall not have to incur the risk

APPENDIX 277

of a possible conflict with European Powers in the Far East (unless there can be arranged a real and working concert between London, Paris, St. Petersburg, and Berlin), it would argue that neither the government nor the people of this country recognise the gravity of our present position in China. On the other hand, granted that position is perfectly understood, and the risk intelligently accepted by the nation, £16,000,000 is a comparatively small sum to stake for British potentialities in the eighteen provinces of the Celestial Empire.

MORE 'COPYBOOK.'

To the Editor of THE WESTMINSTER GAZETTE.

Sir,—Referring to your most sober and reasonable leader of this evening, allow an old 'China hand' to ask why, of all things just now, should Great Britain demand the opening of Talien-wan (within the Russian sphere) and Nan-ning (bordering on French Indo-Chinese conquests) if it were not with the deliberate intention of showing that we are determined to oppose both Powers more than to benefit ourselves? Surely the province of Hu-nan and the Yangtze valley would be enough addition to our trade for the present: that, with security in the shape of control of some branch of the revenue and the strict carrying out of the Tientsin treaty, ought to be sufficient grounds for a loan if we British are so anxious to invest our millions in China.

Can there, Sir, be any doubt that the very fact that our rivals have no coaling stations and a comparatively weak navy will render it inevitable that any conflict concerning our interests in the Far East must be fought out in Europe? We are not the only people in the world who know what we are about.

Doubtless our interests in China are well worth fighting for, considering that we exist by foreign trade and should perish without foreign markets. But is it necessary that the empire should be put to the chance of a general war, which would be a veritable Armageddon? Would it not be wise to secure our needs by a better way? And should not the nation sit quietly down and consult whether with our ten thousands we are prepared to meet those three or four kings who will come against us with their twenty thousands of men?

I am, Sir, yours faithfully,
January 22. FAR CATHAY.

THE CRISIS IN THE FAR EAST.

To the Editor of THE WESTMINSTER GAZETTE.

Sir,—The *Times* leader of this morning on the above subject fully justifies all your arguments as contained in what may be termed the 'Copybook' series of leaders on our real interests in

China. Let us hope that the government is now prepared, if necessary, to waive the demand as to Nan-ning and Talien-wan, as long as the other conditions of the loan are complied with.

The loss of prestige accompanying this modification will indeed be infinitesimal compared with the loss to British influence in the Far East which would ensue were the loan with its other most substantial advantages allowed to fall through.

We must not, however, permit ourselves to vociferate so much as to our disinterested motives and self-denying resolutions regarding the acquisition of additional territory. China and the European powers will take all these professions for what they are worth, and for no more.

We must *always* bear in mind that if we, as a manufacturing nation, intend to profit by the present crisis, we must have a persistent policy of *enforcing the treaty of Tientsin* and any future developments—there must be no relapse into our former state of apathy.

After pocketing our twelve millions the old schemers of the Tsung-li-yamen, in their childish recklessness and cunning, are quite capable of evading their engagements, and of diverting the consequences from themselves, by *freely* giving to Russia and France extension of territory in the north-east and south-west of China, so that the European Powers may be obliged to fight amongst themselves. Supposing such a state of things, Great Britain would be *absolutely obliged in self-defence* to seize Chusan, Shanghai, or some other point whence she could control her sphere of legitimate and vital interests—the central provinces of China lying between the northern boundary of Kiang-su and the southern bank of the Sikiang branch of the Canton River as far as Ng-chau or Wu-chou, and then up the Wu-ling-kiang across into Burmah.

China is already a corpse politically, to be kicked about by Western nations. No amount of sentimental language can disguise this fact. Any real settlement can only be made with Russia and France—perhaps Germany. To fight these Powers or any of them, if we had China as an ally, would be like rushing into war with an 'old man of the sea' on one's back.

Yours faithfully,
January 29. FAR CATHAY.

THE CHINESE PROBLEM.

To the Editor of THE MORNING POST.

Sir,—In this wonderful generation, when the people are ready to believe anything in the world but their Bible, we are all very liable to be deceived by concise and nice-sounding aphorisms. Just at present it seems that there is a tendency on the part of

APPENDIX 279

journalists and political leaders to minimise the gravity of our position in China, by using on every possible occasion the phrase, 'Great Britain's interests are commercial, not territorial.' This sounds very fine, and the saying is easy to remember; but at the same time it is absurd and untrue. On what can our commerce subsist but on the existence of territory which supports the population with whom we have commercial dealings? Our country is now thoroughly aroused with regard to our interests in China; but the zeal now created must be persistent if we wish to reap any permanent advantage from the crisis which has been forced on us by our ignorance and apathy more than by the rapacity of other nations. If we suffer another relapse, the next catchword will be 'Our interests in China are celestial not terrestrial,' and the food and clothing for our toiling millions, which might be drawn from the Far East, will vanish into thin air. There is Russian, French, and German territory now in the Celestial Empire, and unless we secure an influence over the central provinces British commercial interests will most probably be gradually destroyed.

May I put the following questions for the consideration of your readers? 1. Has Great Britain at any time undertaken to defend the integrity of China from the attacks of all other nations? If so, are we not now bound to aid the Pekin government against the designs and encroachments of Russia, Germany, and France in the north, east, and south-west provinces of the empire? If we have not undertaken this obligation, on what grounds of international law can we object to these nations—by diplomacy or by force—taking under their control any part of the empire they may desire for the benefit of their own people? 2. Supposing that France, Russia, or Germany acquires by diplomacy or by other means portions of Chinese territory, by what principles of international law can the British nation claim to demand that the territory so acquired shall be open to the free trade of the whole world? We, having turned our native land into an immense workshop without sufficient food or money, except that dependent on foreign trade, must for our existence believe in and practise free trade. Other nations are not in the same condition, and believe that protection secures their prosperity. What if they were to demand that we place Hong Kong under the rules of protection? Should we obey them, or should we not tell them to mind their own business? Of course, if we are strong enough and ready for the effort, we can enforce what we like in the Far East on the Chinese or on our European rivals; but, if not, we must take what we can get.

At the present moment ought we not to give our whole attention towards securing the sphere of influence left open to us, and to enforce the existing treaty with China in every part of the empire which the Pekin government may be able to keep intact from the encroachments of Germany, France, and Russia? More than this we cannot do, unless we are prepared for a general European war. The time has gone by when we could have secured a well-earned supremacy of influence in the Far East by the presence of a strong minister at Pekin, backed by an energetic admiral and a moderate-sized fleet. When in 1868 the 'free breakfast-table' government handed over British policy in China to the American gentleman, Mr. Burlingham, we entered on a course which has culminated in, or descended to, our present position, *i.e.* we are confined to the alternative of quietly taking what is left to us, or of kindling the flames of a general European war.

February 5.
Yours, etc.
W. A. PICKERING.

To the Editor of THE MORNING POST.

Sir,—The ministerial speeches of last evening have greatly cleared the atmosphere with regard to the state of affairs in the Far East. The specialists and prophets (myself of course included) must feel a little ashamed now they find how little they really knew as to our present position in China. One fact is clearly shown by the government, and that is, our immense commercial interests and treaty rights in the Celestial Empire are in exactly the same state of security as were those in Madagascar and Tunis before the French conqueror 'protected' those countries. In the case of China we have an advantage. Instead of one written guarantee that our treaty rights and trade privileges shall be safeguarded we have two, one each from Russia and Germany. My alarmist views as to a European war seem to be now groundless. But for all that I would suggest to both political parties, and especially to the working classes of this country, that the British nation should keep on the alert, and follow a bold and persistent policy in China. Though peace seems secured in Europe, without the greatest vigilance history may repeat itself in the eastern hemisphere.

February 9.
Yours, etc.
W. A. PICKERING.

ADDENDA TO APPENDIX.

From a leader in the *Times* of this morning it would appear that in my last letter to the *Morning Post* I have been too sanguine as to the validity of the written guarantees given by Russia and Germany.

APPENDIX

If the people of this country do not thoroughly arouse themselves as to the importance of the 'Chinese problem,' some British government, in saving us from the horrors of war, may, by repeated graceful concessions, lose for the masses the means by which they must live in time of peace.

Unless we at once secure our influence over the central provinces of the empire, from the Yangtze to the Canton River, we shall some day awake and find that the Chinese treaty ports, through which, by the payment of a reasonable tariff, British merchants are carrying on an enormous trade—have been transformed into a chain of so-called 'free' ports under Russia, France, or Germany.

These ports, cutting off our own free port Hong Kong, will, it is to be feared, greatly differ from it in character, in that, while all other nationalities are free to reside at, and their vessels to trade with, Hong Kong, on exactly the same conditions as our own people, British merchants and vessels will be freely admitted to enter the Russian, German, or French 'free' ports on the terms of compliance with prohibitive tariffs, specially framed in order to ruin British commerce.

Trusting, however, that these gloomy forebodings may not be realised, still it appears more than probable that for the future Great Britain will not be able to accomplish more than the strict enforcement of the Tientsin treaty, and any additional privileges extorted from China, in that portion of the empire left untouched by the other European Powers.

Holding these opinions, I feel constrained to make a few closing suggestions as to the best mode of dealing with the Chinese government, whether as at present established at Pekin, or, as may yet be the case, removed to the old southern capital Nan-king :

1. That our ambassadors in future be chosen for their strong common sense, absolute justice, firm will, and thorough knowledge of their own language. From what we know of the past, our present minister at Pekin possesses all these qualifications.

2. That they be interdicted from study of the Chinese language, written or spoken, and especially from the study of the classics—knowledge of the language and customs of the natives is most useful for the subordinates, or, as the Chinese term them, 'hands and feet'; but the 'head' has no need of these Oriental accomplishments : his influence is the one thing needful, and it can only be gained by showing the qualities of his race and religion, which have gained for us the foremost rank amongst the nations. The Englishman may well be proud of the monarch whose millenary we are now celebrating ; but had Alfred the Great been fed on no better spiritual food than the Chinese classics Great Britain would now be in no way superior to the Chinese in power or in civilisation. Our ambassador should be furnished

with the English copy of the present and any future more advantageous treaties, and be directed to meditate on these treaties day and night, remembering that his sole *raison d'être* at the Chinese court is the maintenance and furtherance of British interests, in strict accordance with the terms of the treaties signed by the Chinese and British governments.

3. That the ambassador's assistants in the embassy be thoroughly acquainted with the Chinese official language, spoken and written, and that the consuls be chosen and promoted not merely for their capabilities in the court dialect, but for their acquaintance with the local dialects and knowledge of the resources and requirements of their respective districts.

4. That the consuls be instructed that their principal duties are the protection and fostering of British mercantile, missionary, or any other legitimate interests, and the supervision and control of all British subjects in accordance with the provisions of our treaties. Instead of, as in the past, devoting their time to the translation of the old dry-as-dust Chinese philosophical or mystical works, the consuls should be encouraged to devote their leisure to raising the character of our nation in the eyes of the conceited Chinese by translating such works as Shakespeare, Milton, etc., into the language of the Middle Kingdom.

5. That the Admiral on the China station should be permanently furnished with a fleet strong enough not only to enforce all just demands made upon the Chinese government, but also to overcome any alliance of the other European powers, in case they may choose to act as sponsors to the Chinese government in breaches of the treaty, or to make injurious encroachments on our commerce and sphere of influence.

6. That the consuls be instructed to report at once to the minister any breach whatever of the treaties on the part of the Chinese officials, and that in case the Tsung-li-yamen do not at once take in hand and redress all grievances, then our admiral shall be instructed to inquire into the matter, with the assistance of our consul, and to enforce redress at the hands of the highest Chinese local or provincial authorities.

Were the above programme carried out persistently, I feel sure that the central government would at once realise its true position and amend its ways. We should not in any way interfere with other European Powers in their own sphere, acknowledged already by us, and we should within our own particular zone be acquiring an influence over and acquaintance with the viceroys and higher mandarins of the central provinces, which, when the inevitable partition of the Celestial Empire shall arrive, will enable us to organise a separate native government under our direct supervision and control.

As Professor Douglas has wisely stated in a letter to the

APPENDIX

Times, it is easy to conquer China, but difficult to hold and govern the country. A second-rate European Power might without much trouble overrun the empire, but I maintain that the most powerful Western nation would find it impossible to keep in order the teeming population of two or three provinces without using largely the assistance of the Chinese official classes.

March 1, 1898.

NEW WORK BY J. H. E. SECRETAN, C.E.

In 1 vol. large 8vo. with Twenty-four Illustrations. Price 6s.

TO KLONDYKE AND BACK

A JOURNEY DOWN THE YUKON FROM ITS SOURCE TO ITS MOUTH

By J. H. E. SECRETAN, C.E.
OF OTTAWA

WITH HINTS TO INTENDING PROSPECTORS.

NEW WORK BY DR. PARKER

Now Ready, in 1 vol. crown 8vo. 3s. 6d.

CHRISTIAN PROFILES
IN A PAGAN MIRROR

By JOSEPH PARKER, D.D.
MINISTER OF THE CITY TEMPLE, LONDON

An enlightened Pagan Lady comes to England to acquaint herself with the beliefs, the habits, and the customs of Christians. She has long been asking herself such questions as 'Who are the Christians?' 'What do they believe?' 'What life do they lead?' 'How do they conduct themselves towards each other?' Having made inquiry and received impressions, she reports to a friend in India.

HURST & BLACKETT, Ltd., 13 Great Marlborough Street.

NEW WORK BY MR. MACKENZIE BELL

THIRD EDITION now ready, at all Booksellers' and Libraries. In 1 vol. Demy 8vo. with Portraits and Facsimiles, extra cloth, 12s.

CHRISTINA ROSSETTI

A Biographical and Critical Study

By MACKENZIE BELL

Author of 'Spring's Immortality, and other Poems,' 'Charles Whitehead: a Biographical and Critical Monograph,' &c.

This is, in effect, the Authorised Life of the Poetess, being based largely on information and letters supplied by her relatives and intimate friends.

Under the Especial Patronage of Her Majesty

SIXTY-SEVENTH YEAR OF PUBLICATION

Now Ready. In 1 vol. royal 8vo.
With the Arms beautifully engraved, extra cloth, gilt edges, price 31s. 6d.

LODGE'S
PEERAGE & BARONETAGE

For 1898

CORRECTED BY THE NOBILITY

HURST & BLACKETT, Ltd., 13 Great Marlborough Street.

NEW AND POPULAR NOVELS

NEW AND ORIGINAL NOVEL BY ADELINE SERGEANT
Now first published in 1 vol. Crown 8vo. 6s.
SECOND EDITION NOW READY

MISS BETTY'S MISTAKE. By ADELINE SERGEANT, Author of 'The Claim of Anthony Lockhart' &c.

'"Miss Betty's Mistake" can unhesitatingly be entered upon that list which carries the names of Miss Sergeant's happiest efforts to amuse us by means of wholesome fiction. The story is cleverly arranged and capitally written.'—LITERARY WORLD.

'The wholesome sweetness with which the tale is told, and the sensitiveness of touch displayed in the drawing of all the characters, make it pleasant to read.'—DUNDEE ADVERTISER.

MERESIA. By WINIFRED GRAHAM, Author of 'A Strange Solution' &c. In 1 vol. Crown 8vo. 6s.

'I will not divulge the plot, which is original and mystifies the reader. It is not an easy book to lay down when you have taken it up.'—QUEEN.

'There is much that is clever and original in Miss Winifred Graham's latest book. Meresia is an interesting and a lifelike character, and the two Spaniards, Aladros and Serano, are also well drawn. The book is well worth reading, if only for the picture it gives us of "the fascination of hate."'
DAILY TELEGRAPH.

THE CAPRICE OF JULIA. By LEWIS SERGEANT. Now ready, in 1 vol. Crown 8vo. 6s.

'Its plot is good, the character of Julia herself is well realised and adequately portrayed, and many of the scenes interest and convince. Other characters besides Julia's are well imagined and carefully wrought, and the situations are well conceived and brought forth with no lack of strength in the creator or of success in the result. "The Caprice of Julia" is a book to be read.'—PALL MALL GAZETTE.

'There is plenty of imagination to be found in "The Caprice of Julia." Taking the book altogether, it is clever, well-written, and entertaining.'
STANDARD.

A STORM-RENT SKY. Scenes of Love and Revolution. By M. BETHAM-EDWARDS, Author of 'Kitty,' 'Dr. Jacob,' 'Brother Gabriel,' &c. Second Edition now ready, in 1 vol. Crown 8vo. 6s.

A great-nephew of Danton writes :—'Les mœurs de l'époque et du pays sont bien peintes. Le caractère et le patriotisme de mon illustre parent sont mis en relief et décrits d'une façon aussi remarquable que vraie.'
V. SARDIN, Arcis-sur-Aube, 13 March.

'A story of varied charm and more than usual interest.'—WEEKLY SUN.

'Prudent Parisse, the village schoolmaster, is an admirable creation.'
STANDARD.

HURST & BLACKETT, Ltd., 13 Great Marlborough Street.

In One Volume, Demy 8vo.
WITH PORTRAIT OF AUTHOR. PRICE 12s.

An Old Soldier's Memories

By S. H. JONES-PARRY, J.P., D.L.
Late Captain Royal Dublin Fusiliers,
Author of "My Journey Round the World."

CONTENTS.

Parentage and Education—India in 1849—Rangoon—Pegu—Second Defence of Pegu—March to Shoaygheen—Tonghoo—London 1854—The Crimea—Homeward Bound—Lucknow—Alumbagh—Home 1868.

In One Volume, Large Crown 8vo, Gilt Top
WITH PORTRAIT OF LADY HAMILTON IN PHOTOGRAVURE. PRICE 6s.

Lady Hamilton and Lord Nelson

AN HISTORICAL BIOGRAPHY
Based on Letters and other Documents in the Morrison Collection

By JOHN CORDY JEAFFRESON,
Author of "The Real Lord Byron."

NEW EDITION, CONDENSED, REVISED, AND WITH MUCH NEW MATERIAL

HURST AND BLACKETT, Limited,
13 GREAT MARLBOROUGH STREET, LONDON, W.

www.ingramcontent.com/pod-product-compliance
Lightning Source LLC
Chambersburg PA
CBHW030308240426
43673CB00040B/1101